FLIPPING HOMES
LIKE A PRO

FLIPPING HOMES LIKE A PRO

by Stephen Cook
www.Lifeonaire.com

Copyright © 2016 by Stephen Cook

All Rights Reserved

All rights are reserved under State and Federal Copyright Law. No part of this book may be reprinted, reproduced, paraphrased or quoted in whole or in part by any means without the written permission of the publisher and the author.

Legal Disclaimer

This publication is intended to provide accurate and authoritative information with regard to the subject matter covered. It is offered with the understanding that neither the publisher nor the author is engaged in rendering legal, tax or other professional services. If legal, tax or other expert assistance is required; the services of a competent professional should be sought (from a Declaration of Principles jointly adopted by a committee of the American Bar Association and a committee of the Publishers Association).

This book is intended for instructional purposes only. Every effort has been made to reflect the applicable laws as of the date of the publication of this book. However, this is a dynamic field of endeavor in which new laws are enacted, old laws revised and/or reinterpreted on a continuing basis and where statutes, rulings and precedential case law are constantly changing. Readers are advised to proceed with the techniques described herein with caution. Neither the author, printers, licensees nor distributors make any warranties, express or implied, about the merchantability or fitness for any particular use of this product.

ISBN: 978-0-9863228-4-6

Flipping Homes Like A Pro

by
Stephen Cook

TABLE OF CONTENTS

CHAPTER 1:	Introduction	7
CHAPTER 2:	Ethics and Morals	15
CHAPTER 3:	Advantages and Disadvantages of Wholesaling and Rehabbing	29
CHAPTER 4:	How to Get Started	35
CHAPTER 5:	Neighborhoods	49
CHAPTER 6:	Renovation Quality and Style	71
CHAPTER 7:	Building Your Team	79
CHAPTER 8:	Contractors	87
CHAPTER 9:	Real Estate Agents	107
CHAPTER 10:	Finding the Money	119
CHAPTER 11:	Other Sources of Financing	133
CHAPTER 12:	Settlement Attorney / Title Co.	141
CHAPTER 13:	Insurance Agents	147
CHAPTER 14:	Other Team Members	149
CHAPTER 15:	Locating Opportunities	155
CHAPTER 16:	Buying from Bird Dogs	165
CHAPTER 17:	Estimating Values	169
CHAPTER 18:	Estimating Repairs	177

CHAPTER 19:	Making Offers	189
CHAPTER 20:	After Offer Accepted	203
CHAPTER 21:	Rehabbing Start to Finish	209
CHAPTER 22:	Agent Marketing	215
CHAPTER 23:	Individual Marketing	217
CHAPTER 24:	Advertising Methods	229
CHAPTER 25:	Qualifying Buyers	239
CHAPTER 26:	Servicing Wholesale Buyers	245
CHAPTER 27:	Closing a Wholesale Deal	251
CHAPTER 28:	Closing a Retail Deal	259
CHAPTER 29:	Settlement Procedures	273
CHAPTER 30:	Controlling the Process	285
CHAPTER 31:	Two Wholesale Deals	291
CHAPTER 32:	Successful Rehab Story	295
CHAPTER 33:	Quitting Your Day Job	299
Appendix A:	Glossary	303
Appendix B:	Forms	307
Appendix C:	Credit Application	319

CHAPTER I

INTRODUCTION

ABOUT THIS COURSE

This collection will educate you in this lucrative business and explain how to generate money by investing in junk homes. I highly recommend this type of investing to anyone, especially those in the first stages of their career. It is one of the safest and quickest ways to generate cash without spending too much. This course will provide you with all the tools necessary to generate income as a connoisseur of junk homes. Personally, I love fixer upper homes and they continue to be very good to me. Without these junkers, it's quite possible I would still be slaving away in the restaurant business. I've made quick cash over the years and lots of it. Fixer uppers have allowed me to live a better life and I'm happy to pass this education on to anyone willing to listen. These methods have been tested over and over, continuing to be a great source of income. As markets change and new laws are passed, this collaboration will remain the ideal source for becoming a successful real estate flipper. Additional information is market dependent and can be learned by diving in and getting involved. It's a timeless business and these basic principles presented in the collection will never die.

WHAT IS A LIFEONAIRE?

First, let me tell you what it means to you and then I'll tell you who we are as a company. LIFEonaire is like a millionaire, except it describes someone who is full of life, where a millionaire is someone full of money. Many LIFEonaires are millionaires, but few millionaires are LIFEonaires. The goal in life for most people is to accumulate wealth in hopes of one day experiencing an abundant life. The goal of a LIFEonaire is to experience a full and abundant life today, whether our businesses are successful or not.

Life is what we desire, but we've been conditioned to believe that we can't have an abundant life without first having achieved great financial success. Sadly, many have fallen into this trap and traded their lives in pursuit of wealth, hoping their wealth will one day give back their life. For some, this never happens and for others, it's too late. Many achieve great wealth, but it is never enough. These people never get around to truly experiencing abundant lives, but we are here to change that.

At LIFEonaire, we teach people how to design businesses that serve the life they want to live. If you do not know what you want out of life, you can't possibly build a business to help you live that life. Most people pursue careers or build businesses and try to fit life into what is left. We build a life and fit business into what is left. This course is not about LIFEonaire, it is about flipping homes—one of the methods that many LIFEonaire's use.

If you are interested in learning more about becoming a LIFEonaire, please visit us at our website www.LIFEonaire.com and come to one of our events to learn how you can live a great life and build a business that serves you.

MY BACKGROUND

At the age of 19, I bought a copy of Robert Allen's Nothing Down as well as a number of other books on the subject. What particularly intrigued me was the idea of doing deals without using any of my own money. After learning a sufficient amount of information, I began to look for opportunities.

By 21, I bought my first piece of real estate with no money down, but there was one problem. It was a restaurant, so I had apparently bought a job along with a property. I didn't realize this at the time and I felt proud of my accomplishment, happily going to work every day. The happiness dissipated after about six months of working 80 to 90 hours a week, barely making a salary. Soon after, I began to despise the place and was relieved to sell the business after another two months.

I must be hardheaded because I didn't learn my lesson. A few years later, I bought another piece of real estate with no money down. This time it was a $540,000 restaurant. Once again, I had purchased a job with my new investment, but this one was much better. I only needed to work eighty hours each week. What a relief...

After nearly two years, I was tired of the whole mess and I unloaded my restaurant to the first buyer, taking a huge loss. However, this time I realized that my "investments" were liabilities rather than assets. Both times, I had bought jobs equivalent to a prison sentence. In the fall of 1997, I started over again. I got a J.O.B. Having a steady paycheck and relieving myself of the day-to-day drudgery of running the restaurant was a very welcoming alternative...or so I thought.

Eventually, It didn't seem natural to have to show up for work, report to someone else and ask for a paycheck every week. The hours I worked weren't much better than when I owned a restaurant and the financial burden ate up every extra bit of income. On top of everything else, my precarious financial situation continued to worsen as creditors from my restaurants began to track me down.

I felt a need to honor all my obligations, so I worked out payment plans with all my creditors. While this provided some relief, by the time I came to terms with everyone, I didn't have enough at the end of each month to make ends meet. My entire life was taking a turn for the worse, but I wasn't quite sure what to do. I only knew two things—I had to do something and I had always wanted to be a real estate investor.

TURNING TO REAL ESTATE

During these times when I was flat broke, I experienced many sleepless nights and I'd sit up late watching television. And guess who I saw? That's right. Good ol' Carleton Sheets. Once again, Carleton sparked my interests.

The first step to becoming an investor is getting a proper education, so I began seeking information. While I had a basic knowledge of "no money down investing," there was a lot more to learn, including the mechanics of the various types of investing. However, one major obstacle stood in my way: I was broke.

Online, I began searching phrases like "real estate investing" and "no money down" and getting a ton of responses. These sites were nothing short of incredible at the time. I was amazed by all of the information that was available to me and even more astounded by the fact that so much of it was completely free (If you would like free information on Lifeonaire and how I help investors today, visit www.LIFEonaire.com).

I read every article and success story as well as countless posts from various newsgroups. Then, I compiled all of this information into a binder and read it constantly. I studied that binder until I knew the techniques like the back of my hand. I participated on the newsgroup daily and asked hundreds of questions. At some point, I was so well versed in the techniques that I could answer other questions posted on the feed. But one issue remained: I had never done a deal.

TAKING THE PLUNGE

I wasn't the only one who contained the knowledge but had no experience. Several people I came across possessed enough knowledge to get started but were too scared to take the next step. One day, a very personal experience lit a fire under me, that was stronger than my natural fears and I decided to go for it. That fire, for which I will be forever thankful, changed my life for good.

After deciding to take the plunge, my confidence began to take hold of my fear. I had no time to be afraid. Without another source of income, I had to succeed and I knew that failure was not an option. I believed deep in my heart that I was going to be successful and I put myself on the same level as successful investors. If they could experience success in real estate, so could I. All I had to do was use what I learned and I knew that if I didn't make it, I could only blame myself.

With experience, some people may already possess most of the required knowledge from their background or profession. These people will require less education than someone starting from square one. Others will be able to study more than those will more on their plate. Those who are able to absorb more financial missteps can afford to be less cautious and maybe start with less education than someone who is beginning by using a life savings.

Regardless of personal finances, the major aspect to understand is that most of your education will come from doing deals rather than from a book, course or seminar. These materials will, however, teach you the basics to arm yourself before jumping into the marketplace. They will help you to avoid common mistakes that could be devastating to your investment career and can provide the knowledge it takes others years to acquire. After gaining an education, whether you have $2,000 saved or $100,000 saved, it's time to go out and make it happen.

Any investor, new or seasoned, experiences fear, stress and anxiety whenever pushing the limits of their knowledge or ability to venture into uncharted territory. No investor will ever achieve anything without overcoming the stress and anxiety to take action. Educate yourself to minimize known risks. Step out of your comfort zone and begin the journey.

BUT WAIT! THERE'S MORE

Before you run out and buy your first junker house, understand that you need to have a plan. You need goals! You must define what it is that you want to accomplish with real estate investing. Once you know your long-term goals, you can create a plan to reach these goals.

For instance, if you need to begin making cash quickly, rehab projects probably are not the best route. If you have a decent job that pays your day-to-day expenses and you want to develop a stream of passive income, selling homes may not be for you. Take some time to figure out your goals and chart a plan of attack. The "Self Evaluation" survey and "Goal Setting/Action Plan" included with this course will help you set goals to get the most out of your investments.

Real estate investing has been great to me and it can be great for you, too. It has changed my life and provided me with the freedom to live my life on my own terms, through my values. Today, after investing for a short period of time, I have been involved in the purchase and sale of hundreds of homes.

I started with absolutely no money and bad credit, but I did possess a burning desire to succeed. This desire eventually prompted me to take action and use what I had learned to achieve my goals. None of the benefits that I have gained would have been possible without developing a plan and taking action.

MY QUALIFICATIONS

I have bought and sold hundreds of homes since July, 1998. I have done everything from wholesaling, to retailing, to creating and selling paper, to being a landlord. I have gone from being flat broke to enjoying financial independence with countless mistakes along the way. Fortunately for me, the best part about my mistakes is that I'm still here to share them so you will not make the same mistakes. I have also personally tested or experienced everything that you will read or learn in this course and I will provide you with as many details as possible.

> Finally, I manage a website called *www.LIFEonaire.com*, where I have taught thousands of other investors how to start their investing careers. I have also conducted workshops for hundreds of people and personally mentored investors all over the world.

MY HOPE FOR YOU

With this course, I have two desires for my readers. First, I hope to teach you the methods and techniques that I used to complete successful wholesale deals. More importantly, I hope that you will take what you have learned from me and use it to improve your quality of life.

Quality is something that I want to emphasize. Quality doesn't mean that you need to make a million dollars immediately, nor does it mean that you need to be the biggest investor in your area. Whether you would like to make a little extra cash or build the largest wholesale real estate company in your area, I can help. Quality is unique for every individual and something that you must define for yourself.

As I have progressed in my real estate career, I have adopted an approach that differs from my initial approach. No longer do I want to be the biggest investor around, nor do I want to be the most well known. I used to be a "quantity" investor and I thought the key to success was to complete as many transactions as I could. Now, my main goal is to live a quality life and pursue quality deals.

Experience has taught me that doing a high volume of deals not only makes you very busy, it also creates stress which degrades your quality of life and causes my quality of life to fall below my preferred level.

So please remember that the quality of your deals, not the quantity of your deals, will help you to live the quality of life that you desire for yourself and your loved ones. As such, I pray regularly for my students throughout the world that they may improve their lives and I pray that you will one day use my teachings to improve the quality of your life, your family and your community. Then, pass your knowledge and your new and improved attitude along.

CHAPTER 2

ETHICS AND MORALS

Proverbs 10:9 — The man of integrity walks securely, but he who takes crooked paths will be found out.

IN THIS CHAPTER, I will discuss the importance of operating your business with integrity and professionalism. I refuse to advocate any investment practices that are unethical, whether they are geared toward defrauding someone, taking advantage of uninformed people, or being just plain deceitful. I wholeheartedly believe that you should be completely honest with all of the participants in your transactions, even if it means losing a deal. In the long run, your reputation as a person will allow you to participate in many more profitable situations than when being dishonest.

SIGN WITH HONOR AND SETTLE EVERY DEAL

Proverbs 22:1 — A good name is more desirable than great riches…

The first point I would like to make is that as a professional investor, you should be honest with the seller about your position and sign your name with honor. Make every offer with the full intent of settling the deal. If you will not be able to settle on a property, do not present an offer at all. If certain circumstances need to fall into place before settling, present the offer but disclose these circumstances upfront. Above all, be honest with the seller about your position.

This policy has never caused me to lose a deal. Regardless, there have been plenty of other profitable opportunities for me as there will be for you. Anybody can go make several offers, but your name is what is valuable. If you continuously sign contracts without producing, your name will be worthless.

People do not forget when someone backs out of a deal. Bad reputations catch up to investors, even in large cities. On the other hand, if you sign your name with honor, you will reap the benefits. As a result of honoring my contracts, I can offer less than other investors for a home in my area and have my offer accepted over those with a lesser reputation. Sellers know that I will produce. Attaching this type of value to my name has not always been easy, but it has definitely been worthwhile. Another benefit from building a good name is when an investor finds a home run deal that they can't settle; my name is the first on the list to bring assistance. This has become one of my best sources for finding properties.

Building a good name hasn't always been easy. I have had occasions where settling on a deal seemed like it was going to blow up in my face. In all cases, I was able to put the deals together, even though they weren't great deals for me. I broke even on one and made about $500 on the other. But the bottom line is that I settled them. I didn't wait for something to happen. I hit the streets and found buyers to take my place. I didn't wait for the phone to ring. Instead, I started looking for investors who were buying in the areas where I had homes under contract and I started selling. In one case, I found a buyer the day before I was supposed to settle. Granted, we did file for a four-day extension, but I marketed the home up until the last minute and found a buyer who settled in my place.

I've also encountered several situations where I couldn't find a wholesale buyer. Though my intention when I first started investing was to wholesale properties exclusively, I was forced to honor these contracts and settle on the homes myself. In fact, this is the only reason I ever started to rehab houses and if you try to wholesale enough properties, there will come a time when you will be in the same position. When you come to that point, if you are signing your name with honor, you will find a way to settle on the property and rehab the house. If you absolutely must avoid rehabbing and your intentions are to back out of a deal if you cannot wholesale it, I suggest that you put a clause in your contract that will reflect this.

WEASEL CLAUSES — UNETHICAL AND UNNECESSARY

While we are on the subject of adding clauses to your contract, let me take this opportunity to discuss "weasel clauses." Examples include, "Contingent upon the inspection of my partner," when you don't have a partner or, "Contingent upon the inspection of my spouse," when your spouse has already seen the property. I completely disagree with the use of these types of clauses and believe them to be unethical, dishonest and totally unnecessary. Every single time you put your name on a contract to purchase a home, you should do so with the full intent of purchasing that home even if all else fails. Under no circumstances should you tie up someone else's property with the intent of walking away from the deal.

However, only those who are absolutely opposed to rehabbing a property should bother with such a "wholesale only" clause. Presuming that you've educated yourself to properly evaluate the "as-is" condition of a property, you don't need protection from anything else but the possibility that you might not be able to arrange financing. Such a situation may result from the condition, type or location of the property (if you've made your offer sight unseen) or from the fact that your purchase price is too high and you won't be able to borrow enough money to purchase and renovate the property. In either case, you can exercise your financing contingency, which is clearly disclosed upfront to the seller in your offer and, for the most part, the only contingency that you'll ever need.

I say "for the most part," because, on occasion, there will be legitimate unknown factors that will require the insertion of a separate contingency because they can make or break a deal for you. For instance, suppose you are looking at a home that has a well as its water source. If the well is dry, you wouldn't be able to provide water for your new buyers and therefore you should include a contingency, which gives you the opportunity to have a professional check out the well and releases you from the contract if it's dry. Similarly, you may be making an offer on a home specifically because it has extra land, which you think you can subdivide. In this case, you need to check with your county to see if subdivision is possible. In instances such as these, you can clearly identify an unknown piece of information and insert a contingency to give yourself a chance to perform due diligence before committing to purchase the property. Oftentimes, the seller will know or understand this circumstance.

Be careful not to confuse a legitimate contingency such as the ones used in these examples with a "weasel clause." The difference lies in the intent. The first intends to provide you with time to perform further due diligence, often on a particular aspect of a property, while the second serves only to buy yourself time to market the property and provide an exit if you can't wholesale it. Furthermore, even though a contingency such as "subject to inspection by my partner" can be genuine, once you learn how to inspect properties and estimate repairs, you won't need such clauses. In fact, as a wholesaler, you don't want to include them. In many cases, you will be buying most of your properties from banks and other institutions who reject offers with these types of clauses because they have been burned by them in the past. True, you may make some progress with private sellers (whether they are selling the property themselves or listing it through a Realtor), but even so, leave the weasel clauses out. If you've taken the time to educate yourself, they are unnecessary and your offers will be stronger and more acceptable without them.

Furthermore, if there should ever be a time when you need to exercise your "financing contingency" to exit a deal, I recommend procuring a letter from the lender ASAP and requesting a release from your seller as early as possible in the process. Do not wait until the last minute. If you handle the situation properly, you may be able to use the letter to negotiate a better deal with the seller and still settle on time, only for a better price. The reason that sellers get upset is that buyers wait until the day before settlement to dump bad news on them and exit the deal. So if you aren't going to be able to close a deal, let the sellers know as soon as you do.

In sum, my contract says "Stephen Cook agrees to buy the property," and I make every effort to live up to my end of the agreement every single time whether I wholesale the property or not. So should you. If you can't flip a property to someone else, buy it. Don't run scared and back out. There are worse things in the world than fixing and retailing a house for a profit. Yes, I said profit. You've bought the property cheap, so you will make money, in spite of your mistakes, and add another skill to your tool chest to boot. Isn't this a wonderful business?

DON'T TAKE ADVANTAGE OF MOTIVATED SELLERS

Sellers can be motivated for a variety of reasons: medical expenses, a child's education, unpaid bills, unpaid taxes, divorce, pending bankruptcy, settlement of an estate, etc. The more imminent the reason, the more motivated the seller to get something done quickly. If you tell a motivated seller who must have $25,000 in two weeks that you will buy their home within two weeks, they feel an immediate relief. They start to make plans based on that money. They make commitments that they expect to honor because they have placed their trust in you.

Now, what do you do in two weeks if you haven't been able to wholesale their home? Do you exercise your weasel clause, the one that says your partner, who is actually your dog, must approve of the purchase? What happens to the seller at this point? They can't live up to their obligations and commitments. Maybe they'll lose an opportunity. Perhaps their child won't receive a college education. Maybe they'll lose their home and get nothing. Maybe they will have to risk their life and delay a necessary medical procedure. Personally, I don't know how some people do it. I can't sleep at night signing a contract knowing that I'm going to stick the seller if I can't find someone else to buy the home. The moral of the story is not to take advantage of motivated sellers. Trust me, it will come back to haunt you.

AVOID FRAUD

Real estate investing is a business that is becoming well known for the fraud that takes place. The image of a real estate investor is slowly going from a glamorous title to that of a crook. It becomes very tempting at times to commit fraud to close a deal. Especially when the solutions that are presented to you involve fraud. It's not easy to say "no" to something so little, when so much is on the line. But be careful, what seems like something small could put you in jail. Many crooked investors have committed some kind of mortgage fraud and have been fitted for an orange jumpsuit.

Oftentimes beginning investors do not even realize that they are committing fraud. Someone else walks them right through the process. They have done it so often that they tell you, "Oh, this is OK, we do it all the time. Don't worry about a thing," and they just do it. Sometimes it doesn't even seem like a big deal, but it is.

Telling a lender that you are buying a home for personal use as opposed to an investment so that you can get a lower interest rate or qualify for a higher loan to value is fraud. Giving a buyer a couple thousand dollars so that they have enough funds for a down payment and not disclosing it to the lender is fraud. Marking up a purchase contract so the seller can give money back to you at settlement for repairs, and not disclosing it to the lender is fraud. These are scenarios that you will encounter regularly.

When a lender says it's OK to do something shady, chances are high that they won't be the lender who ultimately funds the deal and collects the payments. For example, some lenders have told me that I can give my buyers the money for their down payment and that they just need a relative of the buyer to sign a gift letter stating that the relative gave them the money. These lenders manufacture these paper trails simply so they can close the deal and package the loan in a pool which is then sold to another investor/lender. This investor/lender who buys the loan pool is ultimately the one who must collect the payments and bears the risk of dealing with the borrowers if the loan defaults. The investor isn't being told the whole story. Investors get a bad rap when in most cases, it is in fact the lenders and mortgage brokers who do most of the damage by facilitating fraudulent transactions.

One time, I sat across the table from a loan officer who asked me to sign a gift letter for a buyer. I didn't give the buyer any funds to purchase, so I wasn't going to sign the letter. The loan officer's exact words to me were, "if you sign this letter, we'll settle next week and you'll walk away with $15,000. If you don't, this deal goes bust." I chose to let the deal go bust. A temping proposal, but If I can't do it the right way, I would rather not do it at all.

Now, I'm not saying that all mortgage brokers and lenders are committing fraud and that investors are never guilty. I am merely trying to explain the pitfalls to beginning investors who don't have experience but would like to do the right thing. Sometimes it's very hard to do the right thing, especially when no one is looking, but that's what having integrity and ethics is all about—doing the right thing even when no one is looking. In the long run, doing the right thing ALWAYS pays off.

IS NO MONEY DOWN INVESTING ETHICAL?

Can you invest with no money down and keep your ethics intact? The answer to this question is a 100%, absolute, unequivocal "Yes!"

Many people find this difficult to believe because they feel that we are taking advantage of someone when we buy homes really cheap. In fact, I struggled with this issue myself when I first started, especially when it came to offering less than what a seller was asking. If they were asking $80,000, then offering $60,000 made me uneasy. But, after getting a few offers accepted, I realized that I wasn't the bad guy after all. The sellers were just happy to have someone willing to buy the home.

Another example involves a woman who sold me two homes that had appraised for $100,000 (combined) for $29,000. She was crying when she sold them to me because she was so happy that I had taken them off of her hands. I realized then what a motivated seller was and that to them, I was truly providing a service. Money was not her primary motive for selling the homes, getting rid of her problem is what she desired the most.

As a result of my experience, I have but one comment to make with regard to the sentiment that we are somehow stealing houses. If the seller could get more money or a better deal from some one else, they would take it. The reason the seller is willing to sell you their home really cheap is because no one else is willing to buy it or give them more for it. Most of the properties that I buy really cheap are from banks or government agencies. Do you think they don't know what they're doing? Wouldn't they get more for their homes if they could? Would you feel bad if a bank sold you their home for 50% of FMV?

It's all part of the business of finance and real estate. You are going to get paid for knowing how to buy and fix or buy and wholesale these fixer uppers. You will be helping not only the sellers, but you will help other investors by providing them with a profitable opportunity and the local community by doing something productive with an otherwise vacant home. Eventually, a family will have a home to live in.

Often times, I have new investors come to me who are fortunate enough to have a large nest egg to start with. I'll have people come to me and say, "I have $100k in the bank, how should I invest it?" I always advise them to put their money aside and learn how to do deals without money. Honestly, $100k doesn't go very far when buying homes and if you are relying upon the cash that you have, you will quickly find yourself without any and unable to do anymore deals until something sells. Being able to do deals with no money is a major plus and having cash to fall back on builds even more confidence.

Today, I'm in a different position then I was when I started. Rather then "nothing down" I do deals with no debt today. I won't discuss Debt Free Investing in this course, but you can learn more about it at *www.lifeonaire.com*. Even though you can purchase a home without spending any of your own money, this doesn't mean that you can make a profit on the home without investing any additional money. Soon after you purchase the home, you will begin receiving bills in the mail within a month for many different things—taxes, insurance, utilities, mortgage payments, water and sewer bills, etc. Like it or not, owning property, even vacant property, costs money, and even if you buy homes with nothing down, you must be prepared to cover these holding expenses. Furthermore, if you are renovating the home, you will have even more costs including deposits for contractors and advertising costs. You must have a source for the working capital needed to hold and possibly renovate a property. This source can be your own bank account or, if you want your deal to truly be "nothing down," you must find someone else willing to fund these holding costs. Whichever you choose, you should be sure of your source for working capital before you buy an investment property.

IS "FLIPPING" ILLEGAL?

"Flipping" has become a bad word in the real estate investing world, though it doesn't need to be. Due to the negative connotations created by the media, I don't recommend that you go around telling people that you flip homes for a living. However, I do recommend that you do it right and be proud of what you do. I want to encourage you to do things the right way. You don't need to join the ranks of the deceitful. There is a lot of money to be made honestly and ethically.

Sadly, there are many investors who have done the wrong things. Their judgment becomes clouded by the potential to make a lot of money that they cheat, deceive, manipulate and bribe. Unfortunately, these investors have made life difficult for many others. However, despite their bad acts, they still haven't made flipping illegal.

First, both subjects of this course, wholesaling and retailing, have been called "flipping" by investors and non-investors. So, when you are speaking with someone about flipping, it is important to determine whether they are talking about wholesaling or retailing. Second, neither of these practices is illegal.

WHOLESALING

You will hear some people say that "assigning" contracts is illegal. The contention of those who make this claim is that the investor is acting as a broker and taking a "net listing" which means the broker's fee is not a set amount or percentage but rather equivalent to any sales proceeds generated over and above a certain dollar figure to which the seller and broker agree upfront. For example, if the seller and the broker agree that the seller will accept $200,000 for the property, then the broker will receive anything above $200,000 as commission.

A broker who takes a net listing is particularly similar to a wholesaler who signs a contract to purchase a property for a set price. The broker's commission and the wholesaler's profit are both equivalent to the difference between the final sales price and the price the seller has agreed to accept. However, there is one startling difference. The broker has not signed an agreement to purchase the property and is not obligated in any way to purchase the property. The wholesaler, on the other hand, has signed a contract to purchase. This contract provides the wholesaler with an "equitable" or ownership interest in the property and gives them the right to sell this interest for whatever profit they choose.

An argument could be made that if the wholesaler has no intention of settling the deal unless they find a buyer, then the wholesaler has relinquished their equitable interest and is, in fact, just a broker. I do not advocate this type of wholesaling in any way, shape or form unless the wholesaler's intentions are fully disclosed to the seller. In other words, unless the seller is fully aware that the wholesaler's purchase is contingent upon the wholesaler's finding a buyer, a wholesaler should always intend to settle on their deals one way or another and this is the only approach which will be taught in this course.

RETAILING

Buying a house, fixing it up, and reselling it for a profit is not illegal. To my knowledge, it never has been, and I doubt it ever will be. Adding value to a product is at the core of our nation's economy and retailing homes is just one aspect of that economy.

When the media calls flipping illegal, they are referring to the deals where investors, mortgage brokers and appraisers have individually or collectively defrauded lenders and buyers by doing things such as:

- Giving funds to buyers and writing phony gift letters to meet lender's criteria
- Generating a fraudulent appraisal on the house
- Falsifying the information on a buyer's application for financing such as credit information, rental history or job/income history
- Creating second mortgages that the seller has no intentions of collecting
- Over financing properties and having the seller give monies back to the buyer without notifying the lender.

Basically, their goal is to lie and manufacture whatever information is necessary to obtain financing for a buyer and sell them a house.

Unless you plan to make money by committing fraud, you will not be breaking any laws by buying, renovating and reselling a house.

ETHICAL REHABBING

When I rehab homes, I like to do them "right." I don't cut corners or hide things that should be fixed and if you strive to be an ethical investor, neither should you. If I encounter something that could be costly, I always explore all of my options as long as the final result will provide my customer, the homeowner, with a quality product. Though I'm not opposed to finding the cheapest way to get things done, I want the job done properly rather than just covering up defects, which should really be fixed.

Fixing homes properly can be difficult to do sometimes, especially if you are rehabbing on a shoestring budget. However, you can sleep well at night knowing that you've virtually eliminated any risk of a lawsuit from an angry homeowner and created a good name for yourself in the community to boot. As with settling your deals, this type of reputation can go a long way, particularly if you are focused on rehabbing homes in a particular area.

For those who know the types of rehabs that I do today, don't get caught up in thinking that you have to do full blown gut rehabs to do them right—It's just my preference. Basically, if you know there is a leaky pipe in a wall, but no one can see it, fix it anyway.

REAL LIFE EXPERIENCE

My first rehab and resell was a situation where I wanted to wholesale the home but couldn't find a buyer. The general consensus among the investors was that it needed too much work. So I took on the renovation project myself and hired a crew. I made the rest of the deal work by using a hard money lender to fund the purchase and partner to foot the rehab bill. In the end, I provided a decent home to a buyer and made a respectable profit. I was able to honor my contract and do as I had promised.

Not that long ago I sold a property to someone for $55k through an auction. While he was working on his finances, I found out that he was using a mortgage broker I had bad experiences with in the past. I advised the buyer to go to one of my lenders, but he continued to work with this shady mortgage broker. After months of not settling, he finally told me that they were ready to settle the deal. The buyer then told me that he needed to talk to me about some changes that we needed to make to the deal. I sat back and listened as he told me that we were going to have to raise the price of the home and I was going to have to take back a second mortgage and then I would have to forgive it at the settlement table. I told him he is talking to the wrong seller, that it is fraud and that I would have no part of it. He begged me to do it and it would have closed the deal but I refused. So he said he would work it out and I was then told that settlement was going to take place and that everything had been worked out. I was asking for a HUD 1, but no one would provide me with it.

I showed up for settlement and looked at the HUD 1. The sales price was bumped up to $65k and the title company had a contract, which was cut and pasted that had my signature on a $65k contract. There was a second mortgage reflected on the HUD 1 and the buyer was then telling me that we were just going to rip it up. I told him that if I was going to do the deal, the second mortgage was not going to be ripped up, but I was going to collect on it or I was going to foreclose on the home. I told him that I was upset with them trying to pull the wool over my eyes and that I was going to turn his mortgage broker in. The title company immediately took my side. I do believe he knew the whole time what was going on, but when he saw that I knew what I was doing he backed down very quickly and was advising the buyer to back off. I don't believe that the buyer really knew what was going on. He was instructed by the mortgage broker to do this. The buyer ended up walking away from the settlement table because I refused to budge. They expected me to pay his closing costs and tear up a second, which left me walking with over $4000 less then what I was supposed to walk with. In the end, it was wrong and I wasn't going to do it.

CHAPTER 3

ADVANTAGES AND DISADVANTAGES OF WHOLESALING AND REHABBING

ADVANTAGES AND DISADVANTAGES

Neither wholesaling nor rehabbing is a job in which you have to report to someone else, however they do involve work—sometimes, hard work. And if you choose to do either on a full-time basis, they are both something that you will have to do regularly to make a living. While you do not have to work forty hours per week, more than likely you will. However, you will set your own schedule, perform the majority of work at home and see your free time increase as you learn to integrate personal and work-related business. In short, you'll be working because you enjoy it. You'll also be able to decide whether or not you wish to hire employees to manage.

Other advantages include learning volumes about the business, learning of opportunities in your local market and you earn a very good income in the process. They can both be used as a stepping-stone to help put together a rental portfolio that will enable you to generate a lifetime of passive income. There is little to no risk involved as a wholesaler or rehabber if you buy properties at the right price and you do it on a part-time basis. You also control how much money you make per deal and the number of deals you do. Another advantage is that unlike an automobile salesman or an insurance agent, you don't need to be a fantastic salesperson to make good money—a good deal is a good deal.

As a side note, when rehabbing, I would recommend that you find a reasonably good professional real estate agent to sell your properties. If your homes are done well and priced right, then they will be able to sell themselves. Selling properties is a lot of work and very time consuming. Realtors are well worth the commissions that you have to pay them. A professional realtor will make selling much easier.

Some disadvantages to wholesaling and rehabbing are a lack of passive income. You only get paid if you wholesale or renovate and sell properties. If you want to take a vacation for a few months, you will not have any income for those few months. Also, the market is constantly changing, particularly in a hot area, and you need to keep abreast of those changes by tracking sales prices and talking to other investors. You don't want to have a lot of inventory in a rapidly rising market and get caught when the market turns.

WHOLESALING PROS AND CONS

The major advantage to wholesaling is that you have the opportunity to accumulate cash quickly. I have worked 10 minutes on a deal to make $1,000 and 15 hours on a deal to make $7,000. It used to take me 50 hours per week at a job for two and a half months, or about 500 hours, to make the same $7,000. My best wholesale deal to date consumed about 2 hours of my time and netted me $65,000.

Another attraction of wholesaling is that it requires little to no cash. In fact, as a birddogger, you need zero cash but still have an opportunity to begin generating money immediately. As a wholesaler, you need minimal working capital for items such as earnest money deposits and advertising, yet still far less than a rehabber beginning a project.

Disadvantages unique to wholesaling include the following. First, there is the risk of not always being able to wholesale a property and therefore will end up rehabbing it to rent or resell. Second, it takes some time to learn the market in order to be a full-time wholesaler. Mainly don't expect to be able to go full-time overnight.

Now, I will admit that I started full-time overnight; however, I took the time to educate myself while I was still employed. Even so, by not finding another job, I placed an extraordinary amount of pressure on myself to perform. If I didn't succeed, I wouldn't have been able to eat or pay my mortgage, plain and simple. Worse yet, I would have had to go get another job to pay my bills and the thought of that disgusted me. To be honest, I think this drove me more than anything else. At any rate, I recommend that you do some serious soul-searching before going full-time overnight like I did. Only you can know when the time is right for you to make your move, bearing in mind that the "perfect" opportunity will probably never present itself and you may need to create it.

The advantages to wholesaling outnumber the disadvantages by a fair margin and in my opinion, I think wholesaling or perhaps birddogging is the best way for someone with little resources to get their start in the business. Birddogging is how I began the business. Birddogging is simply finding deals for another investor and getting paid to do so.

REHABBING PROS AND CONS

In the above paragraphs, I discuss how wholesaling is a job which requires a lot of time and effort. Rehabbing can be different. If you use contractors rather than completing the work yourself, then rehabbing is a lot less labor-intensive than wholesaling. It can be much easier to get started in investing as a part-time rehabber than as a part-time wholesaler. With the judicious use of contractors, your role is to simply manage your rehab project, something which can be done on a part-time basis assuming you find good people to work for you.

Another major advantage that rehabbing has over wholesaling is that you can make much more money per deal. Though I have had bad rehabs that have only generated a $5,000 profit, my average rehab nets me about $40,000 and my best rehabs have made me in excess of $70,000. On average, with one crew, my turnaround time for a rehab is roughly 5 months from the day I purchase the home to the day I sell it, averaging about six sales per year. Some of my deals have run 3 months from start to finish, while my longest was 11 months. Today, I rarely have a deal last more than 6 months and most are bought and sold within 5 months. Finally, while you do need money for working capital, you can start rehabbing using other people's money whether they are lenders or partners in your project.

As with wholesaling, rehabbing does have its disadvantages. First, you are not always able to estimate repairs accurately and may end up spending more on the renovation due to hidden problems like clogged sewer lines, burst water lines or extensive termite damage, or the desire to do more than what is necessary. However, if your numbers are right you will be able to absorb the unanticipated and still make a profit. Second, as opposed to bird dogging or wholesaling which require little or no money, completing a rehab project requires some working capital to pay for mortgage payments, insurance, utilities, property taxes, appraisals, advertising and deposits for contractors to buy materials. Third, unlike other forms of investing, a rehab is a project. Without oversight and organization, it can run over time and over budget. And fourth, it takes some time to put some cash in the bank before you have the working capital to support yourself as a full-time rehabber. Don't expect to be able to go full-time overnight unless you have enough cash in the bank to support you and your family through the initial trial and error phase of your business. For a while, a beginning rehabber only has money going out and must wait for a payday.

Like wholesaling, the overall advantages to rehabbing outnumber the disadvantages by a fair margin. Personally, I think rehabbing is one of the best ways for people who have good jobs or people who have money to get their start. Though the quick dollars offered by wholesaling are appealing, I sometimes recommend that these folks start by rehabbing as opposed to wholesaling since rehabbing requires less time and can generate substantial profits by putting your money to work for you.

EVOLUTION FROM WHOLESALER / REHABBER TO INVESTOR

Right or wrong, I don't really consider a wholesaler to be a real estate investor in the true sense of the word. Webster's primary definition of an investor is "one who uses money, by purchase or expenditure, in opportunities with the potential for profit." This coincides with my personal opinion, that an investor is someone who creates, purchases or otherwise procures assets that generate a passive income.

With regard to rehabbers, I have mixed emotions. While I don't consider a wholesaler to be an investor in the true sense of the word, if a rehabber is using their own cash to purchase and renovate homes, then by all means they are investors. A rehabber can also leverage their funds by using someone else's funds. Despite these possibilities, even a rehabber using his own cash doesn't fit my personal definition of a true real estate investor—someone who buys and holds for passive income.

Personally, I see myself as more of a real estate "dealer" when I'm wholesaling or rehabbing. It is my rental properties that make me feel like an investor. After all, a car dealership does the same thing with cars as I do with real estate and yet they don't call themselves "car investors."

Yet, some may say that wholesalers and rehabbers are most certainly investors since they invest their time into learning and running their business. In any case, the goal of either wholesaler or rehabber should be to use the knowledge they acquire along with the healthy income they generate to become an investor who uses their assets to generate a passive income.

Through wholesaling and rehabbing, my goal has always been to generate enough active income, which, when reinvested, would generate enough passive income to support my monthly expenses, therefore making myself financially free. This is something that I believe is worthwhile for everyone to pursue in one way or another. Therefore, I believe it is important for me to make the distinction to you between a real estate dealer who generates active income and a real estate investor who reaps the benefits of passive income.

CHAPTER 4

HOW TO GET STARTED

Proverbs 14:23 — All hard work brings a profit, but mere talk leads only to poverty.

GETTING STARTED REQUIRES A basic education. You need to learn about your neighborhoods, the investment climate, your local investors and the mechanics of a deal. Educating yourself is the only way to gain this knowledge. Many people say that they don't have time to learn the basics. I can assure you that most investors, myself included, didn't have a lot of free time when they first started learning about real estate, but we all made the time to learn. I knew that I couldn't afford not to learn, so I had to pay with other resources such as my time.

I frequently see people enter the game of investing prematurely. They locate a great deal and feel compelled to act immediately because they are afraid of losing the "deal of a lifetime." In reality, there's always another deal and it's fine to pass on one until you know what you're doing. Don't let your fears or someone else push you into investing before you're ready. I'll admit that some people analyze too much and never do anything, but you must spend time learning real estate terms, how to use forms, how to estimate repairs and how to construct offers.

I've also discovered that most successful investors are people who were willing to make sacrifices to become successful. I'll go over this in more detail later in the book, but in terms of my personal experience, my sacrifices involved staying up late every night reading, listening to real estate CD's while I was driving (including CD's I created by reading out loud and recording myself), and spending my free time studying real estate and investing.

To make more time, I slept less, forgot about television and had lunch trading thoughts with other investors or maybe picking the brain of a Realtor. Oftentimes, I sacrificed my lunch hour altogether and met with attorneys, mortgage brokers, and other real estate professionals. I still set aside time to learn about new techniques and grow in my knowledge of the subject. Nothing works without putting in the effort.

People will go to college for four years to get a degree in a particular field, yet often people think they can read one book from the bookstore and be ready to invest in real estate. It's an easy way to make a lot of money, but it is also an easy way to lose a lot of money. Get educated before you start, or the cost will be monumentally more.

HOW TO GET STARTED — WHOLESALING

There are really two ways to get started in making money by finding bargain properties for other investors, as a Bird Dog or as a Wholesaler.

BIRD DOGGING VS. WHOLESALING

Being a Bird Dog simply means that you work to find properties for an experienced investor. There is no risk because you are never signing contracts. You simply find the property, line up the seller with the investor and get paid if they do the deal. It doesn't get any simpler than that.

Sometimes, Bird Dogs—usually the better and more successful Bird Dogs—also negotiate the price with the seller before involving their investor, though in many cases, Bird Dogs aren't required to do so. Of those Bird Dogs who do negotiate the price, many advance to the level of Wholesaler and begin earning more money. In the last year or so, I've seen people just become full time bird dogs. They play the part of a wholesaler, but they never put anything under contract and collect fees from the buyer, the seller and sometimes both.

The downside of being a Bird Dog is that you don't receive as much money as if you wholesale the property yourself. For this reason, bird dogging gets a bad rap from many investors. However, I praise it. As a Bird Dog, you need absolutely no money or credit to get started in real estate and you risk nothing. The only investment you make is your time. I have and will pay bird dogs $10k or more for the right deals.

HOW I GOT STARTED — WHOLESALING

Being a Bird Dog is how I got started. I acquired the rest of the tools that I couldn't learn from experience in a course or book. By being a Bird Dog, I had a risk-free opportunity to learn the market, how to determine good homes from bad homes, how much to pay for homes, how to estimate repairs, how to negotiate, what areas to buy in, what attorneys to use, where to get the money, etc.

Much of the education that you will receive will be tailored to the specific area where you invest. This is one of the main advantages of bird dogging, as no book or course can cover the ins and outs of every neighborhood across the country. What I've done in Baltimore, MD will be different then what is done in Macon, GA. You can't use my title company in Texas. My hard money lenders won't lend in Delaware or any other state outside of Maryland. Repairs in my area may cost more than in other parts of the country. Home values can vary greatly by neighborhood so formulas for determining what to pay for a home can change within an investing area.

As a Bird Dog, I made $1,000 per deal. I did seven of these deals in the first two months. During those two months, I acquired a little money and enough knowledge to become a Wholesaler. Being a Wholesaler may or may not require risk on your part. This is determined by how you are acquiring properties. The primary advantage to being a Wholesaler over a Bird Dog is that you have an opportunity to make much more money per deal. My profits as a Wholesaler have ranged from nothing to $65,000 per deal. The longer I do this, the higher my average profit per deal climbs. Currently, I average about $15,000 profit per deal.

You may find out that being a Wholesaler is not the place to start simply because there can be some risk and some money required on your part. However, being a Bird Dog for a while will help you to overcome these obstacles. The good news is that it can be done.

BIRD DOGGING WITH THE RIGHT INVESTOR

First, find a seasoned investor who does volume. If you deal with a rehabber who only does one or two rehabs per year, then your market exposure is minimal. In my area alone, there are 100's of investors who do twenty or more deals annually. These are the types of people to shadow. They buy two deals per month on average, and if they had a good bird dogger, they might be able to do a third or fourth deal a month. At the very least, they can use your help acquiring two deals per month.

In addition to looking for an investor who does a lot of rehabbing, your prospective mentor needs a track record. You don't want to waste time with someone who has a goal of two houses per month but is struggles to do one every two or three months. Some investors tend to exaggerate when discussing their activities. After speaking a prospect, you'll find that their numbers are inflated and that they did two rehabs, not three, and made $10,000 instead of $30,000.

Unfortunately, newer investors frequently get wrapped up dealing with other newer investors to Bird Dog for them. You want to work for a real investor, someone who can teach you the ropes and be your mentor.

WHEN TO GO FULL-TIME

Going full time as a Wholesaler is a major decision to make. While it's possible to make the same in two weeks at investing as two months of working, it may take several months to make the first deal, especially part time. After your first deal, it may take more time to trade wholesale properties on a consistent basis.

On a positive note, the deals become easier after getting the first under your belt. The more deals you do, the bigger your buyers list will be, the more neighborhoods you will know, the more private lenders you will encounter and the better salesperson and negotiator you will become. In addition, you will have more offers accepted as you become more proficient at identifying good deals. In short, becoming a full-fledged Wholesaler is a learning process, which depends on the time dedicated to learning the business and the amount of relationships, and credibility that you are able to establish with buyers, private lenders and real estate agents who specialize in foreclosure properties.

MY EXPERIENCE

I personally switched to a full-time Wholesaler without making a deal but it was occasionally very stressful and challenging. I placed myself in a "do or die" situation and took my lumps. But I kept moving forward and never questioned my decision to leave my old job. In fact, I shut that door so tight that I had no choice but to move forward just to survive. Your personal circumstances will dictate whether or not you are ready to go full-time. Overall, If you are working a job that is paying the bills and you are able to complete a deal each month, then most likely you will be able to double or triple your production if you become a full-time Wholesaler. The main idea is make sure you are ready to perform before taking the plunge.

HOW TO GET STARTED — REHABBING

There are several keys to being a successful project manager, therefore a successful Rehabber.

1. Have your contractors lined up and ready to go the day you purchase a home. Shopping for contractors and prices after settlement can easily waste a month or two—time you don't want to waste considering holding costs (including mortgage payment, property taxes, insurance and utilities) will range from $400 to $1,000 or more per month. Holding costs less than $400 per month may indicate that you are renovating a home in an area that is hard to sell. Network with contractors and assess levels of professionalism and experience and ask how much to install/replace a typical kitchen, bath, roof, window, heating system, siding, carpet, etc. Once you have a house under contract, use the time before settlement to get bids on the various repairs from these contractors.

2. Find a good real estate agent. They will be a crucial member of your team and, if you haven't already met a competent agent during the course of your networking before you buy a house, work to find one while your rehab is underway.

3. Find a good mortgage broker. This person will pre-qualify potential buyers for your property which come to you or

your agent. If you don't run across a competent broker before you purchase, work to find one during rehab.

4. Learn how to estimate repairs properly. For me, the difference between a good rehab and a bad rehab always goes back to my estimation of repairs. If I underestimated my repairs, I paid too much for the property and didn't borrow enough from my lender to do the job right and do it quickly. This lack of funding resulted in lower profits as the project dragged on, my holding costs ate up my profits until I could make the money somewhere else to get the home completed. Also, I didn't have the money to renovate the home as I would have liked and had to compromise on my sales price to make the sale.

5. Finally, be organized. As your project progresses, there will be a lot of paperwork. Have a central place, even if it's just a notepad, to store names and phone numbers of contractors, potential buyers, settlement attorneys, real estate agents, mortgage brokers, etc. Have a folder to keep letters to and from other parties as well as your personal notes regarding your project. Have another folder for all receipts and invoices related to your project. Have a third folder containing everything related to the settlement when you bought the property. Have a fourth folder containing everything related to the settlement and sale of the property, including listing agreements, ad copy, and any other correspondence you might have with the buyers, or real estate agents involved. I like using the expandable type folders for my properties so that everything is in one place.

Note: I'm not a very technical person and many people utilize different software packages to accomplish the same thing.

I'd like to end this section with a word of warning. A rehab that spins out of control can require a lot of money out of pocket over time. If you are not prepared or if you are not careful, your three to four month project can easily extend to a year or more with your holding costs taking a big bite out of your profits. However, with the proper level of planning, you should be fine. If you do get stuck holding a property longer than you anticipated, don't sweat it. If you've bought the property at the right price, you'll still make money and you can take comfort in the fact that projects have spun out of control for the best of us at one time or another. Make it up next time.

ADVANTAGES OF STARTING PART-TIME

Rehabbing properties on a small scale does not need to be a full-time job to be effective. You can do two or three rehabs per year on a part-time basis and make a very nice supplemental income ($30,000-$75,000). The key is to have a responsible contractor working for you with whom you check in regularly. There are part timers who make in excess of $50,000 per deal; sometimes they make $100,000 and more.

Another issue with part-time rehabs is financing. Holding a salaried job will broaden the scope of lenders and financial partners willing to fund your deals. Many private lenders look solely to the property for loan security, but there are those who seek full-time employees, particularly if you lack credit or experience as a Rehabber. Steady income is an additional security to make the mortgage payment each month. Many lenders look at the whole picture and it helps to include a full-time position.

Another advantage to part-time rehabbing is that your full-time paycheck will provide a safety net for you in case problems arise. The news that the furnace, which looked adequate upon your initial inspection, will, in fact, need to be replaced to the tune of $1600 is a lot easier to take when you're expecting a regular paycheck.

BIRD DOGGING VS. REHABBING

Unlike Bird Dogging, rehabbing may or may not require some risk. This depends on location and payments. The primary advantage to being a Rehabber over a Bird Dog is that you have an opportunity to make more money per deal. My profits as a Rehabber have ranged from

$5,000 to $70,000 per deal. The longer I do this, the higher my average profit per deal climbs. Currently, I average $40,000 profit per deal.

With wholesaling, you may find out that being a Rehabber is not the place to start because there can be risk and money required on your part. However, being a temporary Bird Dog will help you overcome these obstacles and it's a great way for someone with limited funds and experience to get started in real estate.

WHEN TO GO FULL-TIME

While it can be very profitable, being a full-time Rehabber may take a whole year to complete a first deal from searching for to closing a deal. Though this is not meant to scare you, I do want to point out that it takes time to research your market, locate properties, find good contractors and line up financing. Even the best planned projects can run over time and over budget.

Like wholesaling, it becomes easier after the first deal. Completing more deals means a longer list of reliable contractors as well as more neighborhoods and more private lenders. In addition, you will get more offers accepted as you become more knowledgeable about your local market. In short, becoming a Rehabber is a learning process that depends on dedication to learn the business as well as relationships and credibility. As with wholesaling, your personal circumstances will dictate whether or not you are ready to go full-time.

HOW I GOT STARTED — REHABBING

My first ventures into rehabbing came as a result of failed wholesale deals. My partner at the time didn't want to settle for $2,000 wholesaling the property. We bought the home and I did the renovations myself. With no prior experience rehabbing homes, I learned a lot about the process of renovating a house and discovered the work is actually pretty easy. However, I also learned that rehabbing is very time-consuming and someone more experienced could complete the job in a quarter of the time it took me. It didn't cost as much as I thought it would to rehab the home, especially the kitchen. I imagined that kitchen renovations would cost tens of thousands of dollars but I renovated this particular kitchen for under $1,500.

TO INC. OR NOT TO INC.

Many beginners spend too much time determining whether or not they should incorporate. I'm neither an attorney nor an accountant, so I don't like to give detailed advice in this area but I will say that anyone who invests in real estate in his or her personal name is crazy. I urge everyone to seek some form of corporate shelter and I recommend speaking with an attorney and an accountant to find out the best way to structure your venture. This is a business and in addition to shielding yourself and your family from personal liability, you'll want to take advantage of the tax benefits of owning your own business.

Sometimes, the cost of forming a business can be prohibitive for the beginning investor depending on your state. However, even if forming a business and incorporating isn't a costly process, I would suggest that you first focus on generating leads and locating deals. Once you have established that you can locate deals and make money as a rehabber, then you can proceed through the time and expense of starting a company.

EDUCATE YOURSELF QUICKLY

While locating a first deal, educate yourself on the process and expense of forming a business to know how much money it will take for you or your attorney to form some type of business entity to protect your family's assets. After all, you want liability protection from day one get your entity formed so you will not be caught flat-footed in the event you meet the seller that needs to settle ASAP.

You should also determine whether or not your lender, if you are using one to purchase your properties, requires you to hold the property in your personal name. Most private lenders do not care if the property is held by a trust or business entity. Most banks, however, will want you to hold a property in your personal name to have a residential loan. Once you begin to seek financing for a property held by a business entity, they will turn you over to their commercial lending department, where the LTV, interest rate, points and terms are often dramatically different, usually more conservative for the bank in nature.

Personally, if faced with the decision of purchasing a property in my personal name without any liability protection so I could obtain a residential bank loan versus purchasing a property in my company and using a commercial bank loan or private lender, I would buy the home and not worry about the entity. This is especially true if it were a resell property. Many people own properties in their personal names, but if you are uncomfortable, consult with an attorney.

Finally, with regard to choosing the best entity for tax purposes, do not be overwhelmed with this. Get out and do some deals. Unless you are already financially independent, don't worry about the tax consequences of investing and don't be concerned about using the tax benefits of a corporation to shelter your income. Prove you can make money. In the end, if you must pay a few more dollars in taxes than necessary, then I see that as good news. It means that you made money and that you didn't let opportunities slip away while you were trying to arrange everything perfectly to minimize your tax bill. If you are writing large tax checks it means that you are making a lot of money and that's the goal.

FORMING YOUR BUSINESS

After sealing a few deals, feel free to express your needs to a competent attorney and accountant, preferably those used by successful investors and ideally those who personally invest in real estate. Remember that even the best accountants and attorneys hold different opinions on certain issues.

This wide variety of opinions can make the process confusing, but your goal is not to find the perfect tax strategy. As time passes, accounting rules, tax laws and your financial strategy will all change. The key is to find a competent attorney and accountant with whom you feel comfortable. Be sure they have good references and a track record of success.

In addition to providing legal tax avoidance and protection from personal liability, establishing a company will give you credibility, provided that you follow through on all of your commitments. People will recognize your name and feel more comfortable dealing with you than with someone who is starting out.

I will not give any legal advice in this course, though I will tell you that I have chosen to operate my business as an LLC along with another entity that is a corporation. This structure allows me to make the most of tax savings while providing me with protection from personal liability.

PLAN OF ACTION

The first thing to do when contemplating a career in real estate investing is to take a personal inventory of your resources. Be totally honest with yourself and evaluate your strong points.

> You can get free resources at *www.lifeonaire.com* to help with this process. I highly recommend reading my book Lifeonaire.

REAL LIFE EXPERIENCE — BIRD DOGGING

As I mentioned before, I began as a Bird Dog. My first few deals were found for a specific investor. Our agreement was that he would pay me $1,000 for each home that I found and he bought. I stayed on top of the market by checking a dozen homes a day and bringing cheap leads to the investor. In most cases, he made an offer and signed the contract. He cut me a check as soon as the offer was accepted. We did seven of these deals over two months and I put a little money in the bank, found a hard money lender and became comfortable submitting my own offers. The first deal that I wholesaled on my own the following month netted me $7,000. Within eight weeks I had made $14,000. Within my first 3 months, I had made $23,000 as a beginner. There is nothing special about me, you can do it also!.

I highly suggest that every beginner start out as a Bird Dog. Don't worry about how much the investor is profiting from the deals that you bring to them. Whatever their profit, it is far outweighed by the invaluable education you'll receive as a Bird Dog. You will learn and make money at the same time. Working as a Bird Dog for a seasoned investor can cut years off your learning curve and help you find contacts, gain experience and earn money. Knowledge is the most valuable thing you can pick up in this business.

REAL LIFE EXPERIENCE — REHAB & "PRE-SELLING"

My second rehab was a deal that I couldn't wholesale. It needed quite a bit of work so people were shying away from it. With regard to the numbers, I purchased it for $46,000, spent $15,000 in repairs and sold it for $84,900 to make a profit of approximately $6,000 in cash plus a second mortgage in the amount of $11,250. The rest of the money (approximately $7,000) was used to pay holding and closing costs. Many other investors and several other courses always recommend pre-selling homes. I sold this home rather quickly, long before the renovation was done, which was a huge mistake.

My buyers would stop by the job every day and give the rehab crew a hard time. At the time, I didn't know what to do to keep them away.

I was afraid I would blow the deal if I confronted them, so I just let it go. Finally, my contractor called me ranting and raving about the wall being torn down in the living room. Since I had never planned to tear down any walls, I had no idea what he was talking about.

I went to the home to see what was happening and found that a wall had been demolished and now exposed the chimney that ran from the furnace in the basement to the roof. After contacting my buyer to let him know that someone had vandalized the home, I discovered that he had torn out the wall with the intention of turning the chimney into a fireplace. I was completely shocked and at a loss for words. I told him that he should have contacted me before making this decision.

This lack of forcefulness on my part created more work for me. Several days later I received another call from the contractor saying that the siding on the front of the home had been ripped off. The buyer realized that there was wooden clapboard siding under the aluminum siding and decided to start ripping the aluminum down. At this point, I lost it. I was furious. We still hadn't fixed his mess on the inside and his loan was going bad, so he wasn't going to be able to buy the home. Basically, he was sending me backwards. I took the deal away from the buyer and he threatened to sue, but I told him he would surely lose in court and I would get my money out of him. He dropped the issue immediately.

The deal went bust, causing me to sell the house to someone else. When all was said and done, it cost me about $2,500 to fix the damage that he had inflicted. This rehab taught me never to allow the buyers to be involved in the project. Though I did do more pre-selling after I sold this rehab, I wouldn't allow the buyers anywhere near the project until they were complete. I showed future buyers other completed projects, using them as "model" homes, and explained what renovations we were going to do to their prospective home. Today, I use a Realtor to market my homes and no longer need to begin selling them until they are completely renovated. Hopefully, you will all learn a lesson from my mistakes. Keep your buyers away from your renovations in progress!

CHAPTER 5

NEIGHBORHOODS

DECIDING WHERE TO INVEST takes time to research, especially if you are not familiar with your market. You will discover neighborhoods that you never knew existed. When I began, I wanted to invest in the nice properties in nice areas. I searched high and low for properties in my immediate surroundings and neighboring areas. Hundreds of homes later, I had no luck and it became discouraging. I did come across homes in $140,000 neighborhoods that could be bought for about $120,000 and I thought they were great deals. Today, I do not even consider these deals.

To help determine areas near your home to buy, I came up with a Neighborhood Scale (found on page 54). This scale is a pictorial that ranks the different neighborhoods in the Baltimore area from the war zones (Zone 1) to the mega rich communities (Zone 8). There are opportunities all over the scale, though I will say it is more difficult to make money at the ends of the spectrum. You will want to concentrate your efforts somewhere in the middle. Find these areas in your community, educate yourself and determine how to best make money. They will provide you with your greatest success.

When referring to the Neighborhood Scale, keep in mind that different styles of homes can be found within a particular zone and the pictures are only meant as a guide. When determining good and bad neighborhoods, consider the quality of the schools (usually the number one determining factor), accessibility to major roads as well as transportation, shopping, cultural facilities, jobs and quality of housing stock. The best neighborhoods show pride of ownership. Neighbors take good care of their homes and keep the streets clean. The streets are quiet and teenagers are not congregating on the corners. Crime is low, income is usually higher and there is a general sense of peace.

NEIGHBORHOOD SCALE — MEGA WEALTHY

Homes in wealthy neighborhoods are in demand and are maintained very well, so finding a distress sale is tough but not impossible. I found a home in one of Baltimore's most desirable neighborhoods that was a total wreck, but surrounded by homes that retailed for $500,000 and up. This home was listed at $125k so I pursued and offered $75k. I figured that the property needed $250-300k worth of work to be in the same league as it's neighbors. Unfortunately, it was sold to another buyer for $100k. (*Note: this same home sold three years later for $1,050,000.*) Deals do exist in the high-end neighborhoods. They come along infrequently, but if you are lucky enough to get one, the profit potential could literally net you in excess of $100k per deal.

NEIGHBORHOOD SCALE — WAR ZONES

On the lower end of the spectrum in the war zones (zone 1), it is very easy to find homes cheap. In fact, you can get people to literally give you homes in the war zones where some sellers are desperate enough to pay you to take the property. Needless to say, these properties are not always worth pursuing. Even if someone gives you a property, you have to pay taxes and you are responsible for upkeep as well as municipal bills, maintenance and safety issues.

It is very difficult to unload a property in these areas and downright crazy to consider renovating a home in zone 1 or 2. You should renovate homes in areas where homeowners want to live. If people are willing to live there and own there, than others will be willing to buy. Unless you have experienced investor who deal in war zones, then I would recommend you stay out of them. It is much easier to sell a home in a good neighborhood than to give away a home in a war zone.

Finally, please keep in mind that many investors tend to live in zones 5, 6, 7 or even 8. They tend to become very comfortable in their neighborhoods and view zones 3 and 4 as "bad areas." This is not the case. These may be lower income areas, but they are not necessarily "bad areas."

Often, those who live in zones 5 or higher think that zone 3 is a war zone. They have been sheltered and don't realize that just because people make less and live modestly, that doesn't mean they live in bad neighborhoods. War zones are unsafe and down right scary. Some think zone 3 is unsafe but it's just a matter of perspective.

REAL WORLD EXPERIENCE

I have bought many homes for $1,000. They weren't always in the best of areas but some were in decent areas. Frequently, students come to me saying they can't buy homes for $1,000 where they live. So I ask them if they've ever offered $1,000 for a home. Their response is always, "No," and I tell them that they won't ever buy a home for $1,000 if they never offer $1,000 for a home.

Now to the real story—I once bought a home for $1,000 in a war zone. I couldn't wholesale the home, so I decided to sell it at auction to get rid of it. In the end, I lost $750. Though the sale price at auction was $2,000, by the time I paid auction fees and closing costs, I suffered a loss. Even with the cheapest homes, you can lose money.

TARGET AREAS — GENERAL CHARACTERISTICS

Target areas are neighborhoods to concentrate your efforts. Typically, they fall between 3 and 6 on the Neighborhood Scale and exhibit the following characteristics:

1. Blue and white collar, working class demographics.
2. Thirty or more years old, having been around long enough to have properties with deferred maintenance.
3. Property values in the ideal price range for your town or city. A range that is usually slightly below the average selling price of homes in your area. Here in Baltimore, where the average price of homes in the area is approximately $350,000+, I recommend targeting homes that have retail values in the $200,000 to $350,000 price range.
4. Established property values.

Whether you are wholesaling or retailing, it is easier to sell a home in a neighborhood with stable sales. Investors, for instance, will pay more for a home that has several valid comparable sales within a three-block radius than they will for a home that has one suspicious comparable sale in a three-block radius. Generally, I look

for comparable sales, which involve one homeowner selling to another. Investors tend to push the high-end value when selling and foreclosure sales transferring a property from a homeowner to a bank are useless. Similarly, I disregard sales transferring a foreclosure to a homeowner since they often reflect some sort of discount.

I've seen several beginners pay too much because they did not check the legitimacy of their comps. They used a comp where HUD bought back a home for the original mortgage amount plus legal fees, back interest and auction fees. This recorded transfer usually reflects a price substantially higher than the market value of the property, but because the sale is not investigated, they just assume that it is recorded and a legitimate comp when it's not.

IT'S A WAR ZONE...OR IS IT?

Study the neighborhood scale and relate it to your local area. Some of us consider neighborhoods that only rank as a 3 or 4 on the scale as a war zone, but truthfully, these are not war zones. They are areas that many investors (rehabbers or landlords) prefer, and they fall within your ideal range for wholesale deals. As an investor, you can choose to disregard the 3 and 4 areas and only deal in the better neighborhoods, but you would be leaving a great number of deals on the table.

If wholesaling is your primary method of investing, you should become familiar with the lower zones on the scale. These areas provide you with the most opportunities and better your chances of making a deal. While there are deals in the 5 and above zones, the competition is higher and includes homeowners who are willing to outbid investors, which is less likely in lower zone areas.

Finally, I'd like to note that unless you live in a major metropolitan area, you probably don't have an area comparable to the war zones in the bigger cities. Many people who have never been exposed to a war zone believe that a zone 3 neighborhood qualifies because they don't have a true benchmark. Their perception of a war zone might be the one pretty rough street of a smaller city, but this doesn't truthfully compare to those in metropolitan area where they continue block after block.

Neighborhood Scale	
Zone 1	**Zone 5**
War zones, Many board ups. Trash. No pride of ownership. People will give you homes in these areas.	You begin to see much pride. There are few renters but they also take care of the homes and the yards. Good rehab area.
Zone 2	**Zone 6**
Fringe of the war zones. Many homes available in these areas. Usually too close to the war zone to attract homeowners. Mostly rentals.	Hard to come by renters in these areas. Rentals usually command top dollar. Tough to find fixer uppers but worth it when you can.
Zone 3	**Zone 7**
Mix of renters and owners. You begin to see pride. Lower income home buyers will buy here. Most of your rehab and resell opportunities will be here.	Very hard to find fixer uppers. The residents here can usually afford to take care of their homes. Retail buyers will pay top $ for fixer uppers.

Zone 4		Zone 8	
Mostly home-owners but some rentals. Good first time buyer neighborhoods. Pride is evident. Greet rehab potential.		Deals are almost impossible to find. Most never will find one.	

The gray zones are HOT zones. This is where you should search for opportunities.

MY TARGET NEIGHBORHOODS AS A REHABBER

As a wholesaler, I have bought properties in zones 2-6 and sold them to landlords (zones 2-4) and rehabbers (zones 3-6). As a rehabber, my strategy differs. Whenever I consider buying a house and putting money into it, I am much more concerned about the marketability of the neighborhood. Personal preference leads me to look for my opportunities in zones 4 through 6.

If I'm having trouble finding homes in these areas, I will drop down to zone 3 where I can buy homes at will and pick up something to have a project in action. Of course, I still prefer a better area, but I will settle for a property in zone 3 if the purchase price is low enough that I can still achieve my target profit despite over-improving to make it the nicest home in the area. In sum, I prefer to buy in zones 4 to 6, but I do purchase profitable opportunities in zone 3.

This is my strategy, but there are rehabbers out there who deal primarily in zones 3 and 4 and do very well. They are experts at dealing with these neighborhoods and clientele. As an investor, you will have to decide where to focus your efforts. Zones 3 and 4 have more opportunities, but zones 5 and 6 contain better neighborhoods. I prefer zones 5 and 6, but sometimes find myself mostly in zones 3 and 4 due to a lack of opportunities in 5 and 6.

If you can be patient and wait for deals in zones 5 and 6, they tend to be more profitable so you can complete fewer deals per year and make a good living. But don't get stuck trying to get a deal in the upper zones when you are starting out. Go to the lower zones where your odds of getting a deal where the numbers work are better if you are having trouble finding something to buy.

KNOW YOUR NEIGHBORHOODS

As with anything, the key to success in these neighborhoods is education. Talk to other investors and landlords in your area and get to know which neighborhoods they like and which they don't. Use this information to buy homes and don't worry if you haven't memorized your entire city. I discover new neighborhoods all the time, and so will you. Learn one section of your city at a time and go from there.

It's a good idea to identify neighborhoods in your local area that fit into all the different categories on the scale. Once you think you've identified a neighborhood that fits each category, go into the war zone number 1 and then drive directly to the number 2 neighborhood. Take notes and ask yourself, how bad does the number 2 neighborhood look compared to what you just left? Then travel to the number 3 neighborhood. At this point, you may feel you are in a pretty good area.

The purpose of the exercise is to observe the quality of the neighborhoods and gain perspective. People who live in the war zone think that zone 2 is a really good area, zone 3 is an excellent neighborhood, and zone 4 is an upscale place to live. Most of your deals as a rehabber are going to be done in areas 3-6. Talk to the people who live in these areas. They can tell you a whole lot of what is going on in most instances. If you find a police officer patrolling the area, stop and talk to them to learn information about the community.

CHOOSING A TARGET AREA

Once you've done a little bit of research and are prepared to choose a target area, there are a number of factors for you to consider.

1. Your target area should have neighborhoods in the middle of the scale, ranking anywhere from 3 to 6. It doesn't have to contain each of these types of neighborhoods, but it should contain one or more of them.

2. Choose a target area as near your home. This will drastically cut down driving time when looking at homes. There is nothing wrong with travel, but if you decide to make this a full time business, having your target area one hour away is doable but it can be a drag at times.

3. Limit the size of your target area. Find a few good neighborhoods to concentrate your efforts rather than spreading yourself too thin. Many investors make a great living farming a small area. They become experts and are well known enough to make all of their money in a small radius. I chose another route getting started. I know people who have done as well as I have or better and all of their homes were within walking distance of their home. The smaller the hunting grounds, the less time you will spend in your car and the more efficient you will become at identifying opportunites and locating resources. You will get to know the area and people (other investors, title attorneys, contractors, insurance agents, mortgage brokers, other team members, and the public at large) will get to know you. Before long, you will be made aware of deals before anyone else ever knows of them, simply because you are a presence within the area. You will not be able to establish this presence if you are spread too thin.

Having a smaller target area also allows for a greater understanding of market values, urban areas can change block to block and it is imperative that you understand these nuances. You will know how well homes sell in an area and the types of people looking to buy there. You will become familiar with market rents and aware of typical problems such as sewer line blockages or termites.

Once you have learned an area inside and out, you can consider expanding into others. Until then, be careful not to take on too much too soon. Ideally, you should be able to get to your target area in thirty minutes and avoid areas too far away.

AM I IN THE RIGHT PLACE?

As you evaluate neighborhoods and look at properties, you should be able to stand in front of a home and visualize who will live there. If you are scouting for a rehab project to sell, but find yourself at a property best suited for low income tenants, you may want to find a different neighborhood. On the other hand, if the property is in a homeowner neighborhood and the end user will likely be a family, then you are probably in the ideal neighborhood to buy homes for rehabbing.

TYPES OF HOMES TO LOOK FOR

Homes come in all different shapes, sizes, colors, and styles. Therefore, it is important to determine what types of homes are attractive to your end users whether you are a wholesaler selling to landlords and rehabbers or a rehabber selling to homeowners.

THE TRUE REHAB CANDIDATE

Many beginners can't identify a "real fixer upper." This is one of the biggest hurdles for beginners to overcome. The homes that I inspect and determine in good shape are homes that some beginners feel are beyond repair and ready for the bulldozer. Homes that need new paint and a good carpet cleaning are in super condition and usually not a prospective purchase for me.

I look for homes with holes in the roof that allow the sun and rain free access to the home, floors that are warped, ceilings caved in, basements with 2 feet of water, a stench that will knock you over from twenty feet away, broken windows, trashed kitchens, holes in the walls, graffiti everywhere, and/or commodes that are stopped up and overflowing. These are the homes you should be seeking if you are looking for motivated sellers. I can assure you that the owners of these homes don't want them.

PROPERTY REQUIREMENTS OF A REHABBER

Every so often, I run into fixer uppers that I could buy really cheap in areas where homes were selling for good money. Upon further investigation, I discover that the only reason the home is so cheap is that no investor wanted it. Even after it was fixed up, the style of the home, the layout of the floor plan, or some other quirky thing was going to keep retail buyers away. As a wholesaler or a rehabber, you need to be conscious of the fact that you need to find homes that you can sell, the types of homes that your buyers are seeking. They won't purchase homes that don't fit this profile and neither should you.

There are minor advantages and disadvantages to certain homes and the purpose of this section is to point out those qualities that make a home more attractive to your buyers. Keep in mind that even the least attractive homes can be a good deal at the right price. Don't get too hung up on the items outlined below. The most important thing is whether or not you are buying a home for the right price and a cheap price overcomes many obstacles.

1. Safe Neighborhood: You will have a hard time selling to a rehabber or a homeowner if there are boarded up homes on the same block.
2. Established Neighborhood Property Values: From the wholesaler's perspective, it is possible to sell homes in less stable homeowner neighborhoods, but rehabbers will be more conservative when estimating the after repaired value

of the house so your selling price as a wholesaler will be less than usual. Also, it is possible for rehabbers to sell homes in less stable homeowner neighborhoods, but it is harder to get top dollar. If homebuyers can spend a little more, most will choose to live in a more stable homeowner neighborhood versus buying your home.

3. Three Bedrooms or More: Buyers do purchase two-bedroom houses but it is easier to sale homes with three or more bedrooms.

4. Functional Layout: The layout of the home should provide enough space for the homeowner to use everything comfortably. If not, you are going to have a hard time making a sale.

5. Parking: People desire a place to park their car when they return home from work, something that can be difficult on a narrow side street or busy main street.

Besides essentials, there are qualities that should make you avoid a house altogether. Examples include a screwy floor plan (walk-through bedrooms offering no privacy (unless they can be made private), bathrooms off of kitchens, bedrooms directly off of living rooms), kitchens in the basement that can't be easily relocated to the first floor, extremely narrow bathrooms that can't be enlarged or rearranged, one or more low-quality amateur additions, low ceilings that can't be raised, sloping ceilings that make half of a room unusable, houses that are located on an alley, houses that are located among commercial buildings, or huge houses that need a ton of work, unless they are in an area where the values justify the effort. There are areas in Baltimore where the renovation cost exceeds values after repair. Remember, if you can buy for the right price, these issues can be fixed. Don't allow a screwy floor plan in a $400k area that can be bought for $200k deter you.

Be careful with homes that are different from everything else in the neighborhood. I frequently find homes in a decent subdivision that are small, obsolete-looking shacks. The rest of the homes in the neighborhood may be worth $200k or so, but such eyesores might not get $100k on their best day. When you encounter these types of quirky houses, be very conservative when estimating their value and very particular about the types of properties that you use for comps.

A final rule for rehab candidates is to stay away from totally dilapidated houses. Even though you are in the business of fixing homes for profit, try to deal with rehabs where the basic structure is intact as opposed to a "Money Pit." Again, if the home can be bought cheap enough to either tear down and rebuild or to do all necessary repairs, then these homes can be worth buying. Don't get into a dilapidated home without having enough extra cash built into your rehab costs to still make a hefty profit. I always look to buy such properties for less then the value of the land. I would also recommend that you avoid such homes as a beginner unless you have a construction background. I was not capable, nor qualified to take on such large rehabs when I first got started. Through work and experience, I am now able to take on "total gut" rehabs and completely redo everything that needs to be done.

REHABBER REQUIREMENTS AND PERSONAL EXPERIENCE

Personally, I prefer to deal with smaller homes built after the 1950's with at least three bedrooms. To date, my experience with older homes has been more expensive to renovate. Construction standards were not as good before the 1950's and older homes usually have more problems, especially the kind that you can't see. As a result, the cost of renovating seems to be astronomical. I have taken a beating on two homes that I renovated which were over ninety years old. They both had a lot of unexpected damage, particularly structural, and I watched my expected profits of $20,000 per home plummet to roughly $5,000 with much of the profits consumed by holding costs since the homes took so long to renovate. Experienced investors know that older homes pose more problems and will tend to stay away unless they are getting the homes incredibly cheap. I still occasionally rehab older homes but I've learned to be more careful due to the complexity of older homes.

Wholesale or retail, beware of older homes and other undesirable properties, such as homes with a lot of "amateur additions." I have bought a couple of homes where the additions were obviously done by the homeowner, where the work showed no professionalism. Assuming it to be another fix, I found myself to be wrong in this assumption. All of the additions created a lack of flow to the floor plan. Bedrooms were attached to living rooms. Bathrooms were attached to kitchens. I even had one home with a sunroom ceiling that sloped from 8 feet to 5 feet in height making half the space unusable. I will no longer buy such houses unless I am getting them so cheap that I can tear down the whole home and rebuild or at least demolish the additions and rebuild correctly.

Please keep in mind that these are just my preferences and not golden rules. You may find it extremely profitable to pursue something that I would not pursue. Study your market and find the opportunities.

TARGETING RENTAL NEIGHBORHOODS AS A WHOLESALER

For the wholesaler, there are deals in the neighborhoods that rank as a 2 on the scale. Typically, these are primarily rental areas on the fringe of the war zone. If you are a beginner, you should probably treat these neighborhoods as a secondary source until you gain more experience. If you decide to look for properties here, keep in mind that most landlords prefer cosmetic repairs than a total rehab. They want to start receiving income as soon as possible with minimal cash out-of-pocket.

Furthermore, since these are primarily rental areas, if you can't wholesale a property, your worst case tends to be fixing a property and finding a tenant. If this is the case, you may still profit by selling the property to a landlord after it is repaired. Many people would like to own rental property but don't want to go through the trouble of repairing one. "Turn key" rentals are attractive to many prospective landlords. Many rehabbers make a living just renovating, renting and reselling.

PROPERTY REQUIREMENTS OF A LANDLORD

If you begin as a wholesaler and have made the jump to rehabbing, you will most likely continue to find homes in rental neighborhoods. Naturally, you will want to keep homes that you would have normally sold to rehabbers (unless you are overwhelmed), but continue to wholesale properties destined to become rentals.

Landlords tend to be a little less picky than rehabbers when it comes to buying property, especially if they are focused on long-term units. They might not mind a few board-ups on the block (as long as they aren't next to the property they are buying) or a quirky feature such as a walk-through bedroom. Landlords are mainly looking for properties that don't require a whole lot of work for rentable conditions, which allows them to start generating cash flow where people want to live (maybe a 2, 3 or 4 on the Neighborhood Scale but not a total war zone). The bigger the positive cash flow, the better.

The best way to determine types of properties and areas that landlords prefer is to talk to the landlords and investors in your town or city. Ask about areas and property characteristics that they avoid or seek and then act accordingly.

Some areas are referred to as "rental areas." This can have a positive connotation for investors, but a negative connotation for homeowners. A landlord may see a rental area as a lower income area where the homes are reasonably priced and there is an opportunity for positive cash flow. Amongst homeowners, a rental area usually means lower income, run down or crime ridden. Many rental properties in these areas pull down property values because the pride of ownership does not exist.

SAFETY DURING NEIGHBORHOOD INSPECTION

Always keep safety in mind when looking at homes. If you are going into an unfamiliar neighborhood for the first time, you may feel more comfortable taking a partner. If you ever catch yourself in a neighborhood that scares you, keep your car moving and make a mental note not to look at homes in that neighborhood again.

Remain alert when investigating vacant homes. When entering the home, be sure to take a flashlight and a cell phone and watch your step. I've inspected some run down, dilapidated properties where I gingerly walked through, keeping an eye on the stability of the flooring and stairways. Be aware that, particularly in urban properties where the front and back doors aren't boarded, locked or nailed shut and/or the first floor windows are open, homeless people and stray animals may be calling the place home. If you see that a property is not secure, you may not even want to enter. Just assume that the property needs everything and move on. Additional safety measures include mace or pepper spray in case you run into a stray animal or leaving a list of the homes that you are going to visit that day with someone you know.

Keep in mind that none of this is meant to scare you. I've been in lots of homes and never had any trouble, but it's best to always be prepared. Use common sense, be careful, and remember that if you ever feel uncomfortable, exit the home or area as soon as possible. Your well-being is more important than finding a deal.

WILL THIS WORK WHERE I LIVE?

Many people question whether or not they can wholesale or renovate in their town or city. It is possible to wholesale or renovate property anywhere. That is not to say, however, that I would be able to turn as many properties per year in Clarksville, VA as I do in Baltimore, MD. The question becomes, "How many deals or how much volume can I do in an area within a given period of time," and the answer to this question will vary with your individual circumstances. However, if you did live in small town like Clarksville, you can still succeed in investing. Follow these steps to master your area:

1. Dig deeper to find sellers and obtain more intimate knowledge about your sellers. In Baltimore, I can scan the MLS for my deals where others cannot.

2. Consider wholesaling or renovating other types of real estate in addition to single-family homes, like commercial, multi-unit residential, mobile homes, raw land, or even small businesses.
3. Market potential deals to out-of-town investors who think it is tough to find deals in the city they live in, so they pursue your area because they feel that the grass is greener.

The concept of finding a bargain and collecting a profit for finding a buyer or rehabbing the property is the same regardless of the area it is practiced or the type of real estate that is transferred. What you make of this idea, with or without the help of this course, is up to you. Having said that, I do want to reiterate my opinion that striving to close quality deals is more important than striving to close a specific number of deals.

REAL LIFE EXPERIENCE — PROS OF SMALLER TARGET AREA

Focusing on particular neighborhoods has allowed me to really learn the ins and outs of these areas. I once purchased a home and had to replace the sewer line two weeks after a tenant moved in. Afterwards, I purchased another home on the same street and had to replace the sewer line there as well. My contractor determined that the original builder had used a very cheap product for their sewer lines and that most of the ones on the street are collapsing. Now, I automatically include a new sewer line when I'm deciding what to offer on other homes in this neighborhood.

Another example of knowing a neighborhood involves a situation where I purchased a home without a basement. Including this house, I had purchased six homes in the same neighborhood. Four had basements and two did not. Both of the homes without basements were infested with termites and I had to complete major rebuilding to the structure. The area was very close to water and the ground was continuously damp. Without anything between the floor joists and the ground, they were very susceptible to those little wood-eating creatures. Now I know to stay away from homes without basements in this particular neighborhood.

REAL LIFE EXPERIENCE — FINDING MY FIRST DEAL

When I first started looking for investment properties, I lived in a county northwest of Baltimore City. The county was fairly affluent and I had trouble locating deals, so I started traveling further to find properties. My travels eventually brought me to Baltimore City and its neighborhoods. At times, I was traveling an hour and a half each way just to view a property. In the beginning, the traveling seemed necessary. After looking at hundreds of properties, I viewed a FSBO (For Sale By Owner).

The property was in a decent neighborhood, around 4 on the Neighborhood Scale, but the complex was surrounded by a neighborhood that would have been a 5. I wasn't sure what the home was worth and my method of determining value was to inspect other homes for sale in the area, which I now know is the wrong method. The seller of the FSBO was asking $70,000, which seemed like a fair price since I didn't know the value of the neighboring homes. So I began to construct an offer, using my cell phone to call the numbers on other "For Sale" signs in the neighborhood.

On my first call, I got a Realtor by the name of Rob on the phone and asked the selling price of the property. He told me that the house was listed at $64,900, but that it was just reduced to $45,000. I thought, "WHOA! This is a hot deal."

"When can I see it?" I asked.

"Do you have the time this afternoon?" said Rob.

"I sure do."

"How about 3:00?"

"I'll see you then," I said enthusiastically.

It was only around noon at the time, so I grabbed some lunch and came back to the home. I sat out front for three hours waiting for Rob to show up and rehearsed over and over what I was going to say. I wanted to come across as an experienced investor. I didn't want anyone else getting the house before me. I really don't know what I would have done if someone else had come to see it while I was waiting, but the thought of telling them that I was buying the home and it was no longer available did cross my mind. No one else ever stopped to investigate and Rob arrived a few minutes after three. I was nervous as I got out of my car. "Hi, Rob?" is what I said as I reached out to shake his hand.

"Yes," replied Rob as he shook my hand and gave me his card with the other.

"Steve Cook," I said as I reached for his card.

Rob began telling me about the property as he tugged at the screen door. It was really stuck so he had to use both hands to pull it open. Then he retrieved the key for the front door from his pocket and opened it. "Whew!" was Rob's reaction as the door opened. I peered into the house and was shocked.

There was no carpeting on the floor, the walls were all different colors from pink to green to orange to yellow and blue. The house stunk to high heaven. Rob said, "They had a lot of pets." I tried to take everything in stride, but I was disgusted. I couldn't believe that I wasted so much time waiting to get into this dump. Though somewhat dismayed, I left open with Rob the possibility that I might still purchase the house.

The next morning, I had breakfast with a friend of mine who I had met at the local investment club meeting. I told him about the property and he told me to make an offer. My reaction was, "No way. The place is a dump," and went on to explain all of the work that was needed. He had a contracting background and said with confidence, "So it will take about $7,000 to fix it up. Make an offer."

I decided to take my friend's advice and make an offer figuring they would not accept. I offered $36,000 in cash with a $200 earnest money deposit and settlement in 90 days, writing it up with a contract I had bought from an office supply store. There was really no reason to offer $36,000, but it just seemed like a fair number based upon a drive-by appraisal of the property. Rob provided me with the estimated value after repairs of $64,900. I wasn't sure what the comparable sales were, so I took this appraisal at face value and made an offer without using any sort of formula. I thought they would turn it down, which was the outcome I preferred.

A couple of days later I received a call from Rob. He said, "The bank counter offered at $38,000." "Bank? What bank?", I thought, not knowing a bank owned the home. I was actually relieved that they didn't accept my offer but counter offered instead. If they would have accepted, I would have been scared to death. Out of fear, I told Rob, "I'll have to pass. I can't pay that much for the home." Rob sounded dejected, but it made me feel good to pass on a deal.

Later that week, I had breakfast with the contractor again and told him what took place. He told me that I better go buy or he would. At that point, I thought there was no way I was going to let this deal slip away. So I explained to him my fears, including the fact that I didn't have the money to close the deal. My friend told me that he would partner with me if I wanted to buy the house, so I agreed to do it. I called Rob back and said, "Rob, is the property at 4 Chardon Court still available?"

Rob replied, "Yes it is."

I boldly pronounced, "I've given it some thought and I think I'll take it."

"Great!" Rob said with a nervous enthusiasm and we set up a time to wrap up all the paperwork. When Rob and I got together, I discovered that not only did the bank counteroffer on my price, but they also wanted me to take the property "as-is" without an inspection and settle in 30 days. Nor were they happy with the form of my contract and wanted more money for a deposit. Fear rushed over me again. I called my friend who walked me through the situation.

I explained how our standard procedure was to have at least 60 days to close and that we never put more then $200 earnest money deposit down on a home. Rob called in another Realtor by the name of Jim, who ended up being the actual listing agent for the property; Rob his assistant. Jim called up the bank and negotiated the terms right then and there. The bank accepted and I signed the contract.

I was excited and scared, but I had a job to do. I had an opportunity to assign my contract for $2,000, my friend dissuaded me from making "only $2,000." As a result, I would end up rehabbing the home, living there for a year, and then selling it. Looking back, I should have taken the $2,000. Until you have the financial capacity to take on a rehab or the opportunity to wholesale a house, take the money and run.

REAL LIFE EXPERIENCE — WAR ZONES

One time, I decided to experiment on a Neighborhood Scale 2 in my area. I bought a number of houses really cheap (less than $5,000) in areas where some would consider to be not the fringe of the war zone but the war zone itself. I did know that I wouldn't go into these areas at night, but I knew that there were investors who bought there so I figured, "What the heck? I'll give it a shot."

Out of 10 homes that I bought for under $5000, I could only wholesale 5 homes. Nobody was interested in buying the homes from me. I could wholesale homes that I buy for $50,000 and up much easier than cheap ones. The moral of the story; stay away from the really bad areas.

CHAPTER 6

RENOVATION QUALITY AND STYLE

THE END USER AS well as the characteristics and appeal of the neighborhood will determine rehab for a particular property. Unlike a wholesaler, a rehabber must have an idea of the end buyer and how the quality and customs of the neighborhood will affect the quality and style of the renovation.

PICTURING YOUR END USERS — HOMEBUYERS

Envisioning the end buyer is a two-step process. First, try to picture the age, marital status and family size of who may buy your house. For instance, if you have a small two-bedroom ranch, it is very likely that you will have an older couple or a very young couple with a small child interested. With this information, look around the neighborhood to determine the demographics and preferences for renovation.

The demographics will affect your renovation because the functionality of the home needs to be appealing to your potential buyer. I used to stand on the front steps of a home, look around and try to visualize who would call this place home. If I pictured a young bachelor, then my renovation would be different than a family with children. A young bachelor might want a clubroom with a wet bar whereas the family might use the club room as a play area. A bachelor may not mind steps and limited parking while an older couple would not be interested in steps and a mother with children wouldn't want to park too far from the door.

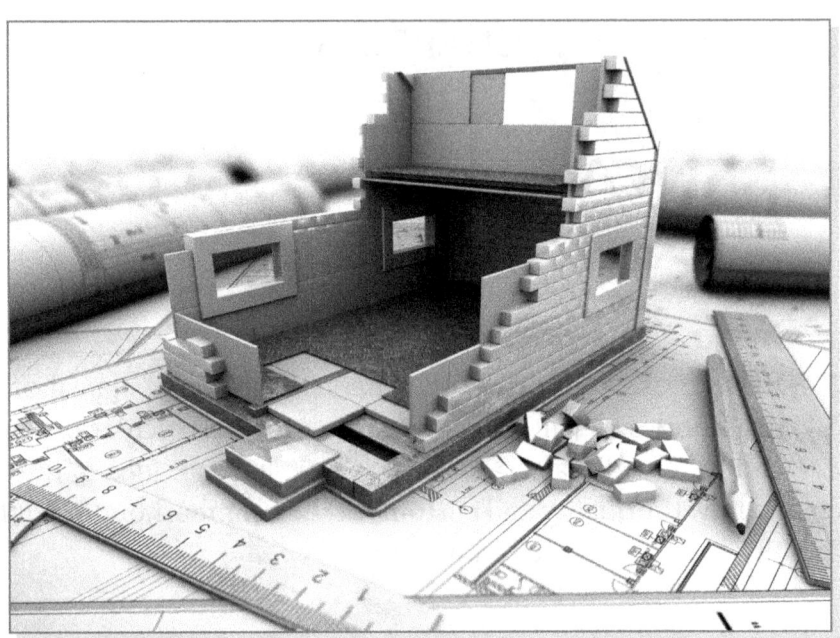

DETERMINING NEIGHBORHOOD PREFERENCES

The preferences of the neighborhood may also affect the renovation. Some neighborhoods feature hardwood floors while others prefer wall-to-wall carpeting. Some like bright, even fluorescent colors while others prefer more modest, dark color schemes. Figuring preferences out isn't always easy. Sometimes you just have to learn this as you go. If all else fails and you feel clueless, go with a neutral décor throughout your rehab. However, try to uncover the preferences of a neighborhood and your potential buyers if possible.

I was once renovating a home that I had presold. It had a basement with unappealing dark paneling. I thought I was doing the home justice by ripping it out, re-sheetrocking the basement and brightening it up by painting it off-white. When the crew began the demolition, my new homebuyer visited and put an immediate stop to it. She demanded that they leave the paneling and I knew at that point that my tastes were different and I should try to learn the differences from neighborhood to neighborhood.

DETERMINING THE QUALITY OF RENOVATION REQUIRED

The "level" of renovation you intend to do and the desirability of the neighborhood impact the necessary repairs for a particular property. These, in turn, determine what should be repaired, replaced, or left alone. There are three general "levels" of rehabbing—low, middle and high-end. Each has a different end-user in mind and each requires a different approach.

LOW-END, BUT NOT LOW QUALITY

A low-end rehab is something I would do to a rental property. My rentals are good, but they are plain vanilla. I don't provide the tenant with anything more than what is necessary. I don't put in the best of everything and I don't replace things that are functional. If the front door works well, I leave it alone rather than replacing it as I do on all the homes that I renovate for resale. I would never do the work to my rental properties that I do to homes that I'm going to resell for top dollar.

HIGH-END REHABBING

A high-end rehab is something an investor does in a hot area. There are two areas near the water in Baltimore where townhomes are selling for $300k-$500k or more. In these instances, an investor will gut the entire home, leaving a shell, and build a brand new home with a lot of high-end amenities. Such a renovation can cost as much as $150,000.

Personally, I operate somewhere in the middle. If I'm going to resell a home, I replace just about everything, just not with the most expensive Italian marble or granite countertops. I always go with a beautiful front door that has decorative glass as a form of high quality, medium-grade material. They show extremely well, are inexpensive and create a great first impression for potential buyers.

NEIGHBORHOODS IMPACT THE QUALITY OF YOUR REHAB

During renovations, the neighborhood plays a role in my decision regarding how much I should or shouldn't do. For instance, if you are working in an area that is becoming "yuppified," then you will need to complete a high quality renovation that will appeal to this type of buyer. Conversely, if you are working in low-income areas, the same type of renovations will not be necessary.

STANDARD AREAS

With a home in a less desirable neighborhood, I will do an extensive renovation, replacing everything, but being careful not to over-improve. On the other hand, with a home in a better neighborhood, I may not spend as much. Let me explain.

I spend more in a less desirable neighborhood to create a reason to move to that neighborhood to a fantastic house. Alternatively, with a home in a better area, many homebuyers are more interested in the location than a house where everything is perfect. Therefore, if I buy a decent home in a good neighborhood, I will do a lighter rehab and only fix what absolutely needs to be done. For example, if the kitchen is in fair shape, then I won't install a completely new one.

HOT AREAS

There is an area in Baltimore where you need to expose bare brick walls, lay or refinish hardwood floors, install granite counter tops, construct rooftop decks and provide stainless steel appliances. To cut corners in any of these areas would be the kiss of death in achieving a successful sale. These same items would throw you over budget in another neighborhood, but they are absolutely essential here.

In a really good neighborhood, it is harder to buy a home at a deep discount, so I have to cut back on the cost of my rehab in order to make a profit. I realize that doing less in the hottest neighborhoods in town is acceptable, but this does not include the "yuppified" areas, more the stable areas where everyone wants to live. Buyers are buying the neighborhood and not the home. The area is hot and there are few homes on the market so people are fighting to live there. Therefore, provided that a home is livable and safe, cosmetically rehabbed homes sell very quickly for close to retail value. In fact, the buyers of these homes often prefer to get a home that needs some work so that they can do it the way that they want it. In a really hot area, I'm not necessarily looking to make my renovation the nicest home in the neighborhood as I still make a good profit by just doing the basics: cleaning, painting, installing new carpet, etc. These people are buying the location, not the home.

Of course, this all depends upon the condition of the existing home. I tend to gravitate toward the homes that need the most work in the low-end areas. This allows me to do large rehabs because I can buy them cheap enough to afford to rehab the entire home. While I do spend more, I don't buy top of the line items for my low-end rehabs and I don't necessarily spend more financially, but I do more of the little things. I have found that doing only a cosmetic rehab in a lower end neighborhood makes it much more difficult to sell a home, where in a high-end neighborhood, cosmetics make it quite easy.

CATERING TO A SPECIFIC BUYER

I no longer presell homes. Instead, I wait until my rehabs are complete before I market them because I don't want to do custom jobs for "pre-qualified" people who may or may not be able to buy the home. I go forward with my renovations and take the demographics and preferences of the neighborhood into consideration, trying to appeal to the tastes of the masses.

I spend a lot on my renovations today and eliminate the need to cater to one buyer. I prefer to buy homes in really bad shape and redo them from top to bottom. Once finished, my totally renovated homes usually sell at top dollar within a short period of time to buyers with good credit.

KNOW THE MINDSET OF HARRY AND HARRIET HOMEBUYER

When people are looking for a home, their thought process usually goes one of two ways. Either they are buying the area with less emphasis on the home or buying the home with less emphasis on the area. If you are renovating a home in a very desirable neighborhood, then you don't need to make it the nicest home on the block. The neighborhood will sell itself. If you are in a good homeowner neighborhood but not a "hot area," then you need to bring your renovation up to a level where the home sells itself. To reiterate, the neighborhood affects the quality of your renovation.

If they could afford to do so, most homebuyers would almost always choose to buy in a more upscale area. In reality, their current income only takes them so far and they begin to look for the nicest home in their price range. More often than not, you are going to be renovating homes in places where people are buying the nicest home they can afford despite the area. For this reason, you should provide them with a home they want since you can't give them the area.

As a result of the Harry and Harriet Homebuyer mentality, I like to make my homes the nicest in the neighborhood. By doing so, I command top dollar for my homes, achieve quick sales and usually multiple offers. I also make an area more appealing to a buyer by giving them a better home. You would be surprised at the exceptions people make for a really nice home.

SELLING WITH EASY TERMS

Selling with easy terms has an effect on the quality required for your renovation. If you are going to offer your end user terms such as owner financing and/or a lease option ("rent-to-own"), you can do almost nothing to your rehab and find someone to buy it from you. Personally, I have gotten away from that end of the business. Though my intent was to sell my homes, I was unsuccessful with the majority of "Rent to Own" customers that I had. In addition, it was very discouraging to totally renovate a home and put someone in it under a rent-to-own program only to get the same home back in a year needing renovations. Now the home that I had just renovated to be a very nice home in an average neighborhood was just an average home in an average neighborhood. Reselling it was tough unless I went with another rent-to-own buyer.

Though I prefer not to use the "rent to own" method to sell my homes and don't recommend it to you, it works well for some people and it is a very good marketing technique in areas where real estate sales are slow. If you think you like the "rent to own" method, you should go into it with the attitude that you are a landlord rather than someone selling homes. If your homes sell, then great, but if they don't, then you are a landlord without any dashed hopes or expectations.

CHAPTER 7

BUILDING YOUR TEAM

Proverbs 15:22 — Plans fail for lack of counsel, but with many advisers they succeed.

ONE OF THE MOST crucial aspects of achieving and maintaining success as a real estate investor is assembling the right team. When it comes to investing, no man is an island. It is absolutely necessary to work with others. I'm not suggesting partners, just business relationships with people who can help you as you help them, like an attorney/title company, a Realtor, a mortgage broker, hard money lenders (private lenders), accountants, contractors, other investors, banks, advertisers, supply companies, etc. Try going it alone and you won't get anywhere. Build a team of professionals and it will pay you dividends for many years.

If you choose to rehab properties, having a stable of good contractors is going to be extremely important. Your job as the operator becomes much easier once you have good contractors on board. Personally, I have used contractors from both ends of the spectrum, from the most reasonably priced to the most expensive. Some crews were diligent while others took two weeks to install a screen door. I discovered that I usually got what paid for, so I came up with two lessons:

First, don't be stingy. Second, don't just sign the first contractor that walks in off the street. Spend some time evaluating various contractors before you hire just anyone.

EMPLOYEES V. SELF-EMPLOYED

While it's true that you could choose to hire employees to perform some of these tasks, I prefer to avoid hiring employees. Instead, I have put together a team of self-employed professionals who don't need me to train them. I like to find independent people who bring something to the table. Hopefully, they will be able to teach me something that will allow me to run my business more smoothly.

So right from the start, you should look at your team as a machine with yourself as the operator of the machine. As operator, it is your job to get the right pieces in place and make sure that each piece functions properly. When one part breaks down, you need to fix or replace it. After you are finally finished building your machine to satisfaction, you will be amazed at how easy this business can be when everyone does their job.

LOCATING TEAM MEMBERS

In assembling your team, you're going to have to meet a lot of people, ask a lot of questions, get a lot of referrals and make a lot of choices. However, don't assume that everyone who claims to know real estate will be able to help you. Hungry professionals have an "I'll figure it out as I go" attitude and won't admit their shortcomings. This isn't good for you or your wallet, as it will cost you dearly if you don't get "experienced" professionals on your team.

Not every attorney who claims to be a real estate attorney can help you. The best way to find the best team is to find out who other experienced investors use. Don't be afraid to take this very important step and ask everyone you know that is already in the business. As you meet other investors and their team members, simply ask who they use for accounting, appraisals, plumbing, etc. They may not always tell you, but if they do, it just saved you a lot of time.

You will be surprised to find out how helpful most people will and after a while, you will hear certain names over and over again. These are the people you want on your team. There is a reason why so many investors use the same title company, go to the same banks or use the same HVAC contractor. They have identified a good source. If someone else has already done the legwork for you, be sure to use it. If the team member is good enough for other experienced investors, they should be good enough for you, especially when you are starting out.

Despite how carefully you may select your team, you don't know everything, especially when you're starting out, and what sounds good when you interview a team member today may change in six months. As a result, you may have to change your team as time passes, but don't let this discourage you. Consider it part of your learning process and move on. I have learned to trust my gut and I'd advise you to do the same. If you are talking with someone and your gut tells you "No," continue the search until you find someone else.

RECRUIT LIKE-MINDED PEOPLE

Choose people on your team that have similar values and goals. Even though your team members may achieve their goals with different vehicles, everyone on the team should share common beliefs on honesty, ethics, integrity and a desire for win/win situations. For example, if you want to produce top quality renovations, you can't work with contractors that cut corners.

I made a conscious decision to run my business with the highest level of morals and values and I expect everyone I work with to do the same. You can't always decipher someone's values during your first visit and you may occasionally bring an undesirable member onto your team. When investing in real estate, there is a lot of money involved. Sometimes, money makes people do foolish things.

If one member of your team falters, you can always find someone new. After two and a half years I am still building my team and it gets better whenever I let someone go to make a new addition.

SPREAD THE WEALTH

It is common for many investors to expect Realtors or contractors to work for less if they become regular customers. I do not advocate this. Your team will become the lifeblood of your business. Your relationships will grow to a point where they can perform tasks without your interaction. Everyone should be compensated fairly for their services for a long, business partnership.

For example, I do not recommend asking your Realtor to list your houses for less money or trying to beat your contractors out of a few hundred dollars. If they do a good job for you, pay accordingly. If they get paid, they will continue to want to work for you. If you start paying the members of your team less, they aren't going to want to work for you and they will give their time to the clients who pay the most.

If your attitude is to always pay people less and expect them to do more because you are a "regular," you will find yourself constantly looking for new team players. It amazes me when I see investors who make $20,000+ per deal but want their entire team to split 10-20 percent. They begin to resent you and just stop working for you.

Alternatively, I prefer to put $10,000 in my pocket for doing nothing while allowing my team to have $10,000 for doing most of the work. But, when I pay my team members more per deal, I also make more money. My team takes care of everything and gives me the time to put more deals together than I would be able to complete if I were beating them up trying to save every penny. I don't have to worry about anything. I find the homes and show up at settlement when the house sells to pick up my check. Of course I have to do a few other things, but for the most part I do very little. My team handles most everything for me and they get paid well. If I tried to keep all of the profits I would be working much harder and constantly looking for new team members, which is the opposite of my win/win situation.

I see investors who use different contractors, switch Realtors and hop from one attorney to another. All of this is time-consuming, unnecessary and very inefficient. With the right team in place, your business will run much more smoothly. The opportunity cost of finding and training new people is much greater than just paying a regular team member what they deserve for a job well done. In short, pay your team what they are worth. The less the team changes, the better off you will be.

I truly believe in spreading the wealth. The more deals I do, the more I pay my team members. They get better, my deals get better, and I do less. Everyone just runs with their part of the job and my end is minimal. I check on my team once in a while, but primarily, I give everyone freedom to do their part.

BE FAIR TO ALL

Proverbs 11:25 — A generous man will prosper; he who refreshes others will himself be refreshed.

Be fair to all of your team members in areas beyond compensation. One of your main considerations should be your team member's time. Don't expect them to do a whole lot for you without receiving anything in return and don't expect them to work nights or weekends if you prefer to have those times off. Ask for favors here and there, but keeping someone on call too much and you will be looking for replacements over and over.

ALWAYS LOOK FOR NEW PLAYERS

I can come up with three good reasons as to why you should always be on the lookout for new and better players.

1. Your team may not always stay intact. People move, change careers or just decide they don't want to do it anymore.

2. You may want to increase the size of your team so that you can do more deals. This applies primarily to rehabbers, but if things are going smoothly with your current team, you may want to assemble another contracting crew so that you can do two renovations at once with relative ease.

3. You want to be able to refer good people to other investors. Giving referrals has always been something that I have done. I've given many more referrals than I have gotten, but when I do need one, someone is always willing to refer a good person to me. Other investors tend to go out of their way to help me when I need it. Plus, as a wholesaler, the buyers that I've helped through referrals return to me more often to buy properties.

REAL LIFE EXPERIENCE

When I find a good team member, I usually offer them incentives. The following story serves as a good example:

Getting started, I realized that my contractor was decent. He always gave me very low quotes, and though he never reached his deadlines he generally finished the project for less money than I had budgeted. So one time he handed me a quote, and I asked him how long it would take for him to finish. Upon hearing his answer, I stated that if he met his deadline, I would pay him an extra $500 for the job.

The next day, I showed up at the job and there were eight guys working on my house. I didn't know his crew was so big. Due to his chronic tardiness, he was accustomed to having people tell him that they would penalize him if he didn't meet the deadline. I elected to use the carrot rather than the stick, offering a bonus if he finished on time. This was a pleasant surprise for him and created a loyalty that still exists today.

Even though I have been in this business for several years, I can honestly say that I've only used a few contractors. I use one exclusively and we have a very good relationship but I keep a few contractors on call as to not put all my eggs in one basket. I try to keep them busy so that I always have access to a few. I make sure that all are well paid so I don't have to worry about my jobs.

I also offer my current contractor incentives as I did with the contractor in the story above. In fact, I offer him quite a bit to work for me exclusively and not on any other jobs. This arrangement works out very well for both of us. He makes more money than he could anywhere else and since he handles everything, I don't need to put much effort into managing my projects.

Finally, I don't advise that others pay their contractors as much as I pay mine until they are able to do so. At my current level, I have the ability to make a mid to high six figure income and therefore can afford to pay my contractor $100-150k per year.

CHAPTER 8

CONTRACTORS

A GOOD CONTRACTOR WILL DO quality work and complete a job according to schedule at a reasonable price. They will show up on time and finish the job rather than leaving it ninety percent done. Keep in mind, however, that just because a contractor is good at one thing doesn't mean he is good at all things. In fact, be wary of those contractors who say they can "do it all." Some can, but many cannot. Some prefer to do one thing since that is what they do best. In any case, I highly recommend that you check referrals of contractors. You'll likely be sorry if you don't.

Wholesaling or not, building a list of reliable contractors is essential. They can help you determine your repair costs and you can refer them to other investors or, if you're wholesaling, buyers. The more you can help other investors, the more likely they are to help you. As a wholesaler, this help often comes in the form of repeat business and higher profits.

If you find someone who is installing carpet and padding for $8 per yard, pass it along to all of your investor friends. They will save a few hundred dollars per property and thank you for it. Or, wholesale a home that needs a furnace to someone and they don't know who to call. You are doing them a favor by providing them with the name of a good heating contractor. Always be on the look out for qualified, professional contractors. Chances are high that someone you know can use them.

YOUR NEW BEST FRIEND

My contractor is my best friend, literally. This is a good thing since I am having him handle all of my rehabs. He knows the way I like my homes to be renovated down to the color of carpeting and the types of kitchen cabinets, so I don't have to get involved with making any decisions involving quality or color of materials used. Once we decide how to tackle the layout of a particular property, he hires all the subcontractors, negotiates the best deals for me and frees me to do what I do best—find cheap homes in good neighborhoods. Our relationship works very well. I can't do his job and he can't do mine, but together we make beautiful homes.

On the other hand, acting as the general contractor yourself can save you money, but it can also cost you money if you make mistakes due to inexperience. For example, if you close in a wall before having the plumbing fixed, then you will waste money tearing it back down to fix the plumbing and rebuilding the wall a second time. This may seem like common sense, but it is only one of a hundred different things to consider when redoing a home.

Contractors who have been through the process before don't typically make these kinds of mistakes. They think ahead, fixing or building things when it is most cost efficient. This is not to say that it is impossible to be your own general contractor. Be prepared to take some lumps as you learn.

YOUR CONTRACTOR — MR. V.I.P.

Though I don't want to lessen the importance of any of your other team members, if you are rehabbing homes, a good contractor is probably your most important team member. As a rehabber, you have nothing until your homes are completed properly. Many contractors can get 95 percent of a job done, but the last 5 percent seem to be impossible to complete. As investors, we tend to hang on to these guys. Once they start a job, it is often easier to let them finish, even though it takes months for them to complete the last few steps. This delay can cost you much of your profit, so I highly recommend locating and holding onto a good contractor.

FINDING AND QUALIFYING A GOOD CONTRACTOR

Contractors can be found in many different ways. Open up the yellow pages, check classified ads, look for business cards at building supply stores, ask for referrals, stop by other jobs or jot down phone numbers off of trucks. No one method of finding a contractor is better or worse than another. However, I would recommend staying away from the big ads in the yellow pages, because they charge the most.

Not that price should be your number one criteria for qualifying contractors. Oftentimes, it pays to spend a little more and though I try to get the best deal, I tend to stay away from the lowest quotes. These quotes are usually much lower than everyone else and I don't feel that the job can be done effectively for such a discount. In most cases, by not taking the lowest quote I am saving the contractor and myself some heartache. If I awarded the contractor the job, he wouldn't make any money and I would have to spend more paying someone else to finish the work. Having another person finish a job almost always costs more than hiring the right person in the first place.

Look for experienced contractors who own their own truck and tools. Find out if they have a line of credit or working capital to purchase materials. Find referrals to see how well they communicate and decide if this will be a long-term working relationship as soon as possible. Some contractors are just "working for the weekend." Check in on current jobs and talk with other owners. With the referrals, check out the names that they give you to see if they include investors who have had experience in dealing with contractors and thereby formed a basis for comparison. Find out if these former clients were satisfied with the quality of the work as well as the time it took to complete the job. Ask if they would use them again.

IS THERE SUCH A THING AS A "GOOD" CONTRACTOR?

Like Realtors and investors, there are good and bad contractors. But few contractors are thoroughly horrible, meaning that most everyone has developed skills. Part of your job as an investor is to coordinate the efforts of your team members, find their strong points and their weak points, and determine who should work which job.

If you identify a weak spot in one of your team members, it is your responsibility to teach them how to do it, if possible, or find someone else to do that job. A lazy investor should get along well with a lazy contractor, someone who hates their job but tolerates it since it pays the bills and may decide to take a week or so off if they make really good money for a few days. In contrast, a hardworking investor will never get along well with a lazy contractor because neither will ever see eye to eye.

PAYMENT SCHEDULE — AVOIDING ADVANCEMENTS

This is a touchy area. I never like paying contractors anything up front simply because I have been burned every time a contractor has owed me because I was ahead. I've done it three times and I have been burned three times. As a result, my policy is to pay after the work is completed. I may pay in draws as certain things are finished, but I don't pay in advance under any circumstances. As long as I owe money, I'm sure they are going to be around. As soon as they owe me money, they usually end up working for someone else who owes them. Though you won't usually have this problem with big companies, they also charge a lot more to cover their overhead, more than I'm normally willing to pay.

CONTRACTS

I recommend that you put your agreements with a contractor into a contract. I didn't do this when I first started and when a home was near completion the contractors claimed the light fixtures were not in their quote. My response would be, "Yes, they were. We were standing right here when we talked about it. Don't you remember? I told you that I wanted this type of light here and that type there?!" The contractor always came back with, "I don't remember," or "We never discussed that." Then I would have to work something out with them to get my light fixtures installed. So, get everything in writing to save yourself some heartache, even after you've established a relationship with someone.

INSURANCE

Make sure that hired contractors are insured for liability as well as workmen's compensation. The work that they do is dangerous and the possibility of someone getting injured while working always exists. If a contractor or one of his workers hurts themselves and they do not have insurance, the person they are going to sue will be you. Even if it's a frivolous lawsuit, the expense may put you and your family in the poor house. Obtain a copy of the contractor's insurance certificate. Although anyone can sue you for anything, you will be in much better shape with this in hand.

RELEASE OF LIENS

For those who don't know, a Release of Liens is essentially an agreement signed by a contractor and given to a property owner at the completion of a job. Basically, it states that the contractor has been paid in full for the work and relinquishes their right to place a mechanic's lien on the property. The release of liens serves as protection for the property owner from an unscrupulous contractor who, though paid in full, might try to claim that they are still owed some money and place a lien on the property for any amount which they claim are owed but have not been paid.

Personally, I have never had one of my contractors sign a release of liens. After talking with various contractors, I have discovered that most wouldn't even know how to put a lien on your property. The one time I did have to threaten a contractor with a lawsuit via a letter from my attorney, I never heard from him again. Therefore, I have never considered obtaining a Release of Liens from any of my contractors.

I am not going to advise against having your contractors sign a Release of Liens upon receiving final payment. Personally, I don't do it, but I'm not aware of the laws in other states. You should always look into this where you live because I know that some investors strongly advocate it.

GENERAL

For my rehabs I prefer a general contractor. Having one person to call for everything is much easier than trying to keep up with several subcontractors. They usually cost more, but the time you save in having them monitor the whole job is well worth it. General contractors are also experienced in the areas that we are not. If a general contractor is paying a subcontractor to work, he will want to get his money's worth and will make sure that the job is done correctly. As real estate investors, we may not know if a job is being completed efficiently. Even if we do, our time is better spent chasing deals than babysitting subcontractors.

I use one general contractor who handles my renovations from start to finish. He does use subcontractors, but he contacts them and negotiates all of the pricing. My general contractor's crew performs about 60 percent of the work to my homes while "subbing out" the other 40 percent. The types of work that we typically sub out include windows, heating and air conditioning, roofs, siding, sheet rock and electrical.

HEATING, VENTILATING AND AIR CONDITIONING (HVAC)

As a rehabber, I can safely say that the heating systems must be replaced in about half of the houses I purchase. Personally, I have found that a new heating and air conditioning system is a major selling point, so I always put new heating systems and central air conditioning into every home. Whether or not you follow this advice, it is important for you as a rehabber to be able to call a good heating contractor.

My heating and air contractor isn't the cheapest guy on the block, but he understands my preferences. As a result, he is concerned about the finished product and uses quality equipment. When placing his ductwork, he takes into consideration how it will affect the next crew coming in behind him and does his best to minimize bulkheads, by impacting the rooms of my homes as little as possible. He also begins and completes jobs quickly. This is vital as the heating system is one of the first things that I do in all of my homes and I need someone who will get in and get out so I can begin the other work.

I am aware that throughout the country there are different types of heating and cooling systems. Various types are predominant in different areas because of differences in average temperature, humidity and altitude. With this in mind, know that when I refer to heating and air systems, I will always be referring to a forced hot air system with a gas furnace and an outdoor compressor for central air conditioning.

ESTIMATED REPAIR COSTS

Typically an HVAC company is going to charge anywhere from $35-70 per hour to come out and do repairs. The price per hour increases as the job gets smaller and decreases with larger jobs.

When taking bids to replace a whole furnace, you'll find that contractors typically have a set price in mind rather than an hourly wage. Expect to spend approximately $1,200-$3,200 with the understanding that I have replaced gas forced hot air furnaces for as little as $4,200 while I have paid as much as $4,200 for a new gas steam boiler.

I also recommend hiring licensed HVAC contractors whenever necessary and having them pull permits for their work—most municipalities will require this. Of course, for smaller repairs not requiring a permit, you may be able to do the work yourself, but use licensed contractors and have them pull permits when necessary.

PLUMBERS

It is inevitable that you will have to do some plumbing work on every job, especially if you are installing new kitchens and updating bathrooms. In most cases, a handyman can take care of minor jobs. However, for those homes with old galvanized pipes that have corroded and reduced water pressure, you will need to tear out all the lines and install new copper, PVC or Pex piping. For a job of this magnitude, I suggest a licensed plumber.

I'm fortunate that my general contractor has an employee who is very experienced and takes care of my plumbing needs, be it repairing minor leaks or re-plumbing an entire home. If you aren't as fortunate, I would recommend finding a small plumbing company (1-2 employees) and establishing a relationship. They do not have the overhead of a large company and can charge less. When pricing jobs with these companies, I usually like to get quotes for the whole job as opposed to paying hourly wages. In my experience, guys with a fixed profit tend to complete a job more quickly.

More important than minor plumbing or even line replacement is the one area that causes me the greatest problems in older homes—clogged drains and sewer lines. Find the best drain opening company in town and be careful because many will come out and tell you to replace your sewer line because they want the bigger job. In my experience, I've called two drain openers when I have a clogged line and the same one tells me that I need a new line while the other can usually clear the line.

Finally, just like HVAC contractors, plumbers will cost more by the hour for small jobs and less for larger jobs. I always recommend obtaining fixed price quotes from plumbers rather than hourly quotes since you will pay much more when hiring someone based on time and materials.

WINDOWS

In many areas, there are companies that specialize in replacement windows. I replace windows in about 80 percent of the homes I renovate. This is both necessary and expensive. I have new windows fully installed for about $200 each, a number which may vary in other parts of the country. Find out the best and most cost-effective supplier of replacement windows in your area. Other investors will appreciate it if you can save them $25 per window, especially when they have to put in twenty or more. I always replace windows in a home unless recently installed, vinyl, double-hung windows are present. Though I have several means of replacing windows, I always choose the one-stop shop. I call a local company who measures the windows, manufactures a custom fit, installs and wraps the windows in aluminum. My cost per window is right around $200 with extras.

This is a little more than if I bought them from a building supply company and had my general contractor install and wrap them. But having my general contractor's crew do the windows would just take them away from other work that they could be doing to move the project along. The people at my window company of choice are experts and they can install an entire home's worth of windows in less than a day. By comparison, my crew, who do not install windows daily, might take up to three days.

FLOORING

Carpeting isn't cheap, but you can get a wide range of pricing for the same product. Find out who works with investors and determine if they have special pricing for investors. On average, I save about 25 percent over the lowest retail pricing in carpet stores by dealing with a company that specializes in corporate accounts.

In my opinion, installing new flooring is one of the most important things that you can do to a home. Along with fresh paint, new vinyl flooring and tile makes the difference between a home looking and smelling new or old. New flooring is something I highly recommend for all renovations. I have a good relationship with two flooring companies and they usually install any carpeting and occasionally install the vinyl flooring in my kitchens and baths when my contractor is busy with other work.

When looking for people to lay carpet, I quickly learned that going into carpet stores was going to be too expensive. I now go directly to a wholesale carpet distributor and pay wholesale prices for the carpeting. These distributors, which can usually be found in industrial warehouse parks, also know moonlighters and the small installers who pick up rolls of carpeting daily. They set me up with someone who will install my carpet for peanuts. Finally, the recommended installers are experts in this area and can usually install an entire home of carpeting in one day.

Prices don't seem to be fixed, but do stay relatively low. In general, I can save from $3 to $7 off of the installed price per square yard by going to these wholesale distributors as opposed to a retail carpet store. The last time I bought carpeting I paid $6.50 per square yard and bought the best padding for $2.25 per square yard. In addition, the wholesaler referred me to an installer who did the job for $3.75 per square yard. My total cost was $12.50 per square yard for a great product.

I usually assume that I will be putting new vinyl flooring or tile in my kitchens and baths. If the bathrooms have good ceramic tile on the floor, I'll leave it alone. Otherwise, new vinyl goes down. Vinyl flooring is cheap and truly helps the appearance of a home.

Hardwood floors are beautiful but are usually too costly. On the other hand, in upscale homes, hardwood floors add to their value and justify the expense of refinishing. A friend of mine redid his floors and was able to rent the sanding machine and buy the materials to do the job in three rooms for less than $300, which seems inexpensive given that I usually get quotes in the neighborhood of $1000 for the same job. His floors were in pretty good shape when he started, so I think that made a big difference. Regardless, I currently only refinish floors in my nicest homes.

The costs below reflect quality flooring, but certainly not the most expensive. You can spend quite a bit on high-end carpeting and tile. I highly recommend sticking with neutral colors.

Estimated Repair Costs:	
Carpet cleaning (minimum 5 rooms)	$30-$70 per room
Carpet installation	$9-$15 per sq. yd.
Refinish hardwood floors	$1.50-$2.50 per sq. ft.
Vinyl floor replacement	$2-$4 per sq. ft.
Ceramic Tile	$6-$12 per sq. ft.
Ceramic Tile (do it yourself)	$4-$8 per sq. ft.

ELECTRICIANS

First and foremost, it is important for you to use licensed contractors and have them pull permits when required. Don't play around with your electrical systems. Everything must be done right or you will spend more later and leave yourself open to liability should an incorrectly wired electrical system cause a fire in the home. Many older homes may need to have the electrical service updated. They may not have grounded outlets or have fuses instead of circuit breakers. If you rehab a home, make sure to have an updated electrical system in order to pass the inspections of your buyer's lender and meet the electrical needs of the new buyers.

I always want my home to have modern electrical systems. If the systems are outdated, I replace them. This isn't cheap but it must be done in order for the home to be sold to a buyer obtaining an FHA loan (meaning repayment to the bank will be insured by FHA, the Federal Housing Administration). Fortunately, most of the homes that I buy have already had their electrical systems updated to meet current standards. I usually just need to install switches and outlets throughout the home.

Installing new switches and outlets makes everything look new, especially when asking top dollar for a home. Potential buyers do not want to see dirty switches or paint-covered outlets. I want them to see new walls, bright light fixtures, shiny switchplates and new switches and outlets, which can be bought for about $.50 each.

Estimated Repair Costs:	
Upgrade service (breakers and amperage)	$1000-$1,700
Rewire entire house	$3,000-$6,000
Replace a light fixture (labor only)	$35-$70
Replace a light fixture (do it yourself)	$0
Replace outlets and switches (labor, 10 or more)	$5-$20 per switch
Replace outlets and switches (do it yourself)	$0

KITCHENS AND BATHS

Probably the most important areas when dealing with renovations, kitchens and baths are usually outdated. What many people perceive as an expensive fix is usually fairly cheap. Kitchen and bathrooms expenses are what earn a rehabber the best returns. I don't use the most expensive stuff available, but I step up a couple of grades of cabinet. Materials cost a few hundred dollars more, but the finished product looks significantly better. I like to make my kitchens bright and airy. It is much more appealing to walk into a bright kitchen and buyers react favorably.

The only appliances that I ever include are a stove and a dishwasher. I install a gas or electric stove because I want the kitchen to be ready and I also include a dishwasher if one was previously installed.

Estimated Repair Costs (Kitchen):	
Cabinet replacements	$2000-$4,500
Countertops and installation	$300-1000
New sink and fixtures	$200-400
Total Kitchen Renovation	**$2,500-$5,900**

Note: While you can spend more than $5,000 on a kitchen, you can have a basic kitchen installed for between $1,500 and $5,000 for a typical rehab.

Estimated Repair Costs (Bath):	
New vanity, sink and cabinet	$200-$500
New tub enclosure	$200-$500
Tub refinishing	$250-$350
Tub Refinishing (do it yourself)	$50
New tub and surround	$300-$1,000
New tile floor and walls	$1,200-$1,700
New toilet	$200
New Toilet (do it yourself)	$100
Total Bath Renovation	**$700-$3,000**

Note: While you can spend as much as $3,000 on a bath, you can have a basic bathroom redone for between $1,000 and $1,500.

PAINTERS

In this area, you can spend or save a lot. Painting contractors usually charge outrageous amounts of money. Despite cheap materials and less than two days of work, I can't find a painter who will quote less than several thousand dollars. As a result, I usually spend about $300-$500 on materials and pay someone $300-500 to paint a home for me in a day or two. I buy quality paint since it requires fewer applications to coat a surface than cheaper paint and also saves money on labor.

To save money on low-end homes, I make sure everything is painted the same color. I don't "cut in" my trim on low-end homes (paint it a different color or different style, glossy vs. flat, of the same color) and I don't paint my ceilings a different color. This saves time and time is money. In terms of color, I basically decided to copy the builder's methods when constructing new home developments with my renovations that are comparable in price.

I noticed that builders were just spraying everything the same color, so I decided to copy this method. In terms of color for my low-end homes, I paint everything with a flat, antique white paint. For my nicer homes, I'll cut in the trim with a semi-gloss white and paint the ceiling "ceiling white" and the walls antique white. In terms of cost, painters usually charge by the square foot or by the room, and pricing from one contractor to another can vary widely:

By the square foot	$1-$4/ sq. ft.
By the room	$100-$400/ room

Skill of the painters can vary drastically from crew to crew. A good crew can perform detailed painting and lots of trim work, but they are typically drastically more expensive. Skilled painters can also complete a job in far less time then unskilled painters, but for most renovations, skillful painters are unnecessary. Finally, I'd like to mention that the key to a good paint job is the preparation. If all the repairs are done and trim is taped off (line walls with tape to avoid painting undesired areas) and caulking is finished, then painting is a breeze. If these things are not completed, the work becomes a chore and the results look unprofessional.

Estimated Repair Costs:	
Paint interior	$150-$250 per room
Paint interior (do it yourself)	$30 per room
Paint exterior	$1,000-$5,000
Paint exterior (do it yourself)	$300-$1,000

Note: Cost of exterior painting will vary with size of home and condition of existing surface. A good exterior paint job takes more time and is almost as costly as new vinyl siding. For these reasons, I prefer vinyl siding.

LANDSCAPERS

Landscapers do everything from cutting grass to hauling trash. Many can repair walkways, cut down trees and tear down old sheds. Though landscaping is a cost that many people ignore, cleaning and hauling trash and cutting down trees can be very expensive. I have spent as much as $3,000 to clean up a lot, cutting down all the overgrown bushes and trees to haul everything away on a quarter acre. In general, I budget about $1,000 for landscaping and trash removal.

Without spending too much, I make sure that the yard is neat and all the trash is picked up. I have a guy who works part time who will go to my homes every two weeks to keep the grass cut and trimmed. He cuts down overgrown bushes, picks up trash and plants grass seed if necessary. At my request, he will put down mulch in front of the home to give it a cleaner appearance, but I never have him plant flowers or bushes. Trimming grass, cleaning the edges and mulching does wonders for a yard.

Other curb appealing techniques include a new mailbox, mounting a porch light, painting trim and posting new address numbers. I also install a decorative front door; usually one manufactured by Stanley with an oval light and priced around $279. While the cost is roughly $100 more than a standard door, the curb appeal added by the door is well worth the additional costs.

Finally, there are times to do concrete work. This can be costly if done professionally, so I've paid handymen to do concrete work in the past. Unfortunately, I've never been happy with the quality of the finished product. I couldn't always afford it in the beginning so I sacrificed quality for price. I now spend more so the job is done right.

ROOF / GUTTERS

Roof expenses depend on the type of roof (flat rubber, pitched shingle, pitched slate), the size of the roof and the extent of the repairs required. In my area, it costs about $1200 to lay a new flat roof on a small home and about $150-$200 per square for a new layer of shingles on a larger home. I normally spend $150 or less per square, which includes tearing off a layer of shingles.

Like most of my subs, good roofers consist of a small crew rather than a large company. My roofers typically finish a job in two days or less and the only reason for a second day is if there is rotten wood to be replaced. A new roof makes a world of difference to the exterior appearance and I put one on every home that needs one. If a roof has any signs of aging, such as curling shingles, I replace it.

To save money, I buy the materials, hire the roofing crew and hire someone else to clean up after the roofing crew. I actually have two crews that will do a roof for me at $100 per square if I supply the materials and have someone else clean up. On average, this saves me about $30 per square; a total of about $500.

Replacing gutters can be expensive or inexpensive, depending on the type. Gutters can be bought in pieces and assembled with caulking, but unless this is done carefully the finished product has a good chance of leaking. When replacing gutters, I prefer to install the seamless variety, which runs about $3 per foot.

SIDING

When I first started, I could never find a siding company with reasonable prices. All of the quotes I received were in the range of $7,500-$8,500 for an average-sized home. As a result, I never put siding on my homes because there wasn't room in my budget.

Today, I can get the same home done for about $3,500. With new siding, my homes look brand new and stand out from all the others on the block. As a result, I estimate that my $3,500 investment enables me to get an extra $7,000-$10,000 per house.

I have been lucky enough to establish the same type of relationship with a siding contractor that I have with my roofing contractor. My siding contractor will install siding at $65 per square if I buy the materials. This saves me about $50 per square, roughly $1000-$2000 for each home I renovate.

Finally, I'd like to mention that a good paint job for the exterior of a home is expensive, primarily due to the labor. The preparation takes a long time, particularly if any scraping is needed, and putting two coats on an exterior could take more time than siding. Since new vinyl siding only costs a little more (and oftentimes less), I spend a little extra and make the exterior look brand new. On the other hand, you could probably paint the outside while you may not be able to install vinyl siding without experience.

SHEET ROCK

In my area, it costs about $35-$60 to install a 4' X 8' piece of sheet rock, depending on the amount being installed. I have a crew that hangs and finishes sheet rock for $18 per board if I buy the materials, which drops my cost to about $25-28 per board.

Many times, gouges, holes and other marks on walls and ceilings can be repaired rather than replaced. Likewise, different textures can be sprayed onto ceilings and sometimes walls to cover imperfections. When estimating repairs, use your best judgment and assume replacement rather than repair.

If you are doing extensive renovations, it is inevitable that you will have to do some sheet rock and/or plaster work. If there isn't much work, you won't be able to justify using a sheet rock contractor. Typically, they like large jobs (hanging 50 sheets or more) and will charge outrageous prices for a small job (as much as $100 or $200 per sheet). This happens because they need to pay their workers a minimal amount (at least $100) just to show up and take their tools off the truck.

For small jobs, use a handyman or carpenter to do light sheetrock work. For large jobs, sheetrock contractors will hang and finish the sheet rock for anywhere from $18 - $50 per sheet. This is a wide range, but most contractors quote $30-35 per sheet.

PLASTER WALLS

With plaster walls, I salvage if possible. If walls are beginning to crumble and separate from the backing, we used to laminate over it with 3/8 inch sheetrock. That was a nightmare. Today, I just rip it out and put in new sheetrock. If plaster walls are not in good shape, I rip them out and replace them with sheetrock.

CARPENTERS / PUNCH OUT

Most of the carpentry work that needs to be done is light and most anyone can do it so I never hire a pure carpenter. I hire Punch Out workers to take care of the most important parts of the renovation process. They perform the tedious tasks, which make the difference between a fair job and a great job. The quality of their work and the diligence is what separates your completed renovation from the rest.

My general contractor and one crewmember handle my punch out items. When I refer to punch out items, jobs include cutting the doors so they open and close smoothly, making sure the door knobs all line up and function properly, installing all the switch plates and outlet covers, painting all areas that need to be trimmed, finalizing the kitchen area (lining up cabinets, installing knobs, installing kick plates, gluing end caps to the countertop, etc.), and installing light fixtures, mailboxes, bathroom vanities and medicine cabinets. This is the last 10 percent of the job and it takes almost as much time to finish as it took to complete the first 90 percent.

These labor intensive, time consuming jobs require a bit of patience so most people just don't want to do it. They would rather do something that makes them feel as if they are accomplishing something. Spending ten minutes changing an outlet and its cover drives many workers batty. Punch Out guys, on the other hand, are patient enough to make sure everything fits right and works accordingly. These finishing touches are the deciding factor when completing a rehab. This part of a renovation is the most important and must be done.

One pitfall during rehab is seeing the job at 90 percent and feeling accomplished because of how hideous the house was before. This, unfortunately, causes a lax attitude, which usually results in unfinished homes. When the punch out of your home isn't complete, your home looks unfinished, making it more difficult to sell, forcing sellers to make concessions on the price.

The test that separates good rehabbers from bad rehabbers is whether or not they can manage their jobs to 100 percent completion. This means that they understand the punch out process of a home, are prepared to finish and have crews ready to jump on the job and finalize it.

The contractor contract should include a final draw containing the "punch list" items. This final draw should be a significant portion of your contract price with your contractor. Most contractors need more than 10 percent to finish this part of the job.

Prior to making your final payment, I recommend going through the entire home and inspecting it. Write down all of the little items that need to be completed, including:

- Sticking doors

- Missing thresholds
- Missing switchplate covers
- Touch up paint
- Missing molding
- Missing or unsecure railings (a must where you have 3 or more steps)
- Knobs on your cabinets
- Toe plates on your cabinets
- Shelves in your closets
- Uncaulked windows
- Missing handles on plumbing fixtures
- Vanities secured to walls
- Commodes tight and secure
- Countertops secure in kitchen
- Kitchen sink plumbing and drain working properly

The list continues, but make sure to provide your contractor with a list of these items upfront and have them sign off on the list. Visualize your completed rehab and take the time to be thorough as this list is very important. Finally, be sure to put everything in writing so there aren't any misunderstandings.

CHAPTER 9

REAL ESTATE AGENTS

UNDERSTANDING THE AGENT

In most cases, you will have to train a Realtor to work for you, since most do not deal with investors so our methods are foreign. Typically, an agent makes more money dealing with pretty houses and good credit buyers, so junker houses are not an area of expertise. If you can find an open-minded agent to teach, you can put together a mutually beneficial relationship. First and foremost, respect the agent's perspective.

An agent gets a license and sells real estate to make a living. A lot of work goes into a putting a deal together and an agent only makes money if someone buys a home. Most agents have been burned over and over by investors who do not produce. These so-called investors have real estate agents scour through listings, make appointments, show them around once or twice, but they never make an offer. Others produce offers so ridiculous that if the agent knew this up front, they would have never agreed to work with the investor. Then there are investors who get offers accepted but never settle on the deal. So the agent, who has about 30-40 hours worth of work into a transaction, will never get paid for their time. It's obvious why most real estate agents pass on new investors.

WHAT TO EXPECT FROM YOUR AGENT

Understand that you are going to be looking at many houses and buying few. You don't need the agent to drive you around, pull up comps on every house or present offers that you can't close on. This is a waste of their time and yours. The only thing I expect from my agents is to provide listings and submit offers. Occasionally I will ask an agent to show me a home or pull comps if I can't find anything on my own.

When receiving listings, I expect to get updated weekly if not daily, especially if I am in an active buying mode. I typically have them pull a list of fixer-uppers for me as well as a list of foreclosures. This list should include every single home that is available, not just the homes that the agent thinks are a good deal.

In terms of submitting offers, I go through every listing and look at every home. Then I will make an offer on every single one of them regardless of the list price. I construct my offer based upon my formula and present it. It doesn't matter if they are asking $100,000 for a property and my formula tells me to offer $50,000. I offer $50,000 and the seller says yes or no. You need to make the agent understand your strategy during your initial meeting as well as the fact that a motivated seller will drastically reduce their price.

I once purchased a home that was bank owned and needed a good bit of work. The bank was asking $93,500, which is what the home was worth after repairs. So I called the listing agent and told her that I wanted the home, but I felt the asking price was outrageous. She agreed and told me that $93,500 was the price at which the bank told her to list it. Nevertheless, I told her to submit an offer on my behalf for $55,000. The next day it was accepted. Actually, I was a little upset that they didn't even counter my offer. I felt I could have offered less.

On another occasion, I offered $45k for a home and the seller, another bank, declined. A month later, I offered $40k for the home and the seller declined. The next month, the seller reduced their price to $39,900, so I offered $34k and the seller declined. Two months later, four months after my initial offer, the seller reduced the price to $34,900 and I offered $29k. This time they accepted, taking $16k less than my original offer of $45k.

A third example involves a property that I bought for $1,000 which was listed at $35,000. All of these were bank owned properties. It makes no sense why they do what they do and I've given up trying to figure it out. I'm just going to enjoy the good fortunes that come my way.

HOW TO FIND A GOOD BUYING AGENT

When interviewing Realtors, you need to have a good idea of what you expect so you can explain exactly what you need. They need to know their role so I tell new agents the following:

"I'm looking for a real estate agent to help me—someone who can provide me with lists of fixer uppers and foreclosures on a daily basis. It won't be necessary for you to run me around town to see all of the houses. Occasionally, I may need to get inside of a home, but not very often. I may also need comps once in a while, but mostly I'll just expect you to submit my offers for which I will provide all of the terms up front. I make a lot of offers and most will be low and most will be turned down, but I usually get one or two. Since you won't have to work too hard for these sales, would you be interested in working with me?"

Most Realtors will say yes and the ones who decline are those who are mega producers and are already busy enough. It is not difficult to find a real estate agent, but it can be difficult to find one that you like and will work with you. The first thing I suggest is to look for someone in a convenient location. You will have to see this person regularly so you don't want to be traveling out of your way all of the time.

HOW TO WORK WELL WITH YOUR BUYING AGENT

The key to working well with an agent is to respect their time. Real estate agents are just like you and me. Their time is their life. If you have an agent spend time running you around town, preparing contracts, talking on the phone with other agents, pulling comps and pulling listings but you don't buy a home, then the agent loses. Be aware of this and respectful of their time. Most investors who go to real estate agents are beginners or wannabes and they never buy a home. This leads to real estate agents avoiding investors so you have to be different.

Next, understand your role in relation to that of the real estate agent. All too often, investors expect real estate agents to do all the work and find good deals. If real estate agents knew how to find the good deals, they would buy them for themselves. It is your job to find the good deals. The job of the real estate agent is to assist you by providing you with the information for you to determine the quality of the deals.

DEALING WITH BUYING AGENTS IN GENERAL

There are a couple of strategies that you can pursue when dealing with agents. You can make offers directly to the listing agent or work with an agent who submits all of the offers on your behalf. The advantage to working with listing agents is that you may get them lobbying harder to get your offer accepted because they will get both sides of the commission. The disadvantage is that you will have to find out when these listings become available on your own. Do not have one agent provide you with listings and comps while using another agent to present your offers. This is unethical.

I suggest searching for newer agents. Experienced agents tend to be set in their ways and unwilling to work with investors. Most new real estate agents do not make it through their first year as a result of lack of sales so your business is welcome. You can mold the agent to work with you while providing them with the income they need to rise above the hurdles of being a beginner agent.

Some agents will ask you to sign a buyer's broker agreement, which essentially states the following:

1. If you buy a property listed on the MLS, it will be through that agent
2. If you buy a listed property through someone else, they have the right to collect a commission from you. Whenever presented with this issue in the past, I always told the Realtor that I do not sign these agreements because I work with anyone who brings a deal to my attention. I go on to assure them that if they bring a deal to me, I will submit an offer on that property through them. However, if someone else brings a deal to my attention, then I will submit an offer through that agent. Furthermore, I state that I believe this is a fair policy and I will not compromise it. To date, no one has ever given me trouble after I explain my position. If they did, I suppose I'd find another agent. There are plenty of agents out there to help us in submitting offers. No sense in working with an uncooperative one.

GAINING ACCESS TO PROPERTIES

However common for investors to enter vacant homes, remember that when you enter a property without the permission of the seller (if it's a FSBO) or the accompaniment of a real estate agent (if listed with a Realtor), you can be arrested for trespassing if the seller wanted to push the issue. Though it is possible that you will find an agent willing to give you the combinations to the lockboxes on vacant properties to inspect without their assistance, it is entirely within your discretion whether or not you choose to enter these properties alone. While I do not recommend going in alone, it has never stopped me.

WHAT TO EXPECT FROM YOUR SELLING AGENT

I expect my agent to give me a feel for the market as a whole. Sometimes we get wrapped up with rehabs and lose touch with how homes are selling and possibly, how they are appreciating. For example, the market may be so healthy before a project is finished that market prices increase beyond what I felt I could get for the home in the beginning. As a result, my Realtor has recommended that I list the home above my original price. At first, I was a little leery since I like to sell my homes quickly, but my agent sits in an office every day where Realtors are crying the blues about not having enough homes to sell to their clients. With this information, she convinced me to raise my price. I have made more money listening to this agent.

Another example involves my agent making money for me by asking for my patience. On two occasions when my home didn't sell in the first two weeks, I was ready to reduce my price but she asked me to wait. Taking her advice, I got a full price contract within two weeks on both occasions.

Next, I expect agents to handle the whole sales process on their own. I believe this is how they earn their commission and my responsibility is to provide a good product to sell. If I do that, my job is done and the rest is up to them. They should follow up with the buyer, making sure that the loan process is moving along, inspections and appraisals are scheduled and a settlement date is set.

HOW TO FIND A GOOD SELLING AGENT

Use the same agent to buy and sell your homes. This will improve your relationship since they don't make much on the buying side (since the prices are so cheap) but they will make decent money on the selling side. If you list your completed renovations, they will look forward to making money on future deals and be more inclined to help you buy homes.

In terms of experience, there are several things to consider. First, your homes are usually going to sell themselves, so you don't need someone who is a good salesperson. However, you do want someone familiar with the process of ushering a deal to completion. They need to be organized and structured.

Second, your agent should have experience in evaluating offers with other agents or have a mentor to guide them. I have seen new investors work with rookie agents to sell their homes. Neither the investor nor the agent knew what they were doing and they accepted contracts that they should not have accepted. The homes were tied up for months and the deals fell apart so the investors eventually went under.

The agent or the mentor should be able to evaluate a good contract from a bad contract and know the reputations of other agents, meaning credibility and experience. My agent knows a contract from a top-producing agent is solid, but a contract from a rookie could go either way. She doesn't want additional work or for a deal to fall short.

HOW TO WORK WELL WITH YOUR SELLING AGENT

When an agent is working in a sales capacity as opposed to a buying capacity, your role is totally different. You should make sure they have a good product to sell and access to it. After that, accept an offer and turn the deal over to them. Now it is their responsibility to work with the buyers or their agent. At this point, your role is limited to providing whatever information your agent needs from you. Since you play such a small part in the sales process, there is no need for you to be as mindful of your agent's time as when buying. Once you have bought and sold a few homes with an agent, you will begin to see the fruits of the relationship. You will become their most important customer and they will take care of you.

LISTING AGREEMENTS

When listing your home with an agent, you are going to have to keep a few things in mind. First, when setting your sales price and figuring anticipated profit, take into consideration that you will need to pay a Realtors commission at settlement when the house is sold and most buyers are going to ask you for assistance with their closing costs. When deriving an asking price, include room to cover these costs.

The market will also determine your price so you can't set it too high. With this limitation, to be assured of profit, budget any Realtor commissions and buyer closing cost assistance into the "Margin for Rehabber's Profit, Holding Costs and Closing Costs" when making your offer to purchase a property.

Second, the agent will ask if you would like to sell your home "as-is" or fill out a disclosure form listing any defects in the home. I always sell my homes "as-is." Since I don't live the home in question, I am not familiar with problems that might exist despite my best efforts to do an extensive renovation. In addition, it is obvious that my homes are completely renovated so they generally don't care that I'm not disclosing anything about the home to them.

Third, your agent may ask if you would like to market your home with a home warranty. On occasion, I will pay for a home warranty to make a home more attractive to prospective buyers. However, if I offer a warranty, I have to pay for it at a cost of approximately $350.

Fourth, you may want to have some input to the remarks that show on the listing. I always ask to see the remarks before the property is actually listed and make sure that my properties are totally renovated. In the past, I have heard comments like: "Gorgeous Home…Totally renovated…Everything is new…Don't let your buyers miss this one!… Bonus family room, all new kitchens and bathrooms, central air conditioning…Home Warranty!…Don't wait—this one won't last."

Fifth, give consideration to whether or not you will offer a selling agent bonus to grab the attention of selling agents who have prospective buyers searching for a home where yours is located. The bonus is modest ($500-$1,000) and given to whichever agent sells the property, including my listing agent. I don't always start out with offering one, but I have offered it periodically when one of my homes was reaching the 30 days on market (DOM) mark.

BE HONEST WITH YOUR AGENT

When dealing with a new agent, be totally honest. If you have never done a deal, tell them that you are a beginning investor and would like to do X deals per year. Don't exaggerate. If you only intend to do three deals in the next year, be honest.

Most agents will be happy if you buy and sell three homes through them. They will collect six more commission checks than without you. If you exaggerate, your inexperience is bound to show and you are sure to lose all credibility.

A real estate agent will be more inclined to work with you if they know your situation up front. If you enlist their services through deception and they discover that you have never done a deal, you will probably never hear from them again.

Overall, real estate agents possess a good heart and they like to see people succeed. Moreover, they would like to be a part of your success story, so be honest and this truthfulness with take you further on the journey to success.

CONCERNS OF A REAL ESTATE AGENT

Real estate agents need to make a living. They earn nothing without selling homes. Whether they sell or not, they have expenses that need to be covered that can be rather costly. If a real estate agent is going to dedicate time and work extended hours with an investor, they will want a payoff. If you take up an agent's time but never buy a home, you can expect for the service to drop off significantly. Most agents are very good at taking buyers with good credit and putting these buyers into nice homes at top dollar. This is where they make the most money and why they will be able to help you with selling your homes.

You will most likely be asking an agent to do something that they have no experience with. Do not assume that they know exactly what you are talking about. Be patient as they learn, and they will be patient as you learn. However, they can help you when you finish your homes and want to sell at top dollar. Understand the methods and the science of buying homes cheap and convey these with your agent. If you lay everything on the table up front, your agent will not be upset with you later because you were honest with them.

REAL LIFE EXPERIENCE

I have never had a problem finding real estate agents to work with me. First, I ask a couple of questions about their experience. For example, "How long have you been an agent?" and, "Have you ever worked with investors?" Then I ask if they are opposed to working with investors and listen to their response. Afterward, I go into my pitch, telling them that I am an investor who buys 3-5 houses per month and sell one house per month on average. I ask if they would be interested in handling my purchases and listings for me, always getting a yes to that question.

Shortly after, I give them something else to get excited about. I tell them that I don't expect them to take me out to show me houses (at this point, their faces usually light up). I tell them what I do expect of them—listings on a regular basis and for them to make my offers. Furthermore, I would like to list all of my finished homes with them. Then I admit that I make about 30-50 offers per month (tailor this number to meet your needs) in order to get 3-5 accepted and I ask if that will be a problem. This usually isn't something they like to hear, but they realize that they don't have to do anything else but make offers, so they agree.

Then I say that I only get about 10 percent of my offers accepted because I offer so low. Most will be turned down but some will be accepted and those are the ones we want. I also explain some of the things that I have learned when it comes to dealing with banks. Most banks pay real estate agents a minimum commission (as opposed to a percentage), so if you are making low offers, your agent can still expect to make decent money. They like to hear that you want them to make money. I bring this up often and tell them that I value their time. Be considerate and they will be loyal.

Finally, don't forget to talk about listing all of your finished homes with them. If you decide to go the Realtor route to market your properties, this is where they would make the most money. It is easy for an agent to get top dollar for a nice home.

CHAPTER 10

FINDING THE MONEY

THERE'S NO WAY AROUND it—real estate investing takes money. The good news is that it doesn't have to be your money. Whether you plan to wholesale or retail, you must locate a source of funding to purchase properties. As a wholesaler, of course, you hope never to purchase a property, but you still need a source of financing not only to prove to sellers that you are capable of settling on a deal (most won't accept an offer without a pre-qualification letter) but also so you can keep your word and purchase the property as promised if absolutely necessary.

Sources of financing include private lenders, lines of credit, cash, banks, finance companies, mortgage lenders or a partner with access to one or more of the above. When you introduce yourself as an investor; sellers, contractors, and other agents assume that you have taken care of this area. After all, how could you consider yourself an investor if you don't know how to fund a deal?

Always have your financing in place. Whether you are currently in the market for a deal or not, you never know when a great deal is going to come your way. Imagine how horrible it would be to see an amazing deal slip through your fingers only because you didn't have the resources available to take advantage of it.

GETTING YOUR FINANCIAL HOUSE IN ORDER

Access to money makes this business tremendously easier. To some degree or another, we can all improve our financial situations. Save more, pay off debt, establish credit and build relationships with banking institutions.

It took years to improve my financial credibility, but the rewards are amazing. Today I can buy just about anything I want. I have bankers willing to give me all the money I need for anything I want to do and I have access to more money for deals than I'll ever need. I can make one phone call and borrow hundreds of thousands of dollars. If you have bad credit, no cash and a ton of debt like I did, you can still invest. It will be tougher but you will be able to overcome these hurdles if you apply yourself.

Most importantly, if you can't handle your finances, you won't be able to handle having more money. I know that most people find this hard to believe, thinking that everything becomes much easier with more money. But more money and poor financial management leads to a bigger disaster. Learn to manage what you have and you'll be able to manage the fortunes that you will make in real estate investing.

REMEMBER WORKING CAPITAL

In my opinion, diving into a project without access to working capital is the primary reason why most people fail as rehabbers. In short, there are holding costs and other expenses incurred while rehabbing a house and people remember to include these when calculating purchase price but neglect to take them into consideration when determining how much cash they will need. Costs include appraisal fees, mortgage payments, property taxes, utilities, lawn maintenance and contractor deposits.

When rehabbing, your working capital to cover these expenses should either be in your bank account before you begin your project. If you can borrow all of this money, great, but most rehabbers cannot borrow all the working capital that they need.

Rehabbers who are working on a shoestring budget usually take a long time to get their rehabs done, if they ever complete them. Their projects languish as they search for contractors who will work cheap enough to fit within their repair budget. They also cut corners, which causes their finished product to linger on the market. Consequently, whatever they may have saved is consumed by holding costs.

I know this from experience. When I first began renovating, I was undercapitalized. I did finish my projects and make money, but my profits didn't come close to what I make now. Today, I have the funds to complete my rehabs quickly and I do them right so they sell quickly. As a result, I make more money.

PRIVATE LENDERS

Private, or "hard money" lenders, are individuals with surplus money available to invest. Some have deep pockets while some have limited resources. Based upon their own personal criteria, they lend this surplus money, primarily on a short-term basis, to real estate investors who use it for a variety of profitable purposes like buying and repairing distressed properties.

TERMS

As you invest, you will discover that terms for private loans will vary from lender to lender and will depend on the experience level of an investor as well as the length of an investor's relationship with a particular lender. Generally, a hard money lender will provide a loan for 50-75 percent of the after-repaired value of a home at an interest rate of 12-18 percent for a period of six months to five years. They will also charge between two and ten points as an upfront financing fee.

Other terms also vary from lender to lender. Some will charge interest only, while others will amortize their loan. Some will lend repair money, while others will not. Some will place the repair money in escrow to be drawn out as the work is completed and others will let you leave with it. Some will lend closing costs and some won't. Some will even lend holding costs. Ultimately, when finding hard money lenders, you will need to determine their terms and how they might fit into your plans as an investor.

Some newer investors refuse to pay the rates required by hard money lenders and never do a deal. To me, this is foolish. The bottom line is that these rates are the cost of opportunity and for many investors, the only alternative if they want to buy homes for pennies on the dollar. For this reason I will never knock hard money lenders. Using their money allowed me to get started and I recommend that everyone without a solid source of funds do the same.

UNDERWRITING CRITERIA

Lending criteria also varies from lender to lender. Each has preferences with regard to whom they will or will not lend. Some will check credit while others will not. Some will do their own appraisals, and perhaps even charge for an appraisal. Some will charge an inspection fee for each draw from the repair escrow. Some will only lend in certain areas. Some are more number driven when it comes to decision-making while others go more on a feeling about you and/or the neighborhood.

ADVANTAGES AND DISADVANTAGES TO THE INVESTOR

Private lenders are probably the best source of financing for beginners and those with no money and/or challenged credit. Generally, they are more concerned with the value of the property than credit and financial, so they will typically lend purchase and rehab money for the deal.

As an investor, strive to find one good private lender but take names of everyone you come across. Hard money lenders are a great resource for all real estate investors and using several will help you become more profitable. They will help you to act quickly and settle deals on time to enhance your reputation in your marketplace. You should be able to get pre-qualification letters from them and make offers with confidence.

Some private money lenders believe it will cost less to fix a home than what I spend. If so, they won't give me all the repair money I request so I am left with a choice to cut corners on my renovation or spend money out of my own pocket. This isn't a problem now, but as a beginning rehabber, I didn't have extra money so my renovations were never quite the quality I wanted them to be when this happened.

Private lenders have their place. I highly recommend that everyone use them when necessary. Even today, though I have cash and lines of credit, if I come across a deal that I need to settle right away but don't have the available funds, I'll make a quick call to one of my private lenders to fund the project.

TWO ADDITIONAL ADVANTAGES FOR WHOLESALERS

There are two main advantages for wholesalers to find hard money lenders, even if you don't intend to buy property. If you do enough volume, you will inevitably find yourself with a property under contract that you can't wholesale, particularly if you are still learning the business. Since your intent as an ethical professional should be to settle every deal, it will be extremely helpful to have a stable of hard money lenders to call on in order to finance the purchase and rehab of the property. The second advantage to developing lending contacts is to develop a reliable source of lenders that your investor buyers can borrow from so that your deals will close and you will get paid.

Many prospective buyers are not cash buyers, whether they claim to be or not. In reality, most cannot write a check from their bank account, but must borrow their money from various sources. Depending on their source of funds, this may or may not be acceptable. If an investor/buyer doesn't have a legitimate source of funds, it is your job to determine if they qualify to work with one of your hard money lenders. Many are capable of making mortgage payments to complete a rehab and would love to buy your properties if they can come up with the cash to purchase it. In this scenario, it is your job to take control of the deal and lead them to the money. Become their financing connection as well as the seller of the property.

Be careful. Maintain control of the transaction and use some discretion in deciding whom to take to your lenders. Don't burn bridges by bringing deadbeat buyers who default regularly. Your buyer's credit report should show intent to repay all debts on time and they should have some source of regular income that gives them the ability to make mortgage payments to your lender.

Ultimately, your goal is to take a potential buyer, assuming they meet minimum criteria, to one of your lenders. I have developed a regular following of investors who buy from me because I find properties and line up the financing. Many investors would like to purchase property if they can find the money. By connecting your wholesale buyers with your lenders, you will make your properties more accessible through financing and ultimately increase your profits.

BECOME THE BANK AND SELL MORE HOUSES

If you choose to use private money to fund a rehab project, one potential advantage is that you can act as a source of financing for your homebuyer. Depending on how you intend to market your completed rehabs, your hard money lenders may be a great resource to help you complete more deals. If you intend to offer owner financing, you might consider selling the properties by wrapping the hard money loans used during purchasing.

To be successful, I borrow money to renovate cheap homes and then mark up prices to make my profit by collecting down payments and the spread between the buyer's mortgage payment and my payment to the lender. Once my buyer refinances, I collect the difference between the principal balances between the two loans. Despite working in the past, wrapping a hard money loan to sell a home is a worst-case scenario. Today, I'll sell the home with owner financing and wrap the mortgage as a safety net. Before making this a primary technique, I strongly suggest you learn a little more about financing in general and the cost of foreclosures in your state. Taking a home back through foreclosure can be a very costly and lengthy process.

HOW TO LOCATE HARD MONEY LENDERS

Finding hard money lenders isn't a mystery. Get out there and take the right steps to locate them. When talking with other professionals, I refer to my lenders as private lenders for the simple reason that everyone is not familiar with the term "hard money" lender. I have found most of my lenders by asking for referrals from other investors, attorneys, accountants or insurance agents who are willing to help because I return the favor. Some of my favorite people to ask are settlement/closing attorneys. They usually prepare the loan documents for hard money lenders and most of them will be able to give you at least one name. Sometimes, the attorney I ask is a hard money lender.

ACCOUNTANTS

Accountants are a good source for locating hard money lenders for three reasons:

1. Many have clients who have cash and need to do something with it.
2. In some cases, they have clients who already hold paper. These clients are great to approach about lending money since they already understand the lending business. They have taken back paper after selling a property or they have lent their funds to another. Real estate paper is a very secure investment and people who understand the business of lending don't mind doing real estate loans, especially when the LTV is low and the interest rate is high.
3. If someone trusts their accountant enough to let them handle their finances, a referral from their accountant should carry a lot of clout.

HOME RENOVATIONS

Another method of finding hard money lenders is to write down the addresses of homes undergoing renovation. With some exceptions, if you go to the courthouse with ten addresses to uncover the lender involved, you will find that a private lender is funding at least one of them. Contact the lenders you discover and add them to the list, especially if they have already lent money in an area where you want to invest.

INSURANCE AGENTS

Insurance agents who sell hazard insurance policies (particularly those agents who specialize in investment properties) must put a "loss payee" on all of the policies where a lender is involved. The lender is the loss payee, and of all the loss payees, the insurance agent can determine which are private lenders. An active agent could probably go through their records and come up with dozens of names of people who have privately lent money on property where they have written policies.

MORTGAGE BROKERS

Hard money lenders can also be found through mortgage brokers, particularly those that work with investors on a routine basis. Any mortgage broker who deals with investors should have a hard money lender in their toolbox. Otherwise, I wouldn't consider them a good mortgage broker. You may have to pay the mortgage broker a fee for the referral, but this is a small price to pay in return for closing a deal.

LOOKING FOR LOOT IN THE WRONG PLACES

Finding a hard money lender has to do with looking in the right circles as well as the type and number of people you ask. Don't ask an employee at Qwiki-Mart when you should be asking an attorney or a title company. Basically, if you don't get anywhere the first time, don't stop asking until you find one.

HARD MONEY LENDERS ARE PEOPLE TOO

When communicating with hard money lenders, keep in mind that most are private individuals. They are not institutional investors who have a set standard guidelines dictated by the Federal Reserve. As individuals, they can be flexible or they can be tough. They can be your neighbor, your doctor, your attorney or your bus driver. They usually don't advertise that they lend money and work through word-of-mouth.

QUESTIONS TO ASK HARD MONEY LENDERS

1) What LTV do you lend up to?
   Typically they will answer 50-75 percent—the more the better.

2) Will you finance 100% of the purchase price?
   Some will, some won't—it depends on the deal.

3) Are there any areas that you won't lend in?
   Some lenders prefer certain areas.

4) What are your terms?
   Usually 12-18 percent and 1-10 points.

5) Do you check credit?
   Some do, some don't.

6) Will you lend repair money?
   Most of the lenders that I know will lend repair money.

7) How much notice do you need to fund a deal?
   I have received enough to cover my purchase and closing costs from a hard money lender in as little as a day. He personally dropped a check off for 41k the next morning.

8) Will you lend money for closing costs?
   Some will, some won't.

9) Do you prefer to work with a certain attorney or title company?
   Most lenders prefer to use one that they have used in the past.

10) Is there an appraisal fee?
    Some charge appraisal/inspection fees, especially larger lenders.

11) Would you be willing to write me a prequalification letter that I can submit with my offers?
    I have asked two lenders to do this for me and they were both happy to do it.

12) If I locate the deals and bring buyers to you, would you be interested in financing these buyers?
    High volume lenders want all the business they can get while those with limited resources are pickier when choosing a lending candidate.

HARD MONEY LENDER QUESTIONNAIRE

Name: _____

Address: _____

_____

Phone Number: _____

Fax Number: _____

1) What LTV do you lend up to?
2) Will you finance 100% of the purchase price?
3) Are there any areas that you won't lend in?
4) What are your terms?
5) Do you check credit?
6) Will you lend repair money?
7) How much notice do you need to fund a deal?
8) Will you lend money for closing costs?
9) Do you prefer to work with a certain attorney or title company?
10) Is there an appraisal fee?
11) Would you be willing to write me a prequalification letter that I can submit with my offers?
12) If I locate the deals and bring buyers to you, would you be interested in financing these buyers?

PREQUALIFICATION LETTERS

You will need a prequalification letter to submit along with your offers on many distressed properties, particularly those owned by institutions. You can obtain a prequalification letter from a hard money lender to help your offer carry more weight, especially when the lender is active and recognizable in your area.

AVOID COMMITMENTS

Be sure to ask your lender for a "Prequalification Letter" and not a "Commitment Letter." A commitment letter locks them into the deal where a prequalification letter gives them an out (usually through a low appraisal) if they don't like the deal. Many newbies have contacted me about having difficulty in obtaining a prequalification letter and they don't seem to understand the difference. Here is a sample of the text from one of my prequalification letters:

"This is to confirm that you have been pre-qualified for financing for the purchase of single family residential home based on a 70 % loan to value appraisal, but with no cash out. The prequalification is good for a period of 60 days from the above date and is renewable by mutual written consent.

As always, final loan commitment is subject to the appraised valuation by our appraiser."

WHY IS IT CALLED HARD MONEY?

Don't be confused by the term "hard money." It does not mean the money is difficult to find or obtain. Quite the contrary, it is actually some of the easiest money to get. In the world of finance, money is either "hard" or "soft." Hard money costs more. Softer money costs less.

In the case of private financing, the terms for hard money loans are exceptionally harsh with very low loan to values (LTV's), higher than market interest rates and a lot of upfront points. With terms so favorable to the lenders, most hard money providers are primarily concerned with the value of the property, placing less emphasis on the credit of the payer. They want to know that if the payer defaults, then they will possess an asset to recoup their original investment if not more.

However, this is not to say that lenders desire to go through the hassle and expense of taking back and reselling a property. Rather to point out that the loans are secure, whether a borrower pays or not.

NO DEBT INVESTING

After reading a chapter on how to borrow money, it would be wrong of me to stop and not include this chapter. In 2006, I made the decision not to borrow to do my deals. This was a decision that I made based off of my Christian beliefs and how debt was affecting my life. I wanted to be free and I did not want to be ruled by debt. Not only did I stop borrowing, I eliminated the $4.5 million in debt that I accumulated.

First, I went back to wholesaling. It doesn't require borrowing and I was good at it so I started redirecting my focus back to it. I needed to evaluate my cash reserves—how much to keep in reserve and how much to put toward buying and renovating houses. I could fund one deal at a time on my own from this account.

My needs were so great that wholesaling and one deal at a time were not going to meet my needs, so I had to come up with another solution. I started joint venturing with other investors. I leveraged my knowledge and used others resources to do more deals. While I was giving up part of my profits, the transformation in my business was incredible. Now I was not limited to how many deals I could do (at least from a financial point of view). I was no longer bound by how many mortgage payments I could afford each month. Those mortgage payments needed to be paid whether or not I had a deal. I was biting my nails some months while swimming in cash in others. Joint venturing on my rehab deals smoothed that out.

The people I borrowed money from were the ones that I made my partners in the deals. As time goes by, you can improve these relationships and give your partners a smaller piece of the pie because they love the returns. Today, many of my students are investing without borrowing a dime. They do everything as joint ventures and are funding many of their deals with their own cash. Not only are they building solid foundations, but it really contributes to their Lifeonaire lifestyle. One of the tenets of being a Lifeonaire is to be debt free.

REAL LIFE EXPERIENCE — PRIVATE LENDERS

I have a list of about twenty-five private lenders who lend money in my area. I have only used five of them, using one for about 90 percent of the deals when I need financial assistance. I use this one lender in particular because he never runs out of money. He also does every deal that I bring to him, it is strictly business. He is concerned about the home and nothing more—his rules stay the same. Many other lenders tend to be fickle, lending in some cases but not others, which doesn't work for me, especially when I'm doing a lot of volume. I need a lender who produces every single time.

CHAPTER 11

OTHER SOURCES OF FINANCING

LINES OF CREDIT

Lines of credit (LOC's) come in all shapes and sizes. They can be secured or unsecured. If secured, they can be collateralized either by assets you already own or by assets that you are going to own. Some lines of credit will require down payments, while others will fund 100 percent of the purchase and rehab costs. Some require appraisals while others do not. Each lender LOC will be different.

When I renovate a home today, I use one of my lines of credit to finance the project. My LOC providers offer lower interest rates than private lenders and are usually more generous with appraisals, something that allows me to pull all the cash I need for repairs. My bank takes my word for the value of the home and only checks the assessed value to see if my estimate is within reason. They lend up to 100 percent of the assessed value, which is great depending on how close to market value the properties in the area are assessed. However, this also seems to be rare since I have only heard of two banks that have done this.

USE LOCAL BANKS

I highly recommend approaching small local banks to obtain this type of credit. National banks are corporations that are more interested in marketing canned products than tailoring something to suit your needs. If you don't fit into a formula, they will not usually create something specifically for your needs. As real estate investors, we are such a small part of a multi-billion dollar banking world that none of the national banks care to take the time to figure out how to help us. On the other hand, a local bank is fighting to get business from the national banks and will usually bend over backwards to help. Steer clear of the big operations and stick with the type of bank where you can talk with the bank president, rather than a branch manager.

Once you have established a good relationship with a bank, they can usually do anything that you need from short-term rehab financing to long-term rental financing/refinancing to working capital loans to signature loans. They are also more flexible, more responsive and even offer personal services. For example, I can call my bank and ask them to wire funds with just my verbal request. If I tried to do this with a major institution, they would tell me to take a hike. Local banks also move quickly and know who you are when you call.

The only possible limitation is the amount of money that they are permitted to lend. Federal guidelines limit the amount that a bank can lend to any one borrower to one percent of the total assets of the bank, meaning smaller banks can only lend so much. With my bank, I'm "limited" to $700,000 with one and $5,000,000 with another. Since I don't do renovations in excess of $500,000, these aren't really limits.

HOW TO OBTAIN AN LOC

I've heard several variations about obtaining lines of credit. Personally, I had to demonstrate experience as a rehabber before any bank would work with me. My first LOC was small at $100k, but my credit was good (not great) and I had only been rehabbing for a year. Though the bank was fairly aggressive, I don't think they would have given me the LOC if I had less experience.

To obtain the LOC that I use today, the bank requires me to have a two-year track record. In addition, my credit for this line had to be excellent. Apparently, these two points of criteria outweighed my financials, which showed that I had been losing money for the previous two years. When I started to explain that we expensed everything we could to show losses, they said, "We know. We see it all the time and we are aware of the way you run your business, so we won't hold it against you." As a result, I received a line of credit, which I use for over 75 percent of my deals.

If you work with the right banks, you can accomplish most deals. With the first bank, I didn't have a track record and fair credit. With the second bank, I had good credit and more of a track record, but was showing losses. In both cases, I obtained the lines of credit I was seeking. The banks viewed themselves like hard money lenders do, keeping their LTV (loan to value) at about 70 percent, figuring they couldn't lose.

CASH

If you happen to have cash to fund your deals, then you're a step ahead of the rest. Now that I have cash, I use it for a variety of reasons.

Occasionally, I'll dip into my pocket to rehab a home, but I prefer to use my line of credit. If a good deal comes along and I have to move quickly, I don't have a problem bringing cash to the table. I use cash to inventory homes, sitting on them until I finish other projects. In these instances, I don't like to use my LOC since the bank starts to ask questions when I don't ask for repair draws for three to four months.

Unlike other teachers, I'm not opposed to using cash if you have it. It makes life as a rehabber much easier. In addition, your risk, if you are buying right, is essentially zero. Even if you had to sell your home through a distress sale to get your money back, it is highly unlikely that you would lose any of your investment if you bought the home right and did a quality renovation.

Make sure you have enough cash on hand versus invested in your rehabs. If you start to fund a few deals out of your own pocket and are not careful, you might find yourself with a ton of equity and no cash in your account—I speak from experience.

I knew my cash was safely sitting in my homes, but it was nerve-wracking to have everything tied up and nothing in the bank. If you intend to use cash to purchase and renovate a home, be sure that you are willing and able to leave your money invested until the project is complete, which for me is an average of five to six months.

PARTNERS

If at all possible, I recommend that you avoid this option. Like many other things, partnerships have their place, but most are unsuccessful for one reason and one reason only: Partners usually do not make their expectations of one another clear.

Many things are left out of the initial discussions and when they become an issue, one partner typically feels the other is responsible. I feel comfortable saying that over 90 percent of the time, either one or both partners end up regretting getting involved in the partnership.

If you find it necessary to have a partner, I suggest you limit it to one deal and only one deal. If that deal works out, then you may decide to do another with the same person, but do yourself a favor and limit your partnership to one deal at first. This is one situation where you should "date" before entering a long-term relationship.

OWNER FINANCING

On occasion, I have had an owner finance my purchase of their property. I know that many people teach this method of acquiring real estate, but I haven't pursued it much. More owners may have offered financing if I had asked, but I don't always look for the best way to purchase a property, just the easiest. For me, the easiest is to offer cash upfront. It's my cookie cutter approach to purchasing and it works really well. I usually don't even consider doing deals another way.

If you prefer owner financing, don't hesitate to ask a seller to finance a home. They might say yes. It has happened to me and I have financed a number of investors who have asked me to finance their purchase of one of my homes.

PURCHASE AND REHAB LOANS FROM COMMERCIAL BANKS

If you can't find a bank to offer you a line of credit, look for a bank that will do purchase and rehab loans. Some national banks and many smaller banks will lend you purchase and rehab money to do renovations. Most will require 10-20 percent down when you purchase the home, but you can usually recover this money as part of the draws that you receive from your repair escrow, provided the amount of your repair escrow exceeds the amount that you actually spend on your renovation.

It's very common for a bank to lend more repair money than is necessary. If I expect to spend $25k on my rehab, I can request and typically borrow $35k from the bank. As I draw this $35k out of my repair escrow, I gradually put $10k ($35k-$25k) into my pocket, which helps me to recoup (legally, mind you) my out-of-pocket expenses from when I settle on the property.

Note that I'm not doing anything wrong here. The bank is making a total loan that falls within their loan-to-value parameters based on their assessment of the value of the property. I am just taking part of those loan proceeds and reimbursing myself for some of my costs, which my bank has advised me to do. They claim that I need to be paid as well.

I can't stress enough the importance of eventually developing a relationship with a bank. Here and there I have "needed" my bank and they were there for me as a result of the relationship. Deal with small banks where you can speak with the president and you'll be just fine.

HOW TO FIND MONEY

Finding any type of money is simply a matter of asking around, calling around and acting on leads. I have referred many to investor-friendly lenders but most just stash the names on their desk to get lost in paperwork. You can't develop a relationship with someone if you don't keep in touch, so be sure to act on the leads that you get.

GOOD, BAD OR UGLY CREDIT

Credit doesn't need to be an issue if you choose to rehab homes. If you are truly determined to succeed, nothing should stand in your way, not even an ugly credit profile. As an investor and small business owner, obtaining financing for your projects is just one of the obstacles in your path. There will be others and it is your job as an entrepreneur to find solutions.

With regard to financing, I have pointed out several avenues of funding, from private lenders to commercial purchase and rehab loans. Some require better credit than others and some require more money than others. Your job is to discover which sources of financing are available to you and how to take advantage of them. While some private lenders take your credit into consideration, many will not. They typically look at the value of the property in relation to the amount you would like to borrow.

If the lenders you encounter want better credit or more money down, you need to find a solution. Educate yourself on the basics of the rehab process and put together a short presentation, either formally on paper or informally in your mind, outlining your plans. Start pitching it to people with resources, offering a nice interest rate and/or a part of the profits when you resell the home in return for the use of their money or the use of their credit to qualify for purchase and rehab financing.

This may seem far-fetched, but once you start intelligently offering people who have money and/or credit a good return for becoming your partner, you'll be surprised at the response you'll get. Some won't listen, but keep trying until someone does. It all comes down to how bad you want to succeed.

With enough effort, anyone can find someone to fund a deal if the numbers makes sense. Some will have to work harder than others and those with no money or credit should arrange financing before putting a property under contract. If you cannot find someone to fund the deal, feel blessed. You probably offered too much and you should be thankful you could use your financing contingency to exit a losing proposition gracefully. Furthermore, you learned a lesson without losing money. If you have good credit, things are easier. You are able to get money at more attractive terms, including better rates and higher loan-to-value ratios. If the numbers are right, both good and bad credit investors can do deals.

REAL LIFE EXPERIENCE

Though I don't use them much anymore, hard money lenders have been a reliable source of financing for me ever since I started rehabbing. My first project involved money from a private lender and throughout one phase of my investing career, I relied on them rather heavily. At one point, I owed a certain lender over $800,000. Oddly enough, this lender wouldn't have recognized me if I walked up to him on the street.

I have never had trouble finding or obtaining money from private lenders despite an average credit rating. Even on my first rehab, it was easy to find private financing. Acting on a lead that I received from another investor, I called a lender and he offered to lend me the money I needed to purchase the property within ten minutes. Since it was my first deal, he didn't lend me repair money, but I funded the rehab with profits from my wholesale deals.

For my second rehab, I partnered with someone with an unsecured line of credit. We borrowed the purchase money from a hard money lender and used my partner's LOC to fund our out-of-pocket expenses at closing and repairs. We were actually so inexperienced that we didn't even ask for repair money from the private lender.

The rehab took longer than expected and we had to cut corners. As a result, the finished product was average quality and the only potential buyers were people with no other options. Our final sales price was significantly lower than the price we originally intended to sell. In the end, we settled for selling the home on a rent-to-own basis (rent with an option to buy) to someone with bad credit. The deal worked out but my deals go much smoother today. I now have resources available to rehab homes correctly and I have identified and use my best funding sources to my advantage.

CHAPTER 12

SETTLEMENT ATTORNEY / TITLE CO.

Whether you renovate or wholesale, a competent real estate attorney will be an important asset on your team. Besides providing referrals of Realtors, lenders (private or conventional) and accountants, a settlement attorney can be instrumental in creatively structuring a deal when the need arises. Use them to handle most or all of your purchases, and call when you have a question or concern. For these reasons, choose your settlement attorney carefully.

Even though an attorney or title company may be accustomed to doing real estate settlements, this doesn't mean they know how to bring a creative deal to fruition. Don't be their guinea pig for a newbie. Find out which attorneys that other investors are using and check them out. You will discover that the more active the investor, the more credible their attorney.

NOT ALL ATTORNEYS ARE CREATED EQUAL

When selecting an attorney or title company, you will find not all are created equal. Many people assume that a settlement attorney is qualified to handle your deals, which just isn't true. More qualified attorneys give better service than others. In addition, not all settlement attorneys work with investors.

As you meet other investors, you will notice that most use the same attorney or, in a highly populated area, you will be able to count the attorneys used by investors on one hand. This is because of the creativity that some real estate transactions require, investors like to use an experienced attorney. Another reason is service. Some attorneys are downright lousy, even with a lot of experience. Be sure to select an attorney who will answer the phone and return messages in a timely manner.

Don't reinvent the wheel. Talk to other investors and pick an experienced attorney that you feel comfortable with and who provides good service. Your investing experience will be much more pleasant.

EXPECT GOOD SERVICE

Some attorneys are very disorganized—not a positive note in a paper intensive business. Some work last minute, make mistakes frequently or just seem generally overwhelmed. Others do not return phone calls and some are downright rude. If any prospective settlement attorneys show these characteristics, avoid them. Find someone who provides good service as well as quality work.

You should also be able to rely on an attorney to move quickly or take an urgent call when necessary. Likewise, the possibility exists that you will find a deal that needs to be closed as soon as possible and you should know your attorney can make the necessary arrangements and close the deal in a matter of days.

Of course you shouldn't make a habit of rushing your attorney to close deals. Check to see how much time they prefer and how fast they can move so you know your limits when negotiating. Then mention that here and there it may be necessary to move really fast in order to take advantage of a good deal. Above all, remember to respect your attorney but if you are not getting good service, find a new attorney.

PRICING

Here's the good news. Despite experience levels, most title attorneys will price themselves within a couple hundred dollars of one another. For this reason, I don't worry much about pricing as long as my deals are getting done without a lot of hassle and neither should you. Most attorneys will charge the same amount for a settlement with a difference of only $250 between the high and low pricing. So don't get too hung up on the costs and place your emphasis on receiving good service.

SEEK EXPERIENCE

Experienced attorneys can save you from your inexperience. When I began as a wholesaler, I only knew the basics. I didn't know every step involved in seeing a deal to the end, nor did I know all of the different methods of doing a deal.

Luckily, I encountered a couple of very experienced attorneys who have experienced just about every kind of deal out there. They taught me a lot. Sometimes I would bring creative deals for them to settle. I thought I had structured a deal perfectly only to have them tell me a better way—one that would make more money. Sometimes I structured deals that couldn't be done and the attorney took the time to figure out a way to get it done. These are just a couple of reasons why you want to draw from the experience of attorneys who have been around for a while.

USING THE SELLER'S TITLE COMPANY

One thing that has changed over the last few years is that sellers (banks) are beginning to mandate that you use their title company to perform the title search and settle on the property. I don't like this...

Apparently, according to the federal RESPA (Real Estate Settlement Procedures Act), it is illegal for them to require this and I usually go against their wish. Both times that I used their companies, I was burned—once with exorbitant closing costs and once with a failure to record any of the documents after settlement. In the second instance, I renovated the home, signed a contract with a buyer and received a call from my buyer's title company who informed me that I didn't own the home I was trying to sell or, at the very least, my ownership wasn't on public record. This was very frustrating and forced me to spend hours of my time communicating with the prior seller's title company to get the problem resolved.

Today, when I have an offer accepted, I go to my title company and get the process started despite signing an addendum from the seller that states I must use their title company. When the selling agent calls to find out why I haven't called their company to arrange settlement, I tell them that I have called my attorney who has everything under control. Usually, they let me go but sometimes they object. Regardless, I continue to move forward in this manner. To date, no one has ever stopped me from using my own title company nor have I had to reimburse the seller's title company for anything they might have spent in vain.

In final analysis, if you find yourself in a position where you absolutely must use a seller's title company or risk losing a good deal, judge for yourself whether or not you want to use their title company. Personally, I would prefer to use my own, but I might use theirs if absolutely necessary, especially if the profit would adequately compensate me for the additional frustrations and potential risks. If I did use their title company, I might have my title attorney review their title work or order a complete set of title work through my attorney. Both of these solutions cost a couple hundred dollars, but at least they would provide me with peace of mind.

Please don't let this debate stop you from doing deals. Not every home is going to have incurable or uncured title problems. Just be aware that it can happen and that I have seen it happen. I would rather see you use a seller's title company than use this as an excuse not to do deals.

CHAPTER 13

INSURANCE AGENTS

WHETHER WHOLESALING OR REHABBING, always collect the names of insurance brokers who act on behalf of low-cost underwriters. Brokers who work with investors and investment properties can be "deal savers" when you need to settle quickly. Whether you are wholesaling or purchasing an investment property, you can call and ask one of the insurers on your list to write a binder and fax it to your settlement table. They can do this quickly in an emergency to solve the problem and make you look like a hero.

Since many insurance agencies aren't willing to write policies on vacant investment properties, obtaining insurance on these properties is not always easy and it can be costly. This area has created some heartache for me.

Some of my policies have been canceled because my homes were vacant and the policies didn't cover vacant homes, even though I was told that everything would be fine when I bought the policies. The insurance agent told me that they were rental policies for investors, but he didn't tell me that I had to have the homes occupied within thirty days. Perhaps I should have read the policies rather than taking the insurance professional at his word.

After receiving notice of these cancellations, I searched for insurance that covered vacant rehabs in progress. Of the policies that I could find, none would provide insurance unless I was spending in the neighborhood of $1,600 per year—an outrageous amount of money. Finally, I found Zurich, a much more reasonable underwriter. Zurich offers a builders' risk policy specifically designed for rehabbers and I currently use them for every rehab policy.

The cost is $4.50 for every $1,000 of after-repair value with a minimum premium, which approximates $350 for the year. It covers loss due to fire and natural disasters. The only disadvantages are no liability, it only covers the property for one year and you don't get anything refunded even if you sell the home within a year. However, you can have the peace of mind knowing that your home is covered at a minimal expense of around $30 per month. For further reassurance, you should seek a blanket liability policy to complement these fire/natural disaster policies.

CHAPTER 14

OTHER TEAM MEMBERS

BANKS

Like other resources, you should stay abreast of the climate in the local banking community. Find out who is working with investors, what types of rehab loans they are doing and rates as well as terms.

If you are wholesaling to landlords or decide to enter into the rental arena, you should find out who is doing unseasoned refinances and purchase money loans for rental properties. If you or your wholesale buyers are using hard money to acquire rental properties, find a lender in your Rolodex who offers unseasoned "cash out" refinances. Once you or your landlord buyer make the necessary repairs, these loans permit you or your buyers to pull cash profits out of a property in the form of loan proceeds and replace your hard money loan with a loan that has more favorable terms. These will keep you and your buyers in business for the long run. If you do begin as a wholesaler, you will find this knowledge useful when you want to use these banks.

ACCOUNTANTS

It is not necessary for you to have an accountant in the beginning, but you will eventually need to find one. It's vital to find an accountant who understands real estate investing. I suggest finding an accountant who also invests in real estate since many are weak when it comes to understanding investors. Don't learn this the hard way like I had to years ago.

Some of my former accountants didn't understand rehabbing and selling or rehabbing and holding. Most of them understood buy, hold and depreciate, but most didn't understand the process of rehabbing, borrowing money to renovate or accounting for rehabbing properties in the same company that I held properties. They got everything mixed up. They didn't understand and never had the desire to figure it out. I recommend that you work with an accountant who has already worked with investors who rehab properties for sale and rental.

Currently, I have a bookkeeper that processes everything for my accountant. Once a month, I give her my bank statements, deposit slips, check stubs and settlement sheets for her to process and give to my accountant. It costs some money to do this, but it saves a lot of time, which is more important to me.

MORTGAGE BROKERS

Be careful when talking with mortgage brokers. They tell you they can do everything, that they produce constantly, that they won't waste your time, that their processors are great and that they have relationships with underwriters and are able to get difficult deals done better than anyone.

In reality, very few of the hundreds of brokers I've met have done a good job without wasting my time. Most mortgage brokers haven't been brokering loans very long. Without any experience, they decide to become mortgage brokers after performing another trade for years. When the industry boomed due to low interest rates, these people began selling mortgages, learning at the expense of the consumer.

ADVANTAGES TO WHOLESALERS

Even a good mortgage broker will have an extremely hard time arranging financing for your wholesale buyers through institutional financing.

Actually, it's nearly impossible. After the media sparking controversy regarding "flipping," most institutional lenders have come up with new guidelines that prevent investors from quick-turning properties.

The majority of institutional lenders will not provide funding to borrowers in cases where an assignment of contract or simultaneous close is involved. If you are selling your property within a year of purchase, lenders back away from the deal. If you ever hear anyone talk about "title seasoning," it usually refers to flipping a property in this manner. Unlike hard money lenders and local banks that don't require title seasoning before financing a new buyer, institutional lenders are requiring six to twelve months seasoning from the seller before financing a new buyer.

Some mortgage brokers will be able to take you to private lenders or local banks that will finance or refinance your wholesale buyers. Also, even if a broker can't finance or refinance your buyers, it pays to have a competent mortgage broker in your repertoire for those wholesale investors who may have a retail buyer for their homes but don't know where to get financing.

ADVANTAGES TO REHABBERS

If rehabbing and marketing on your own, get referrals from other investors who have had success with mortgage brokers. Personally, I do not go this route since I prefer to use real estate agents to sell my homes, letting them bring qualified buyers to me.

But, if you choose to sell your rehabs FSBO (For Sale By Owner), mortgage brokers can help your buyers obtain financing and help you stay on top of the activity in the mortgage markets, which is important. Keep yourself informed to know the current trends as well as obstacles that may arise.

With an ever changing market, it is not uncommon to get a loan commitment for a buyer only to have it withdrawn because the program that existed yesterday no longer exists today. Neither has it been uncommon to get all the way to the settlement table with a deal only to see it fall apart because the lender backed out. There are a lot of mortgage brokers out there. Sift through the pretenders and find a good broker, meaning an experienced professional with references.

BROKERS AND THE SUB-PRIME MARKET

Presently, when reselling rehabs, I deal with prime buyers who typically have their financing in place and have no need for a mortgage broker. Most of the investors I encounter excel with this strategy versus experiencing limited success with the sub-prime market (borrowers with less than perfect credit). While the potential for profit can be good, most investors usually end up making less, particularly if they aren't familiar with all of the issues involved.

I have used mortgage brokers and sold to sub-prime borrowers in the past and I may need to do it again. The industry changes regularly so be prepared to market your completed rehabs in various ways. Even though I market strictly to prime buyers, if the bottom drops out of the real estate market, I may be forced to change gears.

Some investors decide to pursue sub-prime buyers due to the increased number of rehabbing opportunities available in neighborhoods where most buyers have so-so credit and employment histories. But whatever your current or future reason for focusing on the sub-prime market, a good mortgage broker can be a wonderful asset. Make sure you enlist the services of someone with experience you can verify.

Virtually any broker can appear experienced to a beginner investor. Most brokers have access to the same lenders and receive the same rate sheets daily. They literally have access to hundreds of lenders. However, a broker may have only worked with a handful of lenders in their network, which is fine, as long as they have good relationships with that handful.

Good brokers will reveal their experience with these lenders upfront as a selling point, knowing they can keep returning to their proven sources. Less experienced brokers might say, "I have hundreds of investors and I can push any deal through." Beware of these guys. It is extremely difficult for a mortgage broker to establish a new relationship with a lender in the sub-prime market and painful when that relationship develops at your expense.

OTHER INVESTORS

Maintaining working relationships with other investors is something to work towards. I know people who feel everyone is a competitor. Consequently, they won't refer a single person to you nor will they work with you on deals. Their attitude reflects a cutthroat business. In reality, there is more business out there than any one investor can handle, yet these foolish investors ruin the benefits they might gain by networking in a ridiculous endeavor to corner the market.

I regularly help other investors without expecting anything in return. I believe that you should always offer help when asked—unconditionally and regardless of the actions of others. For instance, I have provided assistance to investors who will call or e-mail me for help, even when they won't give me the name of a mortgage broker or contractor. I don't understand why they won't share this information. One way or another, I'll find the resource that I'm seeking, so they aren't hurting me. They are hurting the mortgage broker, the contractor and themselves. The mortgage broker and contractor lose potential business and the investors lose profits from future deals or relationships as a result of their attitude.

Despite this, be sincere when helping others. Don't expect things in return. Expecting a favor returned damages the very relationship you are trying to build. Help other investors freely and sincerely and you will be pleasantly surprised to find that other investors will help you. Outsiders can be the biggest players on your team in referring people to you, buying homes from you, lending money to you, bringing deals to you, bringing other buyers to you or partnering with you. Don't burn bridges and risk losing all of this. Remember, friendly competition is a good thing. If you have no competition, then there isn't any opportunity.

I firmly believe in the saying, "What comes around, goes around." In my life, I feel as though I have witnessed this dozens of times. I believe you should always do unto others, as you would want them to do unto you. This philosophy may cause you to get burned here and there, but in the long run, you will come out way ahead. Even when it doesn't always work out, I would rather be broke and have lots of friends than make a lot of money and have everyone dislike me. If I ever need help in anything at all, business or personal, I feel very comfortable that there will be a slew of investors lining up to give me a helping hand. In addition, many of the friends I have made through investing will surely be lifelong friends, something that is much more rewarding than any money I might make investing in real estate.

CHAPTER 15

LOCATING OPPORTUNITIES

Y**OUR PRIMARY GOAL AS** a real estate investor is to locate moneymaking opportunities. These arrive in the form of distressed properties, which are safe and very lucrative.

DISTRESSED PROPERTIES

When a location is owned but unwanted, it is known as a distressed property. The property may need work or be a foreclosure the bank does not want—it could be an estate sale with a half dozen siblings who can't agree or owned by a tired landlord or an out-of-state proprietor who can't manage the property. Look for properties in these types of situations, particularly single-family homes. The seller doesn't want the property and you are coming to the rescue.

Personally, I have bought homes in move-in condition at wholesale prices and I have bought homes on the brink of being torn down at wholesale prices. In every instance, there was something that chased the retail buyer away. In some cases it was as small as dirty carpeting or peeling paint. In other cases, the home was clearly waiting for a wrecking ball and the owner knew no one else would want the home.

UNAPPEALING HOMES

Most distressed properties are eyesores. They will look and smell awful. Some have nearly burned down, other have holes in the roof, some smell like cesspools, others are filled with trash or have rotted floors and/or boarded windows. Do not be scared of these factors. Most of these repairs are actually cheap to fix.

Once a home does not appeal to the retail buyer, it automatically drops to the wholesale market. Within the wholesale market, there are far fewer buyers than the retail market. You stand a much better chance when there isn't a retail buyer to get a property at your price, leaving enough room for you to make a profit after rehab and retail.

VACANT HOMES

When looking for prospects, search for vacant homes. Out of the hundreds of properties I have bought since 1998, only a handful of properties had someone living in them and most of those should have been vacant.

In most cases, if you find yourself looking at occupied homes, you're looking at the wrong homes to find a deal. In my experience, the most motivated sellers are those who have vacant homes, mainly because vacant homes can only be trouble. Nothing good comes out of a home sitting, doing nothing. They deteriorate, are vandalized, cost money in taxes or in mortgage payments—a bad situation all around, but one to look for. So keep an eye out for vacant homes since they are your best shot for a moneymaker.

MOTIVATED SELLERS

Distressed situations, unappealing homes and vacant homes all point to the type of person you are seeking: the motivated seller.

Problems, whether related to the property or the owner (possibly both), create a motivated seller. Opportunities arise out of these situations because you can provide a solution that benefits both you and the seller. The bigger their problems, the more money you can make because most people lack creativity and patience to find a solution. Do not let unmotivated sellers waste your time. This doesn't mean you shouldn't keep in touch or leave contact information. Time has a way of changing everything and sometimes a non-motivated seller becomes a motivated seller.

Motivated sellers are not hard to recognize once you know the type of person that you are seeking. For many people, this takes a while to really understand. It took quite some time before I encountered a truly motivated seller and everything made sense. After viewing dozens of homes and making hundreds of calls, I finally ran into a motivated seller. After meeting this person, I saw opportunities everywhere. Until that happened, I didn't think investing in my area was plausible.

Also referred to as "don't wanters," some examples of motivated sellers are banks, divorced couples, heirs to an estate, tired landlords and out-of-state owners. The sellers with the highest degree of motivation are willing to do anything to sell their property.

When you make offers on foreclosures through an agent, most motivated sellers will be banks that need to unload the properties due to federal banking regulations. Oftentimes, their properties need more work than a retail buyer is willing to do, so the properties fall into the investor market.

Occasionally, FSBO properties need so much work that the owner is willing to take a big discount to get rid of the property. Personally, I have bought about 90 percent of the properties that I have wholesaled or rehabbed through Realtors and the remainder from FSBO's.

HOW TO ATTRACT OR LOCATE MOTIVATED SELLERS

Personally, my first and primary source of properties is through the MLS (multiple listing service). Realtors have more properties available through MLS than any other source and I take this easy route for the bulk of my properties. My Realtors provide me with a list of all the foreclosures in my buying area, ranging between handful and hundreds of records. My list also includes fixer uppers and updates, meaning all new homes listed since a specific date. However, there are other ways to find motivated sellers.

CLASSIFIEDS

I also scan the classifieds for opportunities. I have bought a number of properties by calling on classified ads online or in print form. It never hurts to call and many times your conversations will become helpful learning experiences where you and the advertiser learn from one another, especially if the advertiser is an investor.

FARMING

When you farm, or cultivate a particular neighborhood, your goal is to turn up every opportunity. You want everyone in the neighborhood to know you are buying homes in that area. By placing signs throughout the neighborhood, sending postcards, dropping business cards, advertising, leaving door hangers, you can pull more deals out of an area. Make yourself a household name in the community and sellers will automatically think of you. If a home becomes vacant, a neighbor may refer you to a potential seller, even before they place a home on the market.

Farming allows you to concentrate on a smaller area and the more adept you become at solving real estate problems, the more deals you will be able to farm. Whether or not these deals will be rehab candidates or other opportunities (commercial deals, "subject to" transactions, lease options, mobile home parks, rental property, raw land, etc.)

depends on the area. There is more opportunity within fifteen minutes of your own residence than you can imagine.

ADVERTISEMENTS

Running "I Buy Houses" ads is another effective way to find properties. However, don't be discouraged if you aren't buying homes right away. I purchase about one out of every twenty homes from callers. As you grow as an investor and increase your ability to negotiate other deals (lease/options, "subject to" deals, deals involving owner financing), ratios will improve. The ad I run reads as follows:

Quick Cash for homes*Any area*Any cond*(xxx)xxx-xxxx

Classified ads are unpredictable. One week, you get ten calls and the next week you may not get any. The key to running a successful ad campaign is to have your ad running continuously. Once a week should be fine. I get better results when I run my ads more frequently. Don't expect to run one ad and have more properties than you can handle. In advertising, repetition is the key.

In the days of the internet, there are many ways to get the word out there and a ton of free options for advertising. But do not discount publications such as the Pennysaver, Thrifty Nickel, or the local newspaper classifieds. They all work.

As an investor, you will be doing a lot of advertising—some for buying property and some for selling property. Run an advertisement every week if not every day stating that you buy houses. Advertise in as many places as your budget allows because the incoming calls received will be directly related to the number of spots that your ad appears. Consider shirts, hats, pins, signs and any other medium you can imagine. Be proud of what you do and let the whole world know that you buy houses.

REALTORS

Realtors are a fantastic source for properties. They have more properties available to than anyone else. There can be tens of thousands of properties listed on the Multiple Listing Service (MLS) in your area. In some areas, investors may use realtors for a very high percentage of the properties that they buy. Even if this isn't the case, you will be able to find some deals among the thousands on the MLS. As you make offers, you will learn which properties to target and how to play the system in your area. After dealing with the same Realtors, you will find out whom they represent and whether or not you are wasting your time with a low offer. For the most part, there still isn't really any rhyme or reason as to what sellers will do so beginners can play the numbers game to their benefit, get some offers accepted, and make some money.

The largest banks in the country—the ones with real estate owned (REO)—list most of their homes with real estate agents. Because of the sensitive nature of the banking industry, it is written in the corporate charters of most banks that all REO's are to be listed with a Realtor. This confirms that the properties are offered in a competitive environment, generating the highest sales price for the bank. In other words, the bank does not want their REO manager discounting houses to friends and family when a higher offer may have come from someone else. So if REO's are what you want to target, you will have to establish a good relationship with a real estate agent.

It is not uncommon for homes to be auctioned of online, in fact it is becoming more popular everyday and this should be an option that you consider.

SHOULD I BECOME A REALTOR?

Being licensed has its advantages and its disadvantages. The two biggest advantages for investors are direct access to property listings and direct access to comparable sales information. You can also submit your own offers and collect a commission check for every house that you buy and sell. If you are doing rehabs, you can list all of them on the MLS yourself and save on commissions. Finally, you might be able to earn a commission check by helping buyers that you encounter with a home even if they don't want to buy one that you own.

Two of the main disadvantages include time for continuing education and the expense involved in terms of dues, fees, and insurance. If you aren't doing many deals or making much money, being licensed will work against you. However, if you are doing a fair amount of deals a year, having your license may pay off. Whether you have your license or not, you can succeed as an investor. Weigh the pros and cons to make your own decision.

The second disadvantage is that you have to disclose you are an agent and you are subject to different rules for advertising and your broker may have a say in how you buy and sell houses.

CARDS, FLYERS AND SIGNS

Passing out "I Buy Houses" business cards has also been an effective form of advertising. People usually keep these cards or pass them along when they know of someone in need. I hand out cards everywhere and I make sure to give one to recent buyers who become very good testimonials. Leave business cards everywhere you go. So many investors hold onto their business cards, reasoning that they shouldn't waste them. Well, having them sit in a box is a big waste of money, mostly because they aren't making you money like they should.

Business cards, flyers and signs are all cheap and effective ways of generating leads. Leaving cards or flyers on the doors of vacant houses has worked for me. I haven't done it much, but I've received calls from the owners of the properties when I have. This strategy could probably generate many leads for me but I've gotten lazy and don't stop to get out to leave a card.

FIND A BIRD DOG OR A WHOLESALER

As I get busier, I do not mind people bringing properties to me for renovation. My time is better spent on things other than riding around to find the best deals, so I don't mind paying someone else to do the legwork for a profitable deal. If you choose to rehab properties, you can find bird dogs and wholesalers by speaking with other investors, networking at a local investment club, running ads or by taking a beginner under your wing.

REAL LIFE EXPERIENCE — AN UNAPPEALING HOME

One home I renovated was one the previous occupant lost to foreclosure. They had their electricity turned off for four years, their water service turned off for six years and their gas service totally abandoned for six years. Without water and electricity, the home couldn't possibly be cleaned. A nauseating potpourri blasted you in the face before you opened the front door.

As you can imagine (or maybe you can't), the inside was absolutely filthy and full of trash—rotten food and stagnant water. The commode and several buckets were filled with excrement and the tub was caked with dirt and grime. The floors were rotten and the kitchen was absolutely disgusting.

The exterior was so bad that the gutters were actually split down the middle from rust. Twelve-foot trees were growing in the pool, making us wary about what might be living at the bottom. In the final analysis, it took not one (as usual) but two forty-five-yard dumpsters just to do the initial demo and remove the trash. Since then, we have hauled away another seven stake body truckloads of trash.

Properties such as these are one of the toughest things for new investors to accept as a moneymaking opportunity. These are actually what you are looking for as an investor. When I do a renovation, I prefer that the home be a disaster area. I'm going to redo the entire home, so I would rather have a total dump. A kitchen that adds value because it was updated ten years ago is useless to me since I'm going to tear it out anyway. That's why I search for complete catastrophes. A home that needs a paint job and the carpets cleaned is not a fixer upper. I'm not suggesting that you only look for total disasters. When I started, I made my money with lighter rehabs. Since then, my preference has just gravitated toward the bigger jobs.

CHAPTER 16

BUYING FROM BIRD DOGS

BIRD DOGS AND WHOLESALERS play a valuable role in the real estate community for rehabbers who want to do something other than legwork to find profitable renovation projects. This chapter covers what a rehabber should consider before using a bird dog or a wholesaler. It is written for the rehabber, but aspiring bird dogs and wholesalers may find it instructive as well.

WORKING WITH A BIRD DOG TO FIND PROPERTIES

Typically, bird dogs are very inexperienced. Because they are less expensive than wholesalers, they look at properties for you in order to learn the ropes. The main disadvantage is that they require a little time to educate.

Bird dogs can be useful when chasing down potential deals, but before using one, it's important to know enough about evaluating properties to ask them the right questions after they examine a home. Their answers will determine if you should make an offer and what the amount should be.

In terms of compensation, I would pay a bird dog $1,000-$2,000 per accepted offer with the money to be paid at settlement. When I was a bird dog, this was the arrangement I had with my mentor/rehabber and I believe it is still fair today.

WORKING WITH A WHOLESALER TO FIND PROPERTIES

Wholesalers make money, sometimes their living, by finding good deals that fit the criteria of their list of buyers. They save you a lot of time by serving up good deals that you might never find from your efforts. Another advantage of using a wholesaler is that there is no need for training. You just need to get on their buyers list by giving them your preferences including area and type of home. They are usually more expensive than bird dog, but this is a cost of doing business.

KEEP IN TOUCH

When using wholesalers, consider calling on occasion to keep in touch and see what they might have for sale. Active wholesalers don't always have time to call everyone on their buyers list when something becomes available, so they might have an ideal property but not a chance to call or email you. If you're lucky, you'll catch them before they've had a chance to market the property to another buyer.

PUT EACH DEAL IN WRITING AND PROVIDE AN EARNEST MONEY DEPOSIT

If you do buy something from a wholesaler, remember that it's not a deal without a signed contract/assignment. Furthermore, when signing a contract, be prepared to give an earnest money deposit just like you would any other seller. This deposit reimburses the wholesaler for their deposit when submitting an offer to the seller and allows them to continue making offers. In addition, your deposit makes you appear legitimate. Wholesalers receive more than enough calls from people wanting to tie up a property for $100—don't let yourself be lumped in with these wannabes.

DETERMINE HOW QUICKLY YOU MUST CLOSE

When buying a property from a wholesaler, consider the time remaining before the closing date on their contract with the seller. If you are using your own cash, this isn't a big deal. If you are using a private lender, they may need time to inspect and appraise the property as well as have their attorney prepare any loan documents and forward them to the title company performing the settlement.

COORDINATE THE DETAILS

In addition to signing a contract, giving a deposit and securing a closing date, one of you—either you or the wholesaler—needs to coordinate and stay on top of the settlement process, keeping the other party informed at all times.

PROVE YOUR WORTH

To establish credibility with a wholesaler, assure them you can settle by revealing your source of funds. If it's cash, give them a statement showing proof of funds. If you borrow from a hard money lender, give them their name and number or provide them with a prequalification letter. Next, be prepared to settle on time. If there's one thing that wholesalers despise, it's buyers who back out of a deal at the last minute. Finally, be kind to your wholesalers. They earn their keep, so let them make their money so they can stay in business and bring you more deals.

REHABBER MINDSET

With more of your own money and resources at risk as a rehabber, you are going to be pickier than a wholesaler. Look for homes in your target area that you are able to fix up and sell quickly to homeowners, criteria that may or may not match a wholesaler's property.

For example, a wholesaler might buy a property on the east side of town, but you prefer to deal on the west side. Wholesalers might pick up a deal in a neighborhood where the numbers will work for somebody, such as a landlord, but you may not want to renovate a home in that area. Wholesalers are looking for homes that they can sell to another investor while you are looking for homes in a target area that you must be able to sell to a homeowner. When a wholesaler brings you a deal, you must decide whether it meets your criteria.

I buy all types of homes in areas ranging from zone 1 on up to zone 6 on the Neighborhood Scale. Of these, if I like the neighborhood and style of a particular home, I renovate it myself. If I don't care for the style or have allocated my resources elsewhere, then I will wholesale the rehab opportunity to another rehabber.

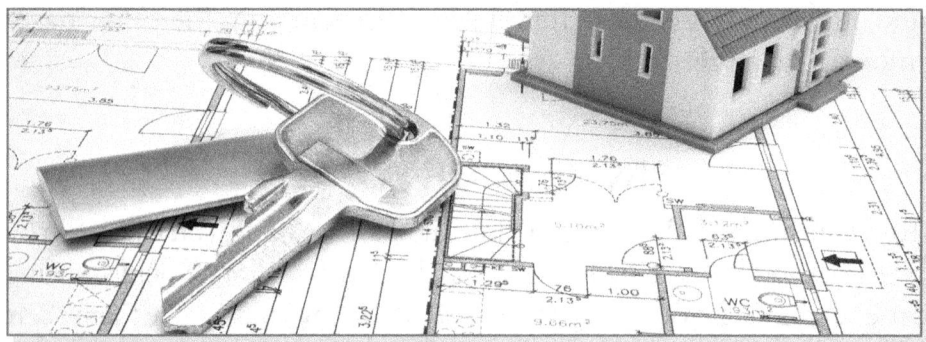

CHAPTER 17

ESTIMATING VALUES

WHAT EXACTLY IS A "COMP"?

"Comp" is short for comparable sales. When determining the value of a home, an appraiser uses recent sales of comparable homes to come up with a realistic value for a subject property. Typically, a good comp is a similar home that has sold within the last six months. By "similar" I mean homes that are close in proximity, have sold recently and are similar in size, style and construction. You don't want to compare a two-year-old, four bedroom, two bath brick home with all the amenities to a three bedroom, one bath frame home built in 1930 that needs updating. Although both may be in the same neighborhood, they are not comparable. Ideally comparable homes should have the same number of bedrooms and approximately the same square footage, give or take 100 square feet. Appraisers can make adjustments for square footage on an appraisal so it isn't an exact science. Stick to comparable sales involving properties roughly the same size. If you can't find a similar home as a comparable, you make adjustments—more on this in the appraisals section.

When I pull comps, I usually review the last couple of years to examine trends in the values of homes in neighborhoods. Some areas are dropping in value despite recent booms in the market. The smaller the area that you decide to work, the faster you will learn the property values and the easier it will be for you to stay on top of the market. You will only need to check comps for updates in a particular neighborhood. I keep a list of web sites that investors throughout the country use to pull comps. I'd also recommend searching the internet for "comp sites".

SOURCES FOR COMPARABLE SALES INFORMATION

There are many different ways to obtain comps. Many local newspapers posts recent sales every Sunday. My state's tax records, including the most recent sales price of every piece of property in the state, are available on the Internet. Real estate agents have access to the Multiple Listing Service that generate comparable sales from the listed homes similar to your subject property. With a real estate license, you will be able to access this data directly. Websites provide you with sales data by street, neighborhood, zip code, etc. Certain information services provide comparable sales data to their users for a fee, sending updates at regular intervals—usually quarterly or monthly. Whichever way you choose, you will need to have a consistent, reliable source to obtain recent sales information to determine the after-repaired value of a property before constructing an offer. This source of recent sales will be both useful and necessary when learning a new area.

BLOCK TO BLOCK

In major cities, it is extremely important that you become knowledgeable with the home values. Home values in Baltimore can range from $100k to $300k for the same home within two blocks. It is very important that you determine values for homes in such areas with comparable sales as close as you can get them. Two or more blocks can cost you a lot of money.

APPRAISALS AND THE APPRAISAL PROCESS

An appraiser accesses different databases like tax records and the MLS to find comparable sales for a subject property. Typically, they look for properties that are comparable in size, style and age to the subject property. They also want these properties to have sold within the last six months that are close to the subject property. The appraiser does a comparison of each home to the subject property noting items for each comp such as condition, size, number of bedrooms and bathrooms; additions such as garages, decks; amenities like thermal windows or central air conditioning and updates and lot size. Taking these advantages and disadvantages for each comp, the appraiser looks at all of the comps and assigns values based on how they stack up against one another. Eventually, the appraiser will choose the three properties most comparable to the subject property—using the sales prices of the three to arrive at a value for the subject property. Finally, the appraiser will incorporate these findings into a written report.

Other factors are days on market, condition of home, noise levels, amount of traffic on the street (residential properties on main streets are worth less than those in quiet neighborhoods), type of heating, proximity to schools, energy efficient items such as thermal windows, updating, additions, parking areas, garages, etc.

ART OR SCIENCE?

Understand that appraisals are not an exact science. Five different appraisals can come up with five different values for the same home. An appraisal is based on the opinions of an appraiser, and each appraiser is going to have a different opinion. Specifically, each appraiser will use different comparable sales and each will have their own viewpoints about the condition of the property. On top of this, appraisers can be swayed by the sales price of a property, particularly if the property is under contract for a specific price and the lender and/or mortgage broker are ready to proceed with the loan.

APPRAISERS AND LENDERS

If appraisers consistently turn in low appraisals that cause borrowers to seek financing elsewhere, they won't get repeat business from the lender who hired them. Lenders make money by writing loans, but the amount they can lend is determined by the appraisal or the sales price on the contract—whichever is lower. If appraisals continually come in below the sales price, the lender will lose a lot of deals.

For example, if someone qualifies for a $90,000 loan and agrees to buy a property for $100,000, then they will need to come to the table with a $10,000 (10 percent) down payment plus closing costs. If an appraiser turns in a report where the value falls around $95,000, the lender can only finance 90 percent of $95,000, or $85,500, rather than the $90,000 originally anticipated. As a result, the prospective borrower has two choices:

1. Come up with an additional $4,500 ($90,000 - $85,500)
2. Find another lender or home

Appraisers do their best to get the value needed to close the deal. Sometimes they have to work hard to find comparable sales, searching a larger area than they would like. If stretched too far, they will come in with a lower value, justifying it by saying that they just couldn't get the value needed. If you are staying close to the top of the market, your homes show well, and your renovations show quality, an appraiser can generally get the value you need when you sell.

GETTING TOP DOLLAR FOR YOUR HOMES

All sellers want top dollar. However, when I first started renovating, my sales prices usually didn't approach the other recent sales in the neighborhood. Since I hadn't done a top-notch renovation, so I didn't feel right asking full market value and typically marketed my homes for 5-10 percent below market.

Today is a different story. I ask for and receive about $5,000-$10,000 above market for a home. Now that I have the resources to do everything right, I feel a sense of pride in asking above what other homes have sold for and increasing the home values in the neighborhoods where I renovate. When I list a home today, I receive numerous contracts and set a new high for values in the neighborhood. This works because my homes are truly the nicest in the neighborhood. In fact, they might as well be new since everything in the homes has been redone. In terms of appraisals, an appraiser never has a problem giving me my value since they can see that my house is better than everything else in the neighborhood.

ALWAYS CHECK THE VALUES YOURSELF

It is very important to position yourself to check home values on your own. Take time getting to know values within your neighborhood. Once you know the values, you won't have to spend the time learning them again. Never take anyone else's word for the value of a home. On a couple of occassions took others at their word and got burned both times. Many investors trust me and I'm usually accurate with my numbers, but my opinion is still only my opinion.

Another reason not to take someone's word for a property value is that if someone has an interest in selling a home to you, they may only give you the comps they want you to see (highest sales prices). Though these are legitimate comps, they are limited in the sense that they don't truly allow you to see the entire picture.

Often, sellers do not provide me with all the comps. Very rarely has a seller given me accurate numbers. They always think their homes are worth more than they are and usually only provide the comparable sales to show the high end of the market. Buyers, on the other hand, tend to be more conservative and estimate values a little on the low side. For example, I told someone about a home worth $35k if I'm standing in the shoes of the buyer but $47k if I'm standing in the shoes of the seller. Our perception of worth changes based on perspective, so do your homework and know what a home is worth to you.

Whenever other investors buy homes from me and ask my opinion of after-repair value, I give them an honest number, but I always tell them to do their own due diligence. In most cases, they don't and it always makes me shudder to think that they probably trust other sellers just like they trust me. This is foolish and bound to get them in trouble one day. The moral of the story is that if you want to know the full story, pull your own comps.

REAL LIFE EXAMPLE — DOING YOUR HOMEWORK

Once, I found a Cape Cod in a really nice neighborhood. The home needed a little work and all the homes on nearby were in the same position, so none had sold in years. There were Cape Cods all over this neighborhood but none were the same style, size or construction. I couldn't determine the value so I asked my Realtor. She asked another person in her office who blurted out that he knew the neighborhood really well. He said the homes were worth about $120k. I felt that was a little high—my personal estimate was about $100k—but when he said $120k, I thought my estimate was conservative.

I went forward and paid $48k for this home that needed quite a bit of work. Estimates for repairs were about $20k. When I tried to wholesale the property, I quickly found out that the homes were only worth about $80k and that I had paid way too much. The home didn't have a basement and it wasn't made of brick like the other homes in the neighborhood. The other homes had a reputation of shoddy construction and were considered very small.

I was terribly upset with myself. I didn't have an out with this one because I made a cash offer with no contingencies and I had to figure out a way to get it done. Ultimately, I sold the home with owner financing and no money down to a couple with really bad credit and I sold the note to a private investor. I didn't make any money on this deal. In fact, in addition to all my wasted time and effort, I lost about $1000. It was my first big mistake, and I want you to learn from it. Don't ever take someone else's word for the value of a home.

CHAPTER 18

ESTIMATING REPAIRS

ESTIMATING REPAIRS IS FAIRLY simple. Once you have established what should be done to renovate a property, it's time to inspect the house, take down general information and add up the numbers. It's that simple.

YOU CAN'T GET INTO A HOUSE

If you can't get into a house, don't worry—no one can. If you are going to redo everything, the problems do not matter, especially if you are buying cheap. Make estimates assuming everything needs to be replaced and move on. After inspecting enough homes, you will become proficient in estimating repairs within a few thousand dollars without even getting inside of the home. Efficiency is more important than getting an exact estimate for repairs.

If miscalculating repairs by a few thousand dollars screws up the whole deal, it was too tight. In fact, I still buy most of my homes "sight unseen," but I do not recommend this until you know your market and repair costs extremely well. If, on the other hand, you only do minor renovations, it is more important for you to see the inside of the house to confirm that no major problems exist.

UNKNOWN REPAIRS

If you aren't sure about the condition of the house, assume the worst. For example, if the utilities are off and you can't test an old furnace, assume it needs to be replaced. If you can't enter a home that was built in the 1960's, assume the bathroom needs to be updated. Remember that your goal is not to get a precise estimate of the repair costs but to make an offer and see if the seller is motivated.

ACTUAL COSTS VS. EDUCATED GUESSTIMATES

Giving actual repair costs is not something I can accomplish in this course, but I can provide guidelines that I use to make an offer. This is all that you need. If you don't feel comfortable making offers without knowing exact repairs costs, you are not ready to move forward. I understand that this is difficult to accept, but I include a fudge factor in all of my estimates to cover mistakes or misjudgments. If the success or failure of your deal hinges on the accuracy of a repair estimate, your offer is too high and your deal is too tight. A few thousand dollars shouldn't make much difference to you.

Once you have done a couple of renovations, you will become very good at estimating repairs. Your numbers will be more precise than those of wholesalers who usually don't renovate homes. Furthermore, if you specialize in renovating homes of the same type, the repairs will almost always be the same amount. If you replace a furnace in one home, it will probably cost the same in another. If a kitchen costs you $3,500 in one home and you do another with a similar floor plan, you can expect to spend about $3,500 again. As a result, your repair estimates will be more accurate, your offers will be less conservative and the number of accepted offers will climb. Soon, you can gauge repair costs from writing checks.

REPAIR GUIDELINES

HEATING, VENTILATING AND AIR CONDITIONING (HVAC)	
Repairs	$35-$70/hour
Forced air furnace (gas or oil)	$1,200-$1,800
Hot water boiler (gas or oil)	$1,800-$2,500
Steam boiler (gas or oil)	$2,500-$3,200
Oil tank removal	$500
General repairs	$300-$1,000
Central air repairs	$300-$1,000
Central air replacement	$1,000-$2,000
Central air duct work	$1,500-$5,000
PLUMBING	
Hourly	$35-70
Entire re-plumb of home	$2,500-$7,000
Replace sewer line	$1,500-$5,500

(Note: the deeper the line and the longer the run, the more this will cost)

Sewer Line cleanout	$150-$250
Hot water heater	$350-$700
Hot water heater (do it yourself)	$250
Well Pumps	$350-$700
Install a vanity (labor only)	$150-250
Install a vanity (do it yourself)	$50
Replace a garbage disposal	$275
Replace a garbage disposal (do it yourself)	$100
Replace a dishwasher	$400-$700
Replace a dishwasher (do it yourself)	$300-$600

(Continues on next page)

WINDOWS	
Replacement windows	$150-$300*
Glass replacement	$30-$100
Scrape and paint per window	$75-$125
Scrape and paint (do it yourself)	$25-$50

*My cost is roughly $200/window with extras.

FLOORING	
Carpet cleaning (minimum 5 rooms)	$30-$70 per room
Carpet installation	$9-$15 per sq. yd.
Refinish hardwood floors	$1.50-$2.50 per sq. ft.
Refinish hardwood floors [Comment: (do it yourself???)]	$0.75 per sq. ft.
Vinyl floor replacement	$2-$4 per sq. ft.
Ceramic tile	$6-$12 per sq. ft.
Ceramic tile (do it yourself)	$4-$8 per sq. ft.

ELECTRIC	
Upgrade service (breakers and amperage)	$800-$1,800
Rewire entire house	$3,000-$5,000
Replace a light fixture (labor only)	$25-$50
Replace a light fixture (do it yourself)	$0
Replace outlets and switches (labor, 10 or more)	$5-$20 per switch
Replace outlets and switches (do it yourself)	$0

KITCHENS	
Cabinet replacements	$2,200-$4,500
Countertops and installation	$300-$700
New sink and fixtures	$200-$400
Total Kitchen Renovation	$1,500-$5,000

Note: While you can spend more than $5,000 on a kitchen, you can have a basic kitchen installed for between $1,500 and $5,000 for a typical rehab.

BATHROOMS	
New vanity, sink and cabinet	$200-$500
New tub enclosure	$200-$500
Tub refinishing	$250-$350
Tub refinishing (do it yourself)	$50
New tub and surround	$300-$1,000
New tile floor and walls	$1,200-$1,700
New toilet	$200
New toilet (do it yourself)	$100
Total Bath Renovation	$700-$3,000

Note: While you can spend as much as $3,000 on a bath, you can have a basic bathroom redone for between $1,000 and $1,500.

PAINTING	
Paint interior (1)	$150-$250 per room
Paint interior (do it yourself)	$30 per room
Paint exterior	$1,000-$5,000
Paint exterior (do it yourself)	$300-$1,000

Notes:

(1) I usually spend about $300-$500 on good quality paint and pay someone $300-500 to paint a home for me over the course of a day or two.

(2) The cost of exterior painting will vary with size of home and condition of existing surface. A good exterior paint job takes more time and is almost as costly as new vinyl siding. For these reasons, I prefer vinyl siding.

LANDSCAPING

I have spent as much as $3,000 to clean up a lot; cutting down overgrown bushes and hauling everything away. This lot was only 1/4 of an acre. In general, I budget about $1,000 for landscaping and trash removal.

ROOF / GUTTERS

The amount for a roof will depend on the type of roof (flat rubber, pitched shingle, pitched slate, etc.), the size of the roof and the extent of necessary repairs. In my area, it costs about $700 to lay a new flat roof on a small home and about $150-$200 per square (100SF) for a new layer of shingles on a larger home. I normally spend $150 or less per square, which includes tearing off a layer of shingles. I actually have two crews that will do a roof for $100 per square if I supply the materials and have someone else clean the area. On average, this saves me about $30 per square or about $500.

Gutters can be expensive or inexpensive to replace, depending on the type. They can be bought in pieces and assembled, but if not placed and caulked properly, the finished product has a chance of leaking. When replacing gutters, I prefer to install the seamless variety that costs about $3 per foot.

SIDING

Today, I can complete an average-sized home for about $3,500. I have been lucky enough to establish the same type of relationship with a siding contractor that I have with my roofing contractor. My siding contractor will install siding at $65 per square if I buy the materials.

SHEET ROCK

In my area, it costs about $35-$60 to install a 4' X 8' piece of sheet rock, depending on the amount you are having installed. I now have a crew that hangs and finishes sheet rock for me for $18 per board if I buy the materials, bringing my costs down to about $25-28 per board. Gouges, holes and marks on walls and ceilings can usually be repaired rather than replaced. Different textures can be sprayed onto ceilings and sometimes walls to cover imperfections. When estimating repairs, assume replacement rather than repair.

PLASTER WALLS

With plaster walls, I salvage if possible. If walls are beginning to crumble and separate from the backing, we used to laminate over it with 3/8 inch sheetrock. That was a nightmare. Today, I just rip it out and put in new sheetrock. If plaster walls are not in good shape, I rip them out and replace them with sheetrock.

CARPENTERS / PUNCH OUT

Most of the carpentry work that needs to be done is light and most anyone can do it so I never hire a pure carpenter. I hire Punch Out workers to take care of the most important parts of the renovation process. They perform the tedious tasks, which make the difference between a fair job and a great job. The quality of their work and the diligence is what separates your completed renovation from the rest.

USE A FUDGE FACTOR

To this day, I still underestimate repairs. Even after estimating repair costs on hundreds of homes, I still miss things that need to be fixed. For this reason, I recommend adding about 30 percent to your figures. This will increase your estimates substantially, especially on big jobs. A "fudge factor" is very important. Somehow or another, I manage to spend it every time. Don't get carried away and estimate so high that you lower your offers and lose deals. One area where I spend more money than I ever thought is the cost of demolition. On my last renovation, I originally budgeted $2,000 but spent over $5,000 paying workers to do the demo work and haul the trash away. Even if you do spend less than you budget on one renovation, you will spend the extra profits that you make as a result on another project.

FIVE-MINUTE "QUICKIE" ESTIMATE

In time, you will be able to walk through the house and have a realistic repair figure in your head before exiting the property. My inspections go something like this:

- **Step 1 (Exterior)** — Check garage, size of lot, condition of roof and gutters, condition of windows (old or new / wood or replacement) and condition of exterior paint/siding as I walk up to the house and once around the outside with a quick check for cracks in the foundation and sags in the porches and roof lines. I also check the outside for a central air conditioning unit or a heat pump to determine the condition and age of the unit.

- **Step 2 (Interior > First Floor > House Locked)** — I look through the windows to determine the type of heating system. Vents indicate at least forced hot air and maybe central air conditioning. Radiators indicate some type of boiler, which adds about $1500-$2000 to my repair estimate since they are more expensive to replace than forced hot air units. I also try to check the condition of the kitchen. In my experience, if the kitchen has been maintained, the rest of the house isn't so bad.

- **Step 3 (Interior > Second Floor / Remainder of First Floor)** — Check condition and layout of bathrooms (need to clean and update or totally gut) and floor plan of the house. Note paint and carpet, but these almost always need to be redone.

- **Step 4 (Basement)** —Check to see if it's finished or not. Look at the type and condition of the heating unit (oil or gas and, if it's a boiler, steam or hot water) and hot water heater. Check the electric panel (if updated or not), plumbing (galvanized or copper), and type and condition of heating system.

This seems like a lot, but it becomes second nature. Look for the big things that jump right out at you. On the exterior, look at the roof, windows, paint/siding and foundation. For the interior, check the major systems (heating, plumbing and electric), and your kitchen and baths. You will almost always need to repaint and put new carpeting, but you don't need to know the exact square footage of each home to come up with a ballpark figure.

Soon, you will be comparing homes that you are inspecting to homes you bought in the past and know exactly what needs to be done. When I wholesale a home, I usually ask my buyer for a repair estimate. I like getting different perspectives from others and it gives me an idea of the buyer's preferences. You will learn what a wide range "repaired" means. I tend not to estimate repairs for others or put a dollar figure on the cost of repairing a home. Instead, I let other investors determine that for themselves.

PROPERTY INSPECTION REPORT

On the following page is a copy of a property inspection report. It covers all of the physical aspects of a property that I take into consideration when estimating repairs. You may find it useful when performing inspections.

PROPERTY INSPECTION REPORT

Property Address _____

Year Built _____

 # Bedrooms _____   **# Bathrooms** _____

Size of House _____   **Size of Lot** _____

1) **Grounds Condition** (include deck, driveway, landscaping, fence, etc.)? **Lots of trash to remove?**
   _____

2) **Exterior**

   Does the foundation need repair?
   _____

   Does the roof need to be replaced?
   _____

   Exterior Type? _____   Repairs, painting, siding?
   _____

   Type of parking, size and condition?
   _____

3) **Interior**

   # of windows?_____   Do they need replacing?
   _____

   # or rooms that need carpet? _____
   # of rooms that need vinyl? _____
   Do hardwood floors need refinishing? _____
   # of Bedrooms? _____   # of Bathrooms _____
   Does the kitchen need replacing? _____ # of cabinets? _____
   Do the bathrooms need cleaning, upgrade, or total remodel?
   _____

   Is there a basement? _____ If so, is it finished? _____

Is basement dry? _____ Does it have a sump pump? _____

Total # of rooms? _____

What is required for painting?
_____

4) Systems

What type of heat does the home have?
☐ Gas   ☐ Oil   ☐ Electric
☐ Radiator   ☐ Forced Hot Air   ☐ Baseboard   ☐ Gravity

Condition of system?
_____

Does the home have central air conditioning?
_____

Does the home have circuit breakers or fuses?
_____

Condition of plumbing?
_____

What condition is the Hot water heater in?
_____

5) Appliances

What usable appliances are included?
_____

What do you estimate total repairs to be?
$_____

Could you enter the home? _____ Is it habitable? _____

What is the condition of the neighboring properties?
_____

Comments:
_____
_____

What comp is most comparable?
_____

REAL LIFE EXPERIENCE — ACTUAL COSTS FOR ONE OF MY REHABS

Below are actual costs for a rehab that I completed. They are about $7,000 higher than my original estimates, which just goes to show that despite my experience, I still make mistakes. In this case, the reason for my error is that I simply underestimated. I think the home was a little larger then I anticipated.

I made my offer sight unseen, figuring that I might spend about $40-45k. I had to hire a concrete contractor and I had never done that before so we underestimated the cost of the concrete work. We also forgot to estimate insulation in the beginning. The concrete and the insulation cost me $4,800 of my $7,000 over run. My actual final numbers are as follows:

HVAC	$ 2,625
Windows	$ 4,188
Concrete Work	$ 3,000
Insulation	$ 1,800
Carpeting	$ 1,696
General Contractor	$39,500
Total Renovation Costs	**$52,809**
Purchase Price	$66,000
Closing Costs Upon Purchase	$ 4,197
Insurance	$ 540
Holding Costs	$ 3,623 (very low rate line of credit)
Utilities	$ 378
Total for Entire Project	**$127,545**

This rehab went very smoothly. I bought, renovated and sold within six months. My sales price was $184,900 and I contributed $5,000 back to the buyers to assist with closing costs. I walked away from settlement with a check for just under $51,000.

CHAPTER 19

MAKING OFFERS

When I first started pursuing real estate, I didn't think the business could work. The real problem was that I wasn't making offers. Making offers is the lifeblood of this business. It's not enough to just look, so do your homework and make some offers.

RATIO OF OFFERS MADE TO OFFERS ACCEPTED

Once I started making offers, I realized the importance of making lots of offers to buy a handful of properties. When I began, my ratio of offers made to offers accepted was about thirty-to-one. This ratio improved greatly as I learned more about the business. Today I'm able to buy about one out of every seven homes.

Keep this in mind when making offers. If your ratios are the same as when I started investing, (look at ten houses per week and make two offers), it could be 15 weeks and 150 homes later before you get your first deal. That can be pretty discouraging, but it's important to move at a comfortable pace.

To move things along faster, overcome your fear of making offers on properties with legitimate potential or do a better job of screening properties before visiting. You should be making offers on most of the properties you visit—at least eight out of ten with the other two having a problem that can't be fixed.

Another business accelerator is to pick up the pace. If you want to do one deal every three months, make ten offers per month. If you want to do one deal every month, then you may have to make thirty offers per month. Most sellers are going to say "no," but you are only looking for the ones that say "yes." The more offers you make, the more homes you can buy.

Eventually, your ratios will improve as mine did. Your knowledge of local neighborhoods will increase along with your understanding of sellers. For instance, now I know when an offer is more likely to be accepted than not—due to the circumstances of the sale—so I started pursuing the deals most likely to be accepted.

These deals have several common characteristics: they are all vacant. I used to make offers that were still occupied, but I found that to be a waste of time. Second, usually they have been on the market for quite some time. Third, they may be brand new listings but listed really low. If they come out low enough, I will offer full price right away. Fourth, I target homes whose price has recently been reduced. And finally, in the neighborhoods that I like the most, I always pursue homes regardless of their listing price, offering what works for me. Some I get, some I don't.

MAKING OFFERS AS A REHABBER VS. AS A WHOLESALER

In the beginning, my primary focus was wholesaling properties. When acting as a wholesaler, my goal was to be efficient at putting together numerous offers and then marketing the properties I bought to all kinds of investors ranging from war zone landlords to high-end rehabbers. The type of property or neighborhood didn't matter so much since I had a customer for whatever I bought as a wholesaler.

Today, I still wholesale my share of properties. But, when I'm looking for homes to renovate, I make far fewer offers because there are fewer properties that meet my criteria as a rehabber. I am very picky about what I renovate. Since I will be sinking a lot of money into a project, I want to be sure it will sell quickly so I prefer certain styles and locations for the homes that I rehab. Rather than making a lot of offers, my goal as a rehabber is to be efficient at purchasing preferential homes at a price that allows me to make my desired profit. If you are a current or future rehabber, I recommend that you use the same strategy.

MAKE OFFERS THAT MAKE SENSE

If you make several offers without doing your homework for the sake of making offers, many of your offers probably won't make sense. Many new investors have taken my shotgun approach to the extreme, making countless offers sight unseen. They do follow the formulas and make offers that will work for investors, but they fail to take into consideration one of the most important details—finding motivated sellers, namely those that own vacant homes.

Some people have blindly offered $65k for beautiful homes occupied by a family with an asking price of $170k. Their offer is rejected and they assume my approach doesn't work. My approach works very well for me, because of my due diligence. Before I submit an offer, I have a good idea that there is some form of motivation from the seller. As I described before, in addition to a vacant home, the price might be low or at least recently reduced and/or it might have been on the market for a long time.

DECIDING WHICH CONTRACT TO USE

New investors have problems finding a good contract to use when making offers. Some use this as an excuse for never starting in real estate investing. They feel they don't have the perfect purchase and sale agreement, so they don't make an offer. For those worried about the quality of your purchase contract, understand that the forms are not that big of a deal. If you really need some peace of mind, get a hold of a contract and have an attorney review it. Let your attorney know your goals and they will make sure that your contract will help you accomplish these goals. Although contracts are legally binding agreement, do not get hung up on having the perfect contract. A standard purchase agreement (example included in Appendix) states the intent of the two parties involved and how they intend to move forward. If one party intends to sell and the other intends to buy, the contract merely describes the manner for this to be done. A contract can get someone into trouble when one party doesn't follow through on their end.

For example, if you sign a contract to buy a home and then back out, the seller will revert back to the contract to determine their rights. Similarly, if the seller backs out, you can revert to the contract to examine your rights under the agreement. In other words, the only time to worry about the language in a contract is when the contract is not followed through with properly. If you sign a contract to buy, you should be prepared to buy. If you sign a contract to sell, be prepared to sell.

WORD OF WARNING TO WHOLESALERS

Once again, I urge wholesalers not to sign purchase contracts without intent to settle and flip the property. This is unethical, immoral and will come back to haunt you. If this is the only way you can operate, I suggest disclosing this to the seller and either:

1. Signing a non-exclusive option to purchase the property that gives you the right to purchase the property but permits the seller to sell it to other people
2. Lock up the exclusive right to buy the property so you don't waste your time, signing an option to purchase that obligates the seller to sell, but does not obligate you to buy. Be sure to make sure the seller understands this agreement.

ENFORCEMENT

Even if the other party blatantly disregards their agreement, it will be too costly to sue for damages unless those damages are significantly greater than the time and money of a court battle, particularly if you are dealing with a sophisticated buyer or seller. Even if you win, you will still need to collect the judgment.

Of course, you can always sue for a huge amount and hope for a settlement. Unless you've lost a lot of money, $100,000 or more, I would think twice about pursuing anything in court. Try to reason with the other party and make an equitable arrangement acceptable to both parties. Otherwise, I would just let it go and start using your time to pursue other profitable endeavors. Time wasted in a dispute is time that could be used to do good deals or grow as an investor.

CONTRACTS AND LISTED PROPERTIES

Oftentimes, local custom will dictate the purchase contract, particularly when you are making offers on properties listed through the MLS. Your local Board of Realtors probably has a form of purchase contract preferred by Realtors in your area that other Realtors will want you to use. You can obtain a copy by contacting any local real estate agent or the Board of Realtors. In the event that you are opposed to using the local contract, you can cross out clauses and make changes, but realize that these changes may hurt the possibility of getting your offer accepted, particularly with bank-owned properties. Private sellers who have enlisted the services of a Realtor may be more accepting of your changes.

Personally, I have never found it necessary to change the standard contract for my state. As long as you intend to keep your word, the form is not really important and by changing the contract, you risk your offer being set aside for other, more "normal" offers. Private sellers may not mind changes, but I've never felt a need to make changes to the standard Maryland contract.

LETTERS OF INTENT

Another, shorter form of an offer is a one-page letter of intent similar to the one found in Appendix B: Forms. Some Realtors prefer to use letters of intent rather than full-blown contracts when receiving offers from potential buyers because it dramatically cuts down the paperwork in their office. Other Realtors will mandate that you use a full-blown contract and won't accept letters of intent. Whether or not you try to use these is up to you. I normally submit offers on the standard Realtor contract for my area unless I know that a Realtor will accept a letter of intent.

CONTRACTS AND FSBO'S

In terms of including clauses and using a preferred form of contract, you have much more leeway when dealing with FSBO's. You will be able to include clauses that you will not be able to insert if you are dealing with banks through Realtors, like "your offer is subject to inspection of the property by your partner." However, let me reemphasize that your intent should still be to settle on the property. Be considerate in having your partner look at the property as soon as possible. Most contracts give ten days for an inspection contingency. Remember, the seller is counting on you to perform, and as an ethical professional, you should produce or exercise your contingency clause as soon as possible if you cannot. If you feel uncomfortable putting this type of pressure on yourself to keep your word, I suggest you continue as a Bird Dog until you have more experience and more money.

CONTINGENCIES AND TERMS OF YOUR OFFER

When attempting to purchase properties, make one offer and only one offer. It should be all cash and totally clean or, if you don't have the cash yourself, contain only one contingency—a financing contingency (notice that you don't need to have the cash yourself in order to make an all cash offer). Forget about making multiple offers and forget about asking the seller to carry financing. This may work with FSBO's, but the vast majority of sellers you encounter will be through Realtors and they will only be asking themselves one question, "Is it enough?"

PREQUALIFICATION LETTER / PROOF OF FUNDS

A Realtor will usually recommend to a seller, who lists a property with them, that the seller make sure any prospective buyers are qualified to buy. This prevents the seller and the Realtor from wasting time with buyers who either aren't serious about making a purchase or don't have any way to obtain the money required to buy the property. As a result, most offers made through a Realtor, particularly those involving bank-owned properties, will require some form of evidence that you can perform. Nearly every bank I deal with these days requires this type of proof. Without it, my offers won't even be entertained. This proof can be shown in two ways—a prequalification letter or a statement showing "proof of funds."

PREQUALIFICATION LETTER

A prequalification letter from a lender (private or institutional) states that you are prequalified for financing, allowing you to buy property. These letters also help if an FSBO ever asks if you are qualified to purchase their home. Whether the property is listed or FSBO, your offer is stronger with a prequalification letter than without one.

PROOF OF FUNDS

If you have cash, you can produce some sort of documentation—such as a bank statement, credit card statement (cash advance limit), or line of credit agreement—proving you have cash available for settlement, or at least unqualified access to it. This is called "proof of funds" and most real estate agents will require it in conjunction with all cash offers that don't include financing contingencies. For example, if you submit a $50,000 cash offer for a home without a financing contingency, the listing agent will want to see that you have direct access to $50,000 in cash. Bank statements or some other type of proof will need to be sent with your offer. If you can't provide proof of funds, your offer will not be entertained. Personally when I got started, I never made all cash offers. All of my offers had a financing contingency and I attached a pre-qualification letter from one of my lenders.

EARNEST MONEY OR "GOOD FAITH" DEPOSITS

When you sign a contract to purchase a property, it is common for the buyer to give the seller a deposit that shows the buyer's intent to act in good faith in completing the purchase of the property. This consideration helps secure the contract and usually comes as cash or check. It is not necessarily required by FSBO's, but will most likely be required when buying through a Realtor. If you are a rehabber and come across a home to renovate, consider making your offer with a higher than normal earnest money deposit to get the seller's attention. This is a good strategy that can set your offers apart from others.

As an investor, you will be making many offers and you may need to make multiple deposits. To conserve working capital, insert a clause in the contract to place the earnest money deposit in escrow with your attorney once the offer is accepted. This eliminates the need to come out of pocket with a deposit for every offer.

Sometimes, the Realtor listing the property will want you to give them the earnest money deposit. I hesitate to do this unless it's a really great deal for a couple of reasons.

1. Losing control over my money.
2. I know I can trust my attorney, but I don't know if I can trust the listing Realtor. One investor friend of mine placed deposits for two properties with another Realtor. This new Realtor found out that he was trying to wholesale the

properties and she relisted them! Turned out to be a big mess. Anyway, my point is that you should be cautious about having deposit checks floating around everywhere. You can exercise more control if your attorney is holding all of them.

MAKE LOTS OF OFFERS / KEEP THE FUNNEL FULL

What you do today pays off one to six months from now. If you do not make offers for the next four weeks, you will experience a drought in the future. I have made offers on properties and never heard back from sellers. Three or four months down the road, they call and ask if I'm still interested in their property. Sometimes I am but not necessarily at the same price. These callbacks happen quite often, so not getting an offer accepted this week doesn't mean it will not be accepted next week.

If you intend to renovate homes continuously, you need to make offers at a pace that keeps you busy. Due to differences in markets and levels of personal experience, this pace will be different for everyone. Since I can always move properties to wholesale buyers, I never stop making offers. If you aren't interested in wholesaling properties, you might have to stop making offers when your plate is full.

You don't want to find yourself holding too many properties and/or trying to renovate too many homes at once, especially with limited resources. I have done it and seen it done all too often. You end up spreading your resources amongst every project and run out of resources before finishing projects. This isn't good and causes sleepless nights. Until you have your systems in place and the resources to accommodate heavy volume, pace your offers accordingly.

OFFER WORKSHEET

The Offer Worksheet is a basic and useful tool to help investors determine the amount to offer on a home. It provides two simple formulas to use when calculating offers, each requiring one or more of the following three figures:

1. After Repaired Value of the Property
2. Margin for Rehabber's Profit, Holding Costs and Closing Costs
3. Repair Estimate
4. Wholesale Profit

AFTER REPAIRED VALUE

Determine this figure by taking five comps, losing the high sale and low sale, followed by averaging the other three. Although many investors will tell you to always work with high comps, it is more prudent to only work with high comps when selling a property. When making offers, protect yourself and work with an average or low comp. Be sure to use realistic sales (ideally homeowner to homeowner sales as investor to homeowner sales tend to be slightly inflated) rather than distress sales as your comps. Otherwise, your offers will be so low that they won't ever be accepted. When I purchase homes, I base my decision on the average after-repaired value in the neighborhood even though I usually sell them above market value.

MARGIN FOR REHABBER'S PROFIT, HOLDING COSTS AND CLOSING COSTS

This number can be modified to conform to the costs in your area. In the state of Maryland, we have some of the highest—if not the highest—closing costs in the country (3% transfer tax). As a result, I figure a larger margin into my deals to accommodate for the increased closing costs. For example, in Method One I use 65 percent of FMV instead of 70 percent, and in Method Two I subtract $25,000 instead of $20,000. It's good to be strict rather than lose with these numbers.

REPAIR ESTIMATE

Calculate this figure after your property inspection. On occasion, I make offers sight unseen and assume that the property needs everything. I do not recommend this until you have an excellent grasp of what it costs to repair various types of homes in your area. As you increase this number, your offer will become more conservative and less likely to be accepted. This is understandable in the beginning and it is better to have an offer rejected than to pay too much. As you get to know your market, your offers will become more precise and accepted more often.

Recently, some of my protégé investors have had trouble buying homes. A number of factors contribute here, but the primary is their fear of buying a home is causing them to be overly conservative when submitting offers. When arriving at an offer price, they are using the low end of the comps to determine their After Repaired Values but estimating repairs for a full-blown rehab. The result of this calculation is that their offers are about $20k too low, causing difficulty when buying homes.

When making offers, try to put things into perspective. If you were planning to spend a fortune on a full blown, high end, quality rehab, you could sell the home for top dollar and your offer worksheet should contain a high repair estimate and a high sales price. On the other hand, if you were planning to spend less on a low-end rehab, you might only sell at a more conservative price and your offer worksheet should reflect a lower repair estimate as well as a lower sales price.

WHOLESALE PROFIT

This figure equals estimated profits when wholesaling the property to another investor. Generally, I like to make this at least $5,000. If I am less familiar with the area or a little uncertain about the after repaired value, I may make it $7,000-8,000 or more. Keep in mind that as you increase this number, your offer will become more conservative and less likely to be accepted.

OFFER WORKSHEET

List Price _____ Listing Agent _____

DOM _____

Fair Market Value Analysis (5 comps, take away highest and lowest, average the rest):

Address _____

Sale Price _____

_____

_____

FAIR MARKET VALUE AFTER REPAIRS (FMV)

_____

Method #1

_____ × 70% = _____ - _____ - _____ = _____

FMV   Repairs   Wholesale   Profit   Offer

Method #2

_____ - $ 20,000 = _____ - _____ - _____ = _____

FMV   Repairs   Wholesale   Profit   Offer

The lowest of the two offers is the one that should be submitted for offer.

Amount of offer _____

Terms included with Offer _____

Date of Offer _____

Response to Offer _____

TRY TO REMAIN CONSERVATIVE WITH YOUR OFFERS

When rehabbing, you will have more flexibility when submitting offers because of larger profit margins. However, whether you are a beginner or a pro, sometimes you will be tempted to offer more to get something accepted. Resist this temptation.

When wholesaling, offering more will cause you to put a property under contract that you can't wholesale and you will be forced to settle and rehab it yourself. Rehabbing can be profitable and you will probably make money, but if you don't have the financial resources, I recommend you do everything imaginable to wholesale the property, even if it means little or no profit. You will be much better off.

If you are rehabbing, giving into this temptation will only result in lower profits or making less profit than intended, something that will likely result in having to tie up more of your own cash than anticipated. Whenever I've found myself in need of a property, I make more offers instead of higher offers—preserving my profits and working capital while ensuring future success.

MAKING OFFERS SIGHT UNSEEN

Several times throughout this course I mention that I occasionally make offers on properties sight unseen. I do not advise this as a beginner, and many people do not advocate it for seasoned investors. In order to make offers sight unseen, you must know your neighborhoods and the repair costs extremely well. I only make sight unseen offers when I know the neighborhoods thoroughly and I've bought numerous homes in the same neighborhoods. Because of my experiences in the neighborhood, I know what I can and can't pay for a home. If one is for sale in a familiar neighborhood, I always make an offer. Whether or not I look at the home before is determined by the price that the seller wants for it.

I have paid $50,000 for homes in a particular neighborhood and made a great profit. I may want to pick up another for about the same price and would be comfortable offering $40,000 (not $50,000) sight unseen. If the asking price of the home is $80,000, rather than spending time to go out and see it, I would just check the seller's motivation by offering $40,000 and waiting for a counteroffer. If a counteroffer comes back in the $50,000 range, I will investigate the home. If the counteroffer comes back in the $70,000 range, I would just let the deal go.

If the asking price of the same home were originally in the $50,000 range, I would take the time to inspect it before I made an offer. I might be able to pay full price if the home is in good shape and I wouldn't want to let it get away because of a lowball offer. If the home came to me priced at $35,000, I would offer full price sight unseen.

I frequently experience all of these scenarios. In many cases, my low offers are used to fish out the most motivated sellers and find out who will come back with a counteroffer that I might be able to negotiate to my preferred purchase price. If the counteroffer is somewhat reasonable, I will spend more time on the home. Despite all of the above, when I look for homes to renovate, I usually go out to see them. The primary reason is that it fits my criteria. If I happen to inspect a home that I don't want to renovate, I'll change gears and view it as a wholesale deal, making my offer so I can wholesale it to someone else.

REAL LIFE EXPERIENCE

Making a lot of offers really works. I have bought as many as nine houses in one day. I remember the first time very clearly. Over the course of a weekend I made about 40 offers on homes—FSBO's, HUD properties, Bank properties, etc. On the following Monday, no less than nine of my offers were accepted. Not a bad ratio. Grow a thick skin in this business, you are going to be told "no" more often then you hear "yes," so get used to it. Play the numbers and make a ton of offers. It works.

CHAPTER 20

AFTER OFFER ACCEPTED

START TITLE WORK

The term "title work" refers to checking the title of the property to ensure that it is clear and marketable. Title companies can check titles, but many hire abstract companies to do so. The "abstracter" performs two main services. They check the historical chain of ownership (or "chain of title") to make sure the previous transfers were performed legally and to determine that the current owner owns the property.

Second, they make sure there are no outstanding liens on the property. Any liens that are found need to be satisfied before the property can be sold to the new buyer (unless, of course, the buyer agrees to take title subject to the existing liens). Liens include mortgages, mechanics liens (work performed but not paid for), and tax liens (unpaid taxes).

I begin title work on homes as soon as possible. I do this because it takes a while to get lien sheets where I live. Also, you cannot record a new deed without obtaining a lien sheet and showing that all prior liens on the home have been satisfied. Second, some title companies get busy, so give your title company time to do their work in order to settle on time. Third, title problems must be fixed by the seller to in order to avoid settlement delays. Lately I have been buying more and more properties with minor title problems that always seem to hold up my purchases. If I were to wait to get the title started, those problems would further delay settlements. And fourth, in the event that I'm wholesaling a property and find a buyer who claims to be ready, I don't want the buyer to use incomplete title work as an excuse not to settle. Even if a cash buyer wants to use their own attorney, I tell them that the title work is done and my attorney will sell it to their attorney. I don't allow my buyers to come up with any excuses for not settling. If you are anxious to get started, get the title work going right away.

FIRST STEPS TO TAKE WHEN WHOLESALING

After contacting your settlement attorney and beginning title work, the main objective as a wholesaler after an offer is accepted is finding a buyer for the property. So, the very first thing to do is crank up your marketing machine. Market, call your buyers list, put out flyers, go to the investment club meeting and call "I Buy Houses" ads. The whole world doesn't automatically know that you picked up a new deal for them. If you don't let everyone know what you have, you won't be able to sell. Once you get a home under contract, it is your duty to make everyone possibly interested to be aware of the sale.

ALWAYS BE PREPARED TO CLOSE A DEAL

When marketing as a wholesaler, always carry blank contracts and assignment forms. If you come across a buyer, don't lose a sale because you are unprepared. If I found myself in a pinch, I would write the contract up on a napkin, take a deposit and follow it up with a contract. However, many buyers won't be willing to do this, so just be sure to carry blank contracts with you as I do and you won't need a napkin.

REAL LIFE EXPERIENCE — WHOLESALING IN A PINCH

In my experience, running an ad in the paper doesn't always work. It is a very effective means of marketing, but not the most effective.

For example, I buy homes all the time, but I rarely scan the classifieds looking for a great deal. On the other hand, if someone takes the time to call me, I might be interested.

When I put my tenth home under contract, I ran into a snag and couldn't wholesale the home. I ran ads in the paper and waited and waited, but buyers seemed shy. I printed flyers for the monthly investment club meeting, but struck out again. At that point, I decided to get on the phone and call everyone I knew who invested in properties. On my fifth call, I spoke to a guy who showed interest. He told me that he would go take a look at it and call me back.

Three days passed with no results, so I called him. He said that he hadn't had a chance to see the property yet. I told him more about the home and, with only four days remaining until the contract expired, I talked him into meeting me there. If he didn't buy, I would have to buy the home or default, which is never acceptable to me. He met me at the home and my persistence paid off. He was totally impressed and we signed the deal right then and there. Whenever you find yourself in a difficult situation, go out and find a buyer. Don't wait for one to find you.

FIRST STEPS TO TAKE WHEN REHABBING

The initial steps as a rehabber after an offer is accepted are a little more involved than if you intend to immediately resell the property as a wholesaler.

CONTACT YOUR LENDER

After placing a property under contract, contact your source of financing. Before submitting an offer, know where and how you are going to finance the purchase and renovation. If you plan to use a lender rather than cash, let the lender know that you have a home under contract and that they need to get the financing process started.

GET ESTIMATES AND FINALIZE PLANS

Have your contractors lined up and ready to roll on purchase day. Even if you are efficient in your search, shopping for contractors/prices after settlement can easily waste a month or two and hundreds (if not thousands) of dollars in holding costs. So, you should use the time between contract signing and settlement wisely. To accomplish this, the second thing is to get bids from the contractors you've met and use their ideas to finalize plans for the new project. Just planning a new project can take a month. If you wait until you settle on one to start another, you will waste a month's payment for taxes, mortgage and insurance before beginning the work. Make your money as a rehabber by completing projects and getting them sold. The longer it takes to get a job done, the less likely you are to make a target profit, if any profit at all. It is vital, especially if you borrow hard money, to get your project started and completed as soon as possible. Holding costs add up very quickly when you are paying in the neighborhood of 15 percent interest.

SCHEDULE YOUR CONTRACTORS

Finally, whether you need to get several bids or learn from experience which contractors to use, the third step to complete your project in a profitable timeframe is to select contractors and notify them of a services-needed timeframe. Schedule them to work in an orderly fashion so they stay out of each other's way. It's best to find one person/contractor to do most of the job, particularly things like painting, light carpentry, kitchens and baths. Personally, I typically sub out for windows, roof, siding, HVAC and electrical and have my general contractor do the rest.

REAL LIFE EXPERIENCE — ALWAYS GET A DEPOSIT

Always collect a deposit check whenever you sell a house to a homebuyer. If you are using an agent, they will take care of this. If you are selling on your own, you will be responsible for obtaining a check. Let your buyer know the purpose of the meeting so they bring their checkbook. When I was first starting out, I had contract-signing meetings where the buyer was not prepared to write a check. I finally realized this was partly my fault because I was afraid to disclose my intent for the meeting for fear of blowing the deal. Often, they signed the contract and promised to give me a check later. In most cases, however, they never did, so these deals never happened. Another example involves a meeting where I had two new investors help close a deal. The seller informed me that it was a done deal and he was ready to sign the documents. The buyer showed up knowing nothing of the sort, or at least that's the way he portrayed it. He was not prepared to write a check and acted as though our meeting was just to discuss the deal. If you want to collect a deposit check from your buyer, make sure your buyer knows the purpose of the meeting.

CHAPTER 21

REHABBING START TO FINISH

This chapter covers the steps involved in completing a renovation from start to finish and I hope you find it useful when tackling your next project. As we discussed in the previous chapter, the remaining steps will be completed once you have the deed.

STEP ONE — MEET WITH CONTRACTOR AND DEFINE JOB

When starting a rehab, I begin with a walkthrough to evaluate the project myself. I meet with my contractor to get his input and finalize my strategy, including how to handle certain repairs and whether or not we're going to make any changes to the layout of the property. Now that I work exclusively with one general contractor, my life is much easier because I only meet with one person. He contacts everyone else and relays the results of his conversations to me. As a result of my experience, I'm becoming fairly adept at determining the best way to do the work. My contractor usually completes the projects how I envision. My contractor does offer advice and I'm always open to suggestions to better or cheaper ways to get the job done.

STEP TWO — DEFINE JOB AND BUY MATERIALS

After determining the amount of work, my contractor and I put together a draw schedule. This is usually required by the lender and lists the order we intend to complete the work required. I shift things around to keep the cash flow coming from the lender and my contractor likes to do things in an order that makes his life easier. We usually settle on something in between.

STEP THREE — PHASE ONE: DEMOLITION

I have learned to do my entire "demo" first. Otherwise, we were constantly working around trash or having to haul it away. Now, I just get a dumpster or two at the very beginning of a job, bring in a crew and rip everything out. We clean all the trash and tear out the kitchen, bath(s), drop ceilings, paneling, flooring and anything else that might get in our way of completing the job properly and efficiently.

STEP FOUR — PHASE TWO: ROOF, WINDOWS, SIDING

The remainder of the work begins on the exterior of the home. We start with the roof to ensure that the interior stays dry. Usually, I'll have the windows and siding done at the same time. I like completing the entire exterior quickly because it starts to attract attention from the neighborhood.

STEP FIVE — PHASE THREE: PLUMBING AND HVAC

The next two items on my list are plumbing and heating as well as air conditioning system. I have had contractors who delayed plumbing, which led to disaster. After they hung and painted the drywall, they turned on the water only to find that there were pipe bursts in the walls. Today, I always make my contractor check out the plumbing first, including the sewer lines. It is important to have a working heating system in the home in the beginning so the interior work, particularly the finishing and painting of the sheet rock, can be completed. While the plumber is working, I'll have an HVAC crew installing a new heating system, consisting of a new gas furnace and central air conditioning. I haven't always replaced functional HVAC systems and even today, if the current system is fairly new, I avoid it. Finally, if the electrical system needs to be updated in any way, I usually do this while the HVAC system is being installed. In many instances, if I am installing central air conditioning in a home that didn't have it previously, the electrical system will need to be updated to accommodate the central air. However, I rarely do any electrical work in my homes.

STEP SIX — PHASE FOUR: FRAMING AND SUBFLOORS

Next, I address areas like rotten wood and replacing walls. If I'm going to remove or build a wall containing plumbing and/or electric, my crew is still in Step Five. I make an effort to finish the basement of every renovation to create more living space. For many of my buyers, my finished basement is the reason for purchase.

STEP SEVEN — PHASE FIVE: SHEET ROCK / DRYWALL

If at all possible, I prefer to skim and patch the walls, but I frequently put new sheet rock in my homes. Hanging and finishing the sheet rock is something that takes a while, but is goes a long way to make an old house look new.

STEP EIGHT — PHASE SIX: PAINTING

Once the sheet rock is done, we paint the walls. First, we'll put a coat of primer or a light first coat of paint on the walls and have the sheet rock crew fix any flaws, which do not show until there is paint on the walls. As soon as the flaws are repaired, we'll apply two more coats of paint.

STEP NINE — PHASE SEVEN: NEW KITCHENS AND BATHS

Next, we lay vinyl floors in the kitchens and baths before installing new cabinets, commode, vanity, etc. We usually take our kitchen dimensions to a home improvement store and have them design the kitchen for us. It makes my contractor's life easier and we always get the right size cabinets with a good fit.

STEP TEN — PHASE EIGHT: PUNCH OUT

After installing kitchens and baths, we begin to wrap everything up. Contractors usually refer to this as their "punch out," consisting of the little details like outlets, switch plates and light fixtures. Often, a homeowner will walk through and create a punch list with the contractor. Since we've worked together for so long, my contractor already knows what needs to be done, so we skip this step. Sometimes it seems like the punch out is the hardest part of the whole renovation since it takes so long to complete every little detail. However, this is also the part of the job that takes your rehab from good to excellent.

STEP ELEVEN — PHASE NINE: CARPETING

We don't want workers ruining the new carpet, so this is the very last thing we install. We usually put new wall-to-wall carpeting throughout the home. As mentioned before, it's possible to find cheap carpet installers at wholesale carpet businesses.

STEP TWELVE — PHASE TEN: CLEAN UP / LANDSCAPING

At this point, the home should be finished and we'll begin the clean up. Since you want the home to stand out, it is important to get it looking like a million bucks. If I'm going to do any landscaping, it is usually done here as the final step.

STEP THIRTEEN — PHASE ELEVEN: MARKETING

Once the home is complete, I immediately begin marketing it. If the area is hot and the home is going to move quickly, I'll start marketing before completion, but most of the time I prefer to have the entire job done before anyone sees the home.

STEP FOURTEEN — PHASE TWELVE: FINAL REPAIRS REQUIRED

Once the home is under contract with a buyer, they may select to use a home inspector and their lender will order an appraisal. As a result of the inspection or appraisal, you may need to do additional repairs. Then, the inspector or appraiser will inspect the property once more to make sure the repairs have been done before issuing a final approval.

CHAPTER 22

AGENT MARKETING

AFTER A RENOVATION, YOU can hire one of two people to expose your home to the marketplace: yourself or a real estate agent. This chapter covers both the advantages and disadvantages of using an agent while the following chapter outlines the various methods available to market a home on your own.

LISTING YOUR PROPERTY WITH AN AGENT

This is now my vehicle of choice for marketing renovated homes. After using every method imaginable, I now prefer to list my homes with a real estate agent. I have a number of investor friends who think I'm crazy for paying the 6-7 percent commission, but the work they do is well worth the expense for several reasons.

First, I have thousands of other agents working for me the day my home is listed and none receives a dime until they perform. Second, most of these new employees have been trained to only deal with qualified buyers, so no one wastes time with buyers who can't make a purchase. Third, as professionals, real estate agents tend to attract qualified homebuyers. Most people who can't qualify for a loan do not visit agents. Fourth, amidst all of this controversy regarding flipping, it helps me remove myself from the marketing process so no one can ever accuse me of any shady dealings. I don't meet the buyers until the settlement day.

Finally, I don't have to spend one single minute marketing any of my homes. The main reason I entered the real estate game was to free myself to do the things I enjoy. Having to wait on people, meet in the evenings or weekends (when you deal with most retail buyers), arrange to show houses only to get stood up, take phone calls, see credit reports with sub-500 scores—all wastes of time for me.

I would rather make a little less and leave my freedom intact, so I can do other things that I enjoy. I still make a good profit on my homes since I factor the cost of marketing through an agent into my offer. Some investors do all this work only to save a few thousand dollars. Not nearly enough to justify all the time and effort.

CHAPTER 23

INDIVIDUAL MARKETING

While I don't recommend it, for those bent on selling rehabs to save on real estate commission, I have included this section. It details the hurdles and pitfalls of the various self-marketing methods. I have experienced success with marketing alone and I have friends who sell everything themselves who do very well.

RENT TO OWN — ADVERTISING

When marketing through newspaper advertisements, the phrase "Rent to Own" works like magic. People come out of the woodwork and your phone rings off the hook. I think the furniture and appliance industry made "rent to own" very easy to understand. People can pick up a sofa for $40 per week and after a year or two of payments, they get to keep it. Since potential homebuyers can relate to this, they become interested in purchasing a home the same way. They are also not intimidated by renting as opposed to purchasing a home. One of my most successful ads reads:

> RENT TO OWN* Main Street, 3 BR, Only $750 per month, low down XXX-XXXX

RENT TO OWN — HANDLING CALLS

Despite an endless number of calls, most had bad credit and had exhausted all other resources before coming to me. However, if you can handle the problems associated with credit-challenged buyers, this method might work for you. Good, bad or ugly credit, most of my callers were somewhat interested in my rent to own programs and a few were ready to act immediately. Historically, these were the people who got me into trouble. I originally had a first-come, first-served policy that caused trouble.

At first, I didn't know how to handle it when someone was ready to write a check and I still had dozens of other calls to return. I usually just said, "OK, since you're the first one, we have a deal." Finally, I made it my company policy to accept all applicants over the course of a week and then take the time to thoroughly evaluate each person (unless I came across someone with stellar credit and enough cash to close).

If you struggle with handling pressure from external people to your business, I suggest you set up "company policies." Even if you are the only person in the company, they give you a rule to follow and a legitimate reason to say, "Hold on" or "Slow down." Sometimes it pays to have policies in place that no one in the company, including you, can violate.

RENT TO OWN — ADVANTAGES

The advantages of a rent to own program are that you can usually get someone in a home immediately and, if you are willing to accept a less than perfect credit history, they may accept a less-than-perfect home. When I had a problem with a home that I couldn't afford to fix, I found a new buyer willing to take the home with the problems if I could handle their troubled credit history. Placing them in the home drastically helped with holding costs because they began making payments.

RENT TO OWN — DISADVANTAGES

The biggest disadvantage to selling a rent to own home is that you are never certain if your tenant/buyer will ever cash out. If they don't qualify for a loan within a year, chances are high that you will end up keeping the house as a rental or kicking the tenant/buyer out and taking possession of a trashed home that you have to start renovating all over again. I have retaken possession of a number of trashed homes and it is terrible. One was in worse shape than any house I had seen before a rehab. I consider using the rent to own method to sell rehabs, but only for homes that I pick up in habitable condition that need minor repairs. In these cases, I put a tenant/buyer who was willing to do the repairs while living there, but I wouldn't have my crew do any work or pay the tenant to do any work.

RENT TO OWN — MY PERSONAL EXPERIENCE

In terms of moving inventory, rent to own programs were my most successful campaign. I couldn't get enough homes to accommodate the number of buyers I had in my system, which was set up to take anyone provided they had the required down payment (it went up as credit scores came down).

When speaking with potential tenant/buyers, I based the purchase price off the annual income of the applicant, trying to emulate what mortgage lenders would require as well as the requisite down payment on their credit score. If someone had terrible credit, I would tell them that they needed 10 percent down if they wanted to rent to own and 20-30 percent down if they wanted owner financing. This angered some, but I had them see what their bank would offer. Since their bank wouldn't give them the time of day, they soon realized it was my way or the highway.

Unlike the bank, if someone had the money, I would give him or her a chance. It's amazing how many people can come up with the money if you ask for it. Someone with poor credit wrote that they could only afford $1,000 for a down payment. Soon after, I sent a postcard of a home that they absolutely loved, saying they needed $13,500 down. After they asked and I refused to lower the down payment, they returned with $13,500.

If someone had good credit, I always made the down payment much lower, as low as one month's rent if they were choosing my rent to own program. My goal was to get someone with good credit into the home so they could cash me out quickly. I did a lot of volume with my rent to own programs. The only problem was that they weren't very profitable.

First, since my buyers had blemishes on their credit, they usually didn't qualify for "good" loans with the best rates and terms. The bank would only lend a certain LTV, so I usually needed to take back a second mortgage instead of cash as part of my profit. Second, since my buyers were cash poor, I usually had to pay their closing costs, which were much higher for these sub prime loans. I did my best to reimburse myself by building the costs into the purchase price, but wasn't always successful.

RENT TO OWN — FINAL ANALYSIS

I built a marketing business on a rent to own basis and I know others who have done the same. However, I now make a better living by cashing out. I would not put rent to own at the top of my marketing methods, but I keep it in the repertoire. Someday, it may come in handy when you have a home that you can't move any other way. The current resale market can always change, warranting a closer look at rent to own. There are plenty of qualified homebuyers and I would rather sell my houses to them than pursue those who can only rent to own.

Make the rent to own decision prior to purchasing a property. This makes a difference in the type of renovation and the financing method. Formerly, I used hard money loans when buying homes and I found tenants through a rent to own program. I couldn't achieve positive cash flow while paying interest at 14.9 percent on my hard money loan and my buyers weren't cashing out as quickly as I hoped—many ended up defaulting. If you need cash for whatever reason (high interest loan, pending balloon payment), be patient and find a good buyer and get your cash.

OWNER FINANCING — ADVERTISING

Like my "rent to own" ads, my owner financing advertisements also made my phone ring off the hook:

OWNER FINANCING, Low down, 3 BR, Must Sell xxx-xxxx

These ads worked well because there are people out there who can't qualify for a bank loan. Meaning, this is their only alternative for buying a house and they call.

OWNER FINANCING — HANDLING CALLS

When getting calls from those interested in owner financing, they ask two key questions: "How much are the payments" and "how much is the down payment?" I always ask how much they can spend each month and how much they can afford to put down. I never give numbers up front. If a person seems like they may be able to afford a home, I ask questions regarding their credit. Very little of the conversation revolves around the house for sale; it is geared toward the financial side of the deal.

OWNER FINANCING — ADVANTAGES

Owner financing is attractive to buyers and allows a seller to move property quickly. There are no banks involved, further expediting the sales process. There are also no inspections involved, so a home that doesn't meet FHA standards can still be sold. The seller can often get extra profit in the form of a higher sales price and interest rate. For an unsophisticated seller, it can be advantageous to "invest" in an asset that they know well (their property), rather than cashing out and trying to invest elsewhere. Unless classified as a real estate "dealer" by the IRS, the seller only pays income taxes on the interest received as opposed to the entire capital gain at once (this may not apply to homeowners who do not pay a tax on any capital gain resulting from the sale of a property they have occupied as a primary residence for at least two of the past five years). Finally, the seller makes profit in the form of interest over and above the sales proceeds.

OWNER FINANCING — DISADVANTAGES

For the average rehabber, there are several disadvantages to owner financing that outweigh any possible advantages.

1. Selling with owner financing doesn't put cash in your pocket unless you extract an unusually large down payment from the buyer. Most homes I sale with owner financing put me in the hole in the beginning. Too many of these will make you paper rich but cash poor.

2. If your intent is to sell your note, it is difficult to create and sell a note to a note buyer at the settlement table (table funding). Note buyers act as if this is easy, but I assure you that it is much easier to find a buyer with good credit than to create and sell a note to a note buyer. They require more paperwork than banks, not less like they advertise, and they typically take months to close, not days. The industry is all but dead when it comes to table funding. If you have

"seasoned" paper (a note for collecting payments), there are some buyers out there, but it still isn't easy. Occasionally, I will still sell seasoned paper that I have created, but primarily to private local investors. If you are interested in creating and selling paper, be prepared to hold it until the paper acquires some seasoning and your payer establishes a timely payment history.

3. From a tax perspective, if you are rehabbing and selling properties on a regular basis, you are acting as a real estate "dealer" in the eyes of the IRS and must pay a tax on any profit you make whether you receive it now or not. This means that if you carry back owner financing and make a $20,000 paper profit, you will need to pay taxes on that $20,000 gain today.

4. Another major disadvantage is that you must foreclose on the borrower to regain control of the property. This process, at least in Maryland, is long (6-14 months) and expensive ($1,500-$5,000), plus loss of payments. And, once you repossess the property, it is often returned to you in deplorable condition.

OWNER FINANCING — MY PERSONAL EXPERIENCE

When the note industry was healthier, I sold dozens of homes via owner financing, an attractive method to buyers that can be advantageous for both the motivated and unmotivated seller. I created notes and sold them to a note buyer either at settlement (table funding) or after pooling and packaging. Though it wasn't terrible, it was more difficult and less lucrative then selling a home to a qualified borrower and cashing out. Today, I would never pursue this method of selling a home. I always ended up giving away most of my profit to the note buyers in the form of discounts.

OWNER FINANCING — FINAL ANALYSIS

Personally, even if creating and selling notes were easy, I would prefer selling rent to own rather than owner financing due to the high cost of foreclosure in my area. While wrapping up a foreclosure, it has taken a year and cost between $14k in attorney fees, advertising and lost payments. The house also needed another rehab job to add a little salt to the wound.

In some states, the foreclosure process is simpler—this wouldn't happen and owner financing might be a viable option. Remember that table funding is extremely difficult and be sure to investigate what it will take to retake possession of the home if the buyer defaults. Owner financing may not be the way to go.

Though it isn't a game for the cash poor, if I had abundant cash resources, I would consider buying homes cheaply before fixing and selling them with owner financing. If you can fund deals with your own cash or that of private investors, this could be a viable and very lucrative option to pursue.

CASHING OUT — ADVERTISING

Cashing out is one of the most difficult types of selling to accomplish alone. You seek a buyer with good credit who can go to a bank, qualify for a loan and buy your house. This happens daily, but it is difficult since most people with good credit know their credit score. They get pre-qualified for a loan and go to a Realtor to shop through the largest selection of homes available. Occasionally, you will attract people with good credit who don't realize they can buy a home without you, but this is rare. There is an exception to this rule. When marketing a home in a very hot area, you can usually put up a sign in the yard and have the home sold to a pre-qualified buyer within days. There are areas in Baltimore where 90 percent of the homes sold are sold from signs or word of mouth, so real estate agents are not as necessary.

CASHING OUT — HANDLING CALLS

When I run ads in an attempt to cash out on a deal, I never put anything to prompt the "motivated buyer" to call me. My ads simply say:

Newly renovated, 3 BR, 123 Main St. $129k xxx-xxx-xxxx

When the calls come in, you will see an assortment of buyers. Some will ask if you are willing to consider rent to own or owner financing. These callers have usually purchased an infomercial course and reading the "questionnaire" contained within. Of the remaining callers, determine which can actually qualify for a loan. This is the biggest concern when wanting to cash out. If they are not prequalified, I may refer them to a loan officer who can prequalify them. Since we've established your primary concern to identify which callers are creditworthy, you can do so by asking a few questions and then pulling a credit report. The questions that I typically ask include:

- How is your credit?
- Do you have any late payments?
- Have you ever filed bankruptcy? If so, how long ago?
- How long have you been on your job?
- How much down payment do you have?
- How much can you afford per month?

For someone with little money, good credit can sometimes prevail. This is the reverse of rent to own or owner financing buyers who must bring a fair amount of money to the table due to poor credit. Also, when someone calls who knows they have good credit and are qualified to purchase, they are much more direct. They ask questions about the house, not your terms. They are ready, willing and able and their only concern is if your house is the right house for them.

CASHING OUT — ADVANTAGES

The primary advantage to cashing out is to get profit without any further time or effort invested on your part. Your investment in the property ends the day you sell it. You are no longer responsible for anything that may go wrong with the home.

CASHING OUT — DISADVANTAGES

There are several disadvantages to cashing out. You may have to accept a lower price for your property, particularly if your renovation isn't top quality. Also, you might have to wait longer to sell than if you sold rent to own or owner financing. I don't consider these first two objections "disadvantages" and they certainly don't outweigh the primary advantage stated above. However, there are two other disadvantages when selling a home yourself to cash out.

First, you will have to sift through unqualified buyers before finding someone qualified to borrow the money to buy your house. Even when taking prospects to a good mortgage broker, this can be very time consuming and somewhat frustrating. I once had a buyer lined up to purchase a house and putting her in on a rent to own basis while working nine months to clean up her credit, she bought a car based on her improved credit rating ten days before settlement, throwing her debt to income ratio out of whack and disqualifying herself for the new loan.

Second, you may have to become adept at helping buyers overcome credit issues. Sometimes the guy who gets the sale is the one willing to take the time to help a buyer straighten out their credit. I know of an investor who regularly works with credit-challenged buyers, spending time each week in an attempt to repair their credit so they can get a loan. As a result, he usually gets a premium and his buyers seem happy to pay because he took the time to get them into a home.

CASHING OUT — PERSONAL EXPERIENCE

Sometimes you can find buyers who are unaware they have good credit. When I was running my ad for rent to own homes, I had people contact me who thought they had bad credit, but they ended up having pretty good credit. Beginning investors tend to get nervous when they don't receive contracts on their homes immediately and consider other routes of marketing like "rent to own." The key is to be patient and wait for the right buyer to cash out. If you have a good home and you know it, the right buyer will come along. You may have to reduce your price if it's too high for the market, but you are better off reducing the price and waiting for a qualified buyer to cash you out instead of trying a rent to own program.

CASHING OUT — FINAL ANALYSIS

Cashing out puts the most cash in your pocket. If you are marketing homes on your own and looking for creditworthy buyers, it can be very tough. Anything is possible, but most people who know they have good credit will go to a Realtor to buy a home. If someone is creditworthy, they can buy anything they want in their price range, so they might as well talk with someone who has the largest inventory.

With that said, I'd like to question why anyone would try to personally market their homes just to save a few thousand dollars. In Maryland, there are approximately 2,700 realtors—each working with 2-3 qualified buyers, trying to find homes as well as 5,400-8,100 potential qualified buyers at my disposal by listing homes. With all of this, I only need one. In my view, cashing out by using a Realtor is the best way to sell a renovated home.

CHAPTER 24

ADVERTISING METHODS

THIS CHAPTER CONTAINS A discussion on the various methods of advertising as a FSBO (For Sale By Owner). As a wholesaler and a rehabber, I have used all of them, some with better success than others.

CLASSIFIED ADS

If you are a wholesaler or choose to personally sell your rehabs, you need to advertise. Historically, I have had the most success by advertising through my local both online and print. After spending thousands of dollars on all kinds of advertising—short ads, long ads, specific ads, generic ads, ads that made me seem desperate, and ads that made me seem totally unmotivated—I have discovered what works best.

When trying to sell a completed rehab, the two ads in the "Sample Ads — Rehabbing" section drew the most calls. When wholesaling, I have yet to pin down one failsafe ad that works all the time. I've also discovered that when running my wholesale ads, I need to change them on occasion so they do not become stale. Repetition is good for most advertising, but if the ad seems to show the same home each week, it receives fewer calls over time. Alternatively, when I run generic ads

(ads to purchase properties) and run them continuously (once a week), that does well for me. Ultimately, only trial and error will determine what works best for you.

I have placed ads that have brought in hundreds of calls and then used the same ad only to get a couple of calls. It's tough to determine the most effective method. While the two sample ads below did very well for me, I still don't believe there is a magic ad to run for fantastic results. When you write your ads, try to get as many callers as you can and weed through all the respondents. If I have a property for sale in a good area and I list the name of the area in the ad, I usually get a lot of calls regardless of what else the ad says.

SAMPLE ADS — WHOLESALING

As I said, there is no magic ad that draws hundreds of calls. Below I share the ads that have been the most productive for me, and I hope they work as well for you. If one of my ads is more successful then any others it is the following:

123 Main St. * 3 BR, $80k area, only $45k! Financing Available (xxx) xxx-xxxx

Another ad that I've used with success is:

Fixer Upper*123 Main St., $80k comps, only $40k

(xxx)xxx-xxxx

Two ads that can help you to build your buyers list are:

Wholesale Properties, seeking serious cash investors! (xxx) xxx-xxxx

Or

Fixer Uppers*Cheap, All Areas*Financing Available, (xxx)xxx-xxxx

SAMPLE ADS — REHABBING

Unlike my ads for wholesaling, neither stood apart from the rest, two of the ads that I used for retailing not only got unique results, but blew the doors off all my other ads. Here is the first:

Owner Desperate*Must Sell!*Westside 4BR*Low Down*Owner may finance* (xxx)xxx-xxxx

The second was a very generic ad. It read as follows:

Rent to Own*We Finance Anyone*Many Homes to Choose From*Low Down*Call Now (xxx)xxx-xxxx

This second ad drew over 120 completed applications with credit reports per month, and it kept up that pace for two months after I stopped advertising. If you are in the owner finance or rent to own business, I highly recommend this ad:

HOW OFTEN YOU SHOULD RUN YOUR ADS

I only run my ads once a week. I don't believe in spending the money to advertise every single day. In many areas, that can be a very expensive proposition. If you can advertise for free online, do it more often, even daily.

WHERE TO RUN YOUR ADS

I've experienced the most success in my weekly shopper. Papers like the "Thrifty Nickel" or the "Pennysaver" are papers that people tend to keep around longer. This may be contrary to what other investors say, but I can undoubtedly say that my most successful ads come from my local Pennysaver. Craigslist is free and should be in everyones toolbox.

FLYERS

Occasionally, when wholesaling, I put flyers at our local investment club meeting. Each one lists a number of properties and offers very attractive terms. Every once in a while, I sell a home as a result of distributing these flyers, but I wouldn't use them outside of my investment club. On the whole, I have found them ineffective. In addition, early in my investing career, I took some advice from "the gurus" and attempted to advertise my rehabs via flyers in the surrounding neighborhood. I don't think I received a single call from one of those flyers. As a result, I have never done it since nor would I recommend this method of advertising a rehab to anyone else.

SIGNS

Producing a number of sales, signs have been a very effective form of advertising. Use cheap signs or spend the money to have them professionally done. I have aluminum signs produced at $23 each. Whenever I put one of these signs in front of a completed rehab, my phone rang off the hook. I've never used roadside or "bandit" signs, but I imagine these would work as well.

Signs usually work best on streets with high traffic or in really hot areas where people are driving the streets looking for homes. When marketing a home on a high traffic street, I always put a sign in front of the house because they generate calls that could sell homes for me in other areas.

Post signs work better than metal frames stuck in the ground. They look more professional and are higher off the ground while being more visible to drivers. With regard to putting them up and taking them down, we have a sign service in town that put the posts in the ground and take them up when the home is sold.

INTERNET

With technology as it is today, I highly recommend that wholesalers and rehabbers consider using the Internet when marketing on their own. In time, it will outpace other marketing vehicles. Once your website becomes well-known in your area, buyers will visit daily to check for new endeavors. You won't have to call or e-mail and they will know how often you update with new inventory. Posting a new home may result in calls from people who want to schedule appointments immediately.

When I post homes through my rent to own program, it works extremely well. After advertising the site on my rent to own signs, the newspaper and business cards, I was receiving over 100 visitors per day within the first two months. I actually couldn't supply enough homes to all the interested buyers. At the moment, I do not use the website because I no longer market homes myself. In a low-interest rate environment, I market completed rehabs through a real estate agent. This allows me to cash out and let someone else do the work while eliminating need for a website.

PHONE SCAN AND FAX SYSTEM

If you intend to get heavily involved in real estate investing, it is important that you have one phone number dedicated to your business. This number should be equipped with a voicemail system and a professional greeting. When answering the phone personally, answer with a clear and confident greeting, mentioning your name and the name of your company.

In addition to a dedicated phone line, you should also have a dedicated fax number and scanner. This is a document sensitive business, so it is inevitable to use a fax and scanner frequently. If you do not have this equipment readily available, you may lose deals on occasion. This is not meant to say that you need all of this from the start. Today, you can do most everything with a cell phone. You can scan documents, sign documents, fax and receive documents and mange your voicemail all from your pocket. It's a much different business and technology is making it easier.

TAKE CALLS PERSONALLY IF POSSIBLE

Don't allow your voicemail system to catch every call. By using an answering service, I determined that 30 percent of callers were hanging up when they got an answering machine or voicemail. That's 30 potential buyers out of 100 that you lose.

Due to the volume of calls, I have also experienced tremendous difficulty in getting back to everyone who has left messages in the past. It is not uncommon that I never get to speak with someone after they leave a message. At times, it seems almost impossible to get back in touch with some people when convenient for both of us. Despite past issues, I recommend you make a concerted effort to call back all of the people who call on your ads. You never know good buyers from bad buyers without personally speaking with someone.

Due to time constraints, I have not returned phone calls based on how a person sounded when they left a message, which is downright foolish. Several times I returned a phone call that I was tempted to skip over only to find out that the caller had $20,000 cash to put down. This shows that you should call back everyone who calls you. You pay for advertising, so take advantage of the results.

Returning calls is sometimes a grueling task and it's usually least convenient for you. Unfortunately, people are waiting for your call when you are home and ready to relax. When I was selling homes myself, this is one thing that I hated. Contacting people had to be done on their time and I like for things to be done on my time. The reason I got into this business was for freedom so that is why I now use a Realtor. I don't like for other people's schedules to dictate when I have to work.

KEEPING A BUYERS LIST

Whether you choose to wholesale or retail properties, keeping a list of potential buyers is going to be one of the most important things you do.

WHOLESALERS

If you wholesale properties, developing a buyers list is absolutely critical for your business. Once you have a decent buyers list, you can cut back on your advertising. You can notify everyone on your list about all of your new deals and delay advertising a property until everyone on your list has passed it up. You will also need to continuously add to your buyers list. Someone may buy a number of properties, but it's best to have a longer list. Ultimately, your goal should be to develop a regular customer base. Personally, I have regular, aggressive buyers who buy most of my properties. I either sell the other properties to other investors or buy and renovate them myself.

REHABBERS

Developing a list is also important for those who renovate and resell properties. Unlike a wholesaler's buyers list, which consists mainly of investors, a rehabber's list doesn't have a very long shelf-life. Most of these people will only be in the market for a few months. In addition to being qualified, they are typically motivated to buy something and will buy a home from someone else if you don't have one available right now. Oftentimes, they will go through a Realtor and select from the hundreds of homes available on the MLS from other investors or homeowners.

There's not much to do to keep a qualified, motivated buyer from going elsewhere to find a home, but that didn't stop me from trying. The way I looked at it, I had just as much right to work with a good credit buyer as the next person. I would do anything legal or ethical to keep them loyal to me. I tried to be as convincing as possible when telling them that if they worked with me, I could get them a home. However, I never misled or lied to anybody. When I discovered that they had good credit, I simply let them know that we could work together and it was just a matter of me finding the right home for them.

MARKETING TO YOUR BUYERS LIST

When marketing homes on your own, you will start to reach more and more qualified buyers. Develop a list of these buyers and begin to market your future homes to them. As your list grows, it will become difficult to notify all of your buyers by telephone whenever you have a new property for sale. I suggest obtaining fax numbers and e-mail addresses from everyone. By doing so, you can reach dozens or even hundreds of people with very little effort on your part, distributing information on a property whenever one becomes available or possibly keeping in touch with a weekly list of properties.

As a rehabber, I've marketed to my buyers list using color postcards. I enlisted the services of a company that would design and print the cards for me in small quantities for $.40 each. This was a little pricey, but the postcards were extremely effective. Whether you choose to wholesale or retail, if you are successful in maintaining a list of your prospects with the pertinent information, you can target better buyers by notifying them of new opportunities. I put postcards in the mail and have people show up at my office in the morning, waiting to buy a home.

I'd also like to mention that if you are rehabbing, depending on your activity level, you might have two or three homes in progress with another two or three in the pipeline. If so, consider using one project as a model home to convince one of the qualified buyers on your list to put a deposit down on a home that you haven't started yet. When you tell someone that a home will be ready in two months, they will rely on your word when making decisions regarding moving out of and possibly selling their current residence, so be ready to roll. Otherwise, you could lose the sale, especially if they need to move somewhere and your house isn't complete.

CHAPTER 25

QUALIFYING BUYERS

ONCE YOU HAVE A potential buyer, determine if they are legitimate or if you can make them legitimate. The last thing you need is to have someone else put your property under contract so that they can flip it to someone else. It is imperative that you know whether or not your buyers are capable of performing. If they cannot perform, you need to identify whether or not you can help them. Since the process for qualifying buyers is somewhat dependent on whether you are wholesaling the property or retailing the property, this chapter discusses both perspectives.

QUALIFYING WHEN WHOLESALING

From my experience, most callers for investment properties are beginners who have never done a deal. In many cases, they can't pull off a deal despite helping them. You can identify who is serious and who is not by asking a few questions. If you determine that you have a serious buyer on your hands who lacks some of the knowledge required to close (he doesn't know where to get the purchase and rehab money), you can help put the deal together.

QUALIFYING PROCESS

The first question to ask any investor is, "How do you intend to pay for the property?" This catches newbies off guard and they usually stumble. You need to be versed from this point forward. When they answer, you need to take control. If they answer by saying "cash," you need to respond by saying, "Where is the cash coming from? Are you borrowing the money or do you have cash of your own?" If they say that they have their own cash (bank accounts, mutual funds, 401k) or line of credit (home equity or other), you should make them provide you with proof of funds or a sizeable earnest money deposit, if not both. Neither should be a problem. If they say that they are borrowing the cash, proceed as follows:

Ask for the name of their lender. It should be a private lender (not a bank) that you recognize as a proven source of funds. Call the lender to verify that they are willing to work with your prospective buyer and determine if they are going to lend money on the property and at what loan-to-value (LTV). Once you have assured yourself that your buyer will be able to obtain financing, get together to sign a contract and collect a deposit. Don't sign a contract until you are sure that your prospective buyer can get financing. You don't want to bind yourself to someone who can't perform. When you do collect a deposit, it should be large enough to reassure yourself that your buyer will show up at settlement. I collect enough to reimburse myself for my earnest money deposit and sometimes more, particularly if I've never dealt with the person before. After signing the contract and getting a deposit, start the appraisal process with the lender as soon as possible.

If you don't recognize their private lender, satisfy yourself by contacting them directly. Verify that they are willing to work with your prospective buyer and determine if they are going to lend money on the property and at what loan-to-value (LTV). Sign a contract and collect a deposit.

Your second option is to line them up with one of your own hard money lenders. Verify that your lender will play ball and sign a contract to collect a deposit. At this point, depending on the lender, you will need a copy of their credit report—pull it yourself or have them provide it. If you must pull it yourself, your buyer needs to fill out a credit application similar to the one in Appendix C. Then, you can pull his or her credit, if you belong to a service that gives you the ability to do so (there are plenty of these on the Internet), or have someone that you know do it for you (mortgage broker). If your buyer is inexperienced with rehabs, you will need to hold their hand through the rehab process, making sure that they complete the rehab and pay off your lender. Otherwise, they may default on their loan and jeopardize your relationship with the lender.

PRIVATE VS. CONVENTIONAL LENDERS

Beware if an investor is planning to get a rehab or construction loan from a bank. Due to the abusive and fraudulent practices of some investors, "title seasoning" has become an issue and most conventional lenders will not finance properties purchased and resold through assignments or simultaneous closings. Therefore, most banks are not a reliable source of funds.

Private lenders, on the other hand, understand the business and are more flexible than conventional lenders. Buyers can borrow money without a problem. If you are not satisfied with a prospective buyer's source of funds, take them to a private lender or do not deal with them at all. Personally, I will not wholesale properties to investors who want to get a bank loan. I let them know they can't buy my house, regardless of whether they are prequalified or not. Some get mad when I say this, but it's my policy. If they are prequalified or know the bank president, they can use them to refinance or to finance their retail buyer. I've been burned by banks who pull out at the last minute and I refuse to sell to investors who want to use them to get the money to buy my wholesale deals. I'd rather have an investor walk away mad than be left holding the bag before settlement.

STAY IN CONTROL

Basically, qualifying your buyer is your job to make sure deals settle. In addition to staying on top of your deals, know exactly where the money to purchase your home is coming from and that this source is reliable. My preference is to take buyers who need financing to lenders I already know, since I feel comfortable and it offers me control. Whatever you decide to do, stay in control and make sure that your deals make it through settlement.

QUALIFYING WHEN RETAILING

When speaking with potential homebuyers, quickly determine who has a legitimate chance of buying your home and who does not. The following paragraphs outline what you need to know to qualify a potential buyer.

KNOWING FINANCING REQUIREMENTS

It is nearly impossible to successfully qualify homebuyers if you don't know what is required for them to obtain financing. Acquaint yourself with a number of different financing programs, particularly if you are selling or plan to sell to sub-prime buyers. Three criteria common to most loan programs are:

1. A buyer should not have any late payments on their credit report for the last twelve months
2. A buyer should have been on their job for the last two years (or moved up to a better job)
3. A buyer's debt to income ratio should be in line.

PULLING CREDIT REPORTS

I have had the ability to pull credit reports since my first day of investing. Different programs give you this ability. When I began, I was paying $15 per report and waited up to two days before receiving it. My last service charged me $3 per report and enabled me to pull them immediately from my desk. If you are going to market your homes and do volume, I strongly suggest you obtain a means of pulling credit reports on your prospects. It is important for you to know if a potential buyer is real or not and a credit report will let you know whether that prospect is worth your time. You must get sufficient information from each caller to pull a credit report. Taking down a name and phone number is not enough and you will be surprised at the number of people who might tell you they have good credit but in reality couldn't get a credit card with a $200 limit.

PROFILE OF A GOOD RETAIL BUYER

A good buyer is simply a trustworthy individual who can hold up their end of the bargain. Whether you are selling a home on a rent to own basis, with owner financing or cashing out, this means a buyer will perform and follow through on their commitments. The main question becomes, "How do I know if someone will keep the promises they've made to me?"

Those who keep their word usually have a track record of doing so—steady job, good credit history and sound money management with a reasonable debt to income ratio. It really isn't that difficult to get financing for someone like this who wants to buy a home from you. They are mature and motivated enough to cooperate throughout the home-buying process.

If you find yourself dealing with someone who can't find their tax returns, doesn't have their bank statements or falls short on anything else required for financing, chances are high that you're headed for trouble. The inability to complete such simple tasks demonstrates a lack of organization on their part that will usually reflect in the way they handle their money. It is extremely difficult to close loans with people such as these who are disorganized, credit-challenged and unreliable.

CHAPTER 26

SERVICING WHOLESALE BUYERS

For the wholesalers among you, this chapter describes what your buyers list will look like and how you can best service the buyers on your list.

"ALL CASH" BUYERS DEBATE

Not all buyers need to be "all cash" buyers. If you have creditworthy buyers who possess enough income, they don't need cash. You can provide financing for them by taking them to the hard money lenders who fund your buyers. Cash buyers are tough to find and very hard to take on as loyal customers. Since they are in a position to do whatever they want, whenever they want, they buy their homes wherever they can get a deal. Furthermore, they usually like to make the rules, so it is harder for you to control the transaction. If a cash buyer wants to use their own title company, I require a substantial earnest money deposit until they have proven themselves. I do occasionally sell to cash buyers, but I don't have a single one as a regular customer.

INVESTORS WHO CAN AND INVESTORS WHO CAN'T

Investors who call come from different backgrounds. You will find investors who have rehabbed hundreds of homes to people who have never bought a home. It is up to you to determine whether or not you will be able to do business with someone. The following three profiles of potential buyers are meant to guide you:

ALL CASH / EXPERIENCED INVESTORS

You can tell when you are talking to an experienced investor. They know what they are talking about and get right to the point. They want to know the cash price of the home, the address and how to gain access so that they can go out to see it. They may ask a few basic questions regarding number of bedrooms, style and construction (frame or brick) of the property to determine whether the home fits their profile and is worth further investigation, but they won't waste time asking things like "How big are the rooms?" or "Is there a garage?" Furthermore, if they decide to purchase it, they know where to get the cash and they will not have a problem giving a deposit.

INTERMEDIATE INVESTORS

These investors possess some of the knowledge needed to put a deal together, but need help with the other pieces. They may need the name of a good contractor, or they may have good credit but not know where to get the money. Evaluate each intermediate investor and their situation on a case-by-case basis, particularly if you are going to refer them to one of your hard money lenders. Judge whether or not they can successfully complete a rehab project, even if they have good credit. Otherwise, they may screw up the project and default on their loan, damaging your credibility with the lender. If I don't think someone is ready to tackle a rehab project, I tell him. I'd rather be honest than sell a home and set them up for failure. If they are persistent and have their own cash, I may or may not sell the house to them. It's a judgment call, but if I did, I would collect a substantial deposit ($3,000 to $5,000) upfront to ensure that they show up at settlement.

NOVICE INVESTORS

Newbies tend to have an infomercial script and ask questions like, "May I please have your name?" They ask dozens of inane questions about your home and I usually cut them off by the third question and let them know that "my house needs work and I'm asking fifty cents on the dollar for it." Also, "if they are interested and have cash, please feel free to call me back." I'm sure I come across unfriendly, but people who buy wholesale properties don't need to know all the details. Furthermore, I honestly can't answer most of the questions asked for the homes that I wholesale.

I've never stepped in many of the homes and couldn't tell someone if there is a heating system in the house if my life depended on it, much less when it was last serviced. The homes are cheap and that is what matters most to the wholesale buyer. They realize that the amount of your mortgage, the last time you had your furnace serviced, or the color of your carpeting are all irrelevant when you are buying a home at a deep discount. Unless the person asking all the questions has a pile of cash and is willing to part with a substantial deposit, move on to your next prospect.

TYPES OF BUYERS ON YOUR LIST:

REHABBERS (NON-CONTRACTORS)

Rehabbers tend to look for homes in better neighborhoods and most prefer light cosmetic work. However, some like homes completely dilapidated because they prefer to redo the entire home. Important details for rehabbers are location and number of bedrooms. Most rehabbers want at least three bedrooms. Though I have sold a number of two bedroom homes over the last couple of years, I have either rehabbed myself and sold to end users or wholesaled "as-is" to landlords. Two bedroom homes are also easy to rent where I live so it depends on the area.

REHABBERS (CONTRACTORS)
Contractors are also a great source as buyers. They have the skills and resources to fix homes, but many do not have the money to buy. If you have a home and can line them up with money, they might become a regular customer.

LANDLORDS
Landlords tend to look for homes in cheaper areas. This isn't always the case, but most want homes in cheap areas that need very little work, providing them with a high, positive cash flow in a short period of time. Landlords want to put a tenant in the home and start producing positive cash flow as soon as possible. They tend to stay away from big rehabs that cause negative cash flow every month (mortgage payments, taxes, insurance, utilities) before they are ready for occupancy.

HOMEOWNERS
I can recall four occasions where I have wholesaled homes to people who bought the home and fixed it up for themselves. In this lending environment, these people will need to bring their own cash to the table. They probably won't be able to get a loan to purchase your property from a conventional lender and you will not be able to take them to a private lender. While it is fine for your hard money lenders to provide commercial loans to investors, most will not be properly licensed to provide residential loans to owner occupants.

MY FAVORITE BUYER
My favorite type of buyer is the person who has reasonable credit and a good income. They can afford monthly mortgage payments, but they can't always come up with a lot of cash at one time. Many have jobs and don't have the time to find homes or learn the ropes, two needs that I help fulfill. Since they have decent credit and a good income, these are exactly the people that my hard money lenders prefer. These

buyers like to use my private lenders because they want to purchase homes with no money down and preserve what cash they have. I usually build as many closing costs as possible into the deal so they don't need to come to the settlement table with too much of their own cash. As a result, these buyers like to deal with me and they are able to buy more homes from me. The majority of my wholesale profits come from dealing with these types of buyers. I help them find a property, get their purchase and rehab money, get the home refinanced and get it sold, so they can buy another.

BE A FULL SERVICE WHOLESALER TO YOUR BUYERS

As a wholesaler, your job is to sell houses. Many potential buyers have little to no experience and have yet to develop relationships with hard money lenders, attorneys, contractors, mortgage brokers or real estate agents. Even those investors who have already renovated several properties or purchased several rentals will need help in one or more areas. If you can assist these prospective customers, you will dramatically increase your chances of selling houses to them now and in the future.

I provide houses and other services to other investors. I line them up with money to do deals, put them in touch with a good settlement attorney, refer contractors to fix the property, refer real estate agents to sell their completed rehab, pass on the name of a good mortgage broker to get their buyers financed or themselves refinanced, etc. I give my buyers every reason to deal with me on current and future transactions.

This strategy helps me to ensure that my deals close successfully since I maintain control of the whole process. I know where the money is coming from and who is performing the settlement. After the sale, I make sure that my investors are successful in completing their rehab and getting the home sold. I want them to buy another home from me and the majority become regular customers because they are successful when dealing with me.

KEEP ABREAST OF YOUR BUYERS' NEEDS

Your buyers list will become one of your biggest assets as a wholesaler. I do maintain a buyers list, even though I deal primarily with a handful of buyers. At this point, I know who is going to be interested in which home as well as what they will pay and whether or not they are in a buying mode. I stay in constant contact with my regular buyers. If they haven't called me in a while (some call me on a daily basis looking for homes if they are in a buying mode), I will call to see how they are doing and if I can help them with something. As a result, I always have a feel for what is going on with them and with the market at large. Nothing feels better than knowing when you buy a home that it is already sold and all you have to do is make a phone call. I now have about half of the homes I buy sold within minutes of getting them under contract.

REAL LIFE EXPERIENCE

In the first 45 days of 2001, I bought 27 homes. By the end of February, I decided I was going to rehab three of the homes for resale and keep one for my rental portfolio. I was able to buy 27 homes and sell 23 of in two months because I have a good buyers list. Most of my buyers are not cash buyers. They buy from me because I find the homes they like, line up all the financing, get them their rehab money, line them up with contractors to do their rehabs (in some cases, not all), and advise them through the whole process. Some have been investing longer than I have, but because I spend much of my time looking for better homes, better money, and better contractors, I can provide value to them. My average profit on the 23 homes was just over $6,000 per property. Most of my buyers know exactly how much money I make from these sales, but they don't care. I always put them into profitable deals and help them get out of them as soon as possible so they can buy another home from me.

CHAPTER 27

CLOSING A WHOLESALE DEAL

WHETHER WHOLESALING OR RETAILING, this is one area that is a complete mystery to many beginning investors. This chapter and the next help to demystify these processes by addressing the steps you need to close a wholesale deal and a retail deal.

ALWAYS GET A CONTRACT SIGNED AND COLLECT A DEPOSIT

Once you have an interested wholesale buyer, it is time to sign a contract. You do not have a deal without a signed contract. You need to understand this. In the beginning, it was tough for me to ask my buyer to sign a contract and give me an earnest money deposit. Since I wanted to avoid putting money up when I signed a contract, I didn't feel right asking for one from my buyers. You must do this to protect yourself.

After I stopped birddogging, getting contracts signed and collecting deposits scared me. I was shaking when getting the first few contracts signed—so much I only got one check out of my first three deals. With the first one, I was so nervous I forgot to ask. With the second, I was too scared to ask. With the third deal, I finally got a check. The results of these deals were as follows:

The first deal didn't go through and I had to find another buyer (I got a check that time). The second deal didn't go through and I had to find another buyer (I got a check this time, too). The third deal went through without any problems. The moral of the story is that you should always collect a deposit check to protect yourself.

Even if you trust your buyer, you will sleep better knowing they have something at stake. My success ratio without getting a check is zero. My success ratio at getting a deal closed after getting an earnest money check is probably around 98 percent.

Make it perfectly clear that your home is still for sale until you have a check from them in the amount of $1,000. I usually make my buyers give me what I put down on the home. Most people who can't come up with earnest money on a home will not be capable of completing their purchase and you are better off letting them get away now than finding out they can't buy the home right before settlement.

ASSIGNMENT AGREEMENT — ALTERNATIVE TO CONTRACT

Rather than signing a contract, you might choose to execute an assignment agreement. This is a simple one-page form that conveys your interest in a contract to your assignee. The consideration for transferring this right is outlined within the agreement and is known as the assignment fee. This is a simple process, basically accomplished with the phrase, "I, (insert your name) agree to assign my rights in this contract to (insert the name of your buyer) for the sum of $X,XXX."

ASSIGNMENT OR SIMULTANEOUS CLOSING

Whether you choose to execute another contract of sale with your buyer or an assignment agreement is entirely up to you. If you execute a second contract of sale, the title company will perform a simultaneous closing at settlement. The downside of is that there are two sets of closing costs. The upside is that your buyer won't know your profit.

If you execute an assignment agreement with your buyer, assigning your rights in the contract to them, there will only be one closing (the purchase from the original seller) and one set of closing costs. The downside is that your profit will appear on the settlement sheet.

In my area, closing costs are very high (2.5 percent transfer tax alone), so I almost always do an assignment. Furthermore, the majority of my buyers don't care how much I make as long as it's a good deal for them. Use your best judgment to determine what works for you.

CONVERTING NON-ASSIGNABLE CONTRACTS — DIRECTIONS FOR WHOLESALERS

While you will probably be able to include an assignability clause in a purchase contract, most banks will not allow you to assign their contracts. Basically, they have been burned by investors who do not settle when they can't wholesale the property. As a result, they won't accept offers that don't include a non-assignability clause.

However, there is a way to make a non-assignable contract assignable. Make the offer in the name of an entity such as an LLC, land trust or corporation whose membership interest, beneficial interest, or stock can be assigned or sold. Once your offer is accepted, go down to your state department and form the entity whose name is on the purchase contract. Then, assign or sell the entity to your buyer.

You aren't assigning the purchase contract, but you are assigning or selling the entity that owns the rights to the purchase contract. The same objective is achieved but in a slightly different way. In terms of obtaining documents required to form and assign/sell an entity, consult with an attorney to confirm you are using correct forms.

When you form the new entity, be sure that the registered name of the new entity is exactly as it appears on the contract. Otherwise, it will not match the name of the entity as it appears on the new deed prepared by the closing agent. A new deed can be prepared, but this causes unnecessary delays and may raise questions from the seller, who signs the deed. Take time to double check and get it right the first time.

MAKING A NON-ASSIGNABLE CONTRACT ASSIGNABLE —- MY METHOD

In Maryland, I have started making all of my offers in new entities. If I am making an offer on a property at 345 Main Street, the buyer on my contract will be 345 Main Street, LLC. When my offer is accepted, I immediately set up my new LLC.

After forming the LLC, I start marketing the property to other investors. Once I find a buyer, I transfer my membership rights in the newly created LLC to them. This is done in lieu of assigning the contract with the bank. As far as the bank is concerned, their buyer is still the LLC, the same entity they originally agreed to sell the property.

When transferring the membership interest, I have an Assignment of Membership Interest and Substitution of Member agreement that I use over and over. Everything is simplified because the LLC's I create are single member LLC's (my corporation is the only member, although any person or entity can be a member) that do not require operating agreements (operating agreements usually set up the rules that the members of the LLC must abide, including the means for its liquidation or dissolution). As a single member of a Maryland LLC, I have no need for an operating agreement because I make the rules. I can sell my LLC whenever and however I want.

Among other things, my Assignment of Membership Interest and Substitution of Member agreement mentions the following:

1. Name and address of LLC
2. Corporation as the existing member and assignor
3. Buyer or company as the assignee
4. Any assets owned by the LLC (contract to purchase)
5. Consideration that I receive for transferring membership interest
6. Terms regarding how and when I am to be paid

My agreement states that I am to be paid upon settlement of the property that the LLC has a contract to purchase. Once signing the agreement with my buyer, I give a copy to my attorney and collect a check at settlement, which is performed by my attorney in his office. Purchasing membership interest of an LLC is easy. It works well for my buyers because the cost setup in Maryland is reasonable and less expensive than doing a simultaneous close. In other states, where cost is more expensive, I would recommend using the same technique but with a land trust or corporation.

Whichever entity your wholesaler wants you to purchase, I seriously urge you to check with your attorney to make sure it is legal and easy to do in your state. I purposely have not gone into every detail because I'm not an attorney and I'm not familiar with the rules regarding LLC's on a state-by-state basis. Therefore, I must reiterate that although I have told you what I do, I very strongly recommend that whatever entity you might purchase (LLC, land trust, corporation, etc.), you should talk with your attorney and enlist their help in reviewing the documents used for creating and assigning the entity in your state.

Finally, keep in mind that this method of buying property is not for everyone. Insist on a simultaneous close if you feel uncomfortable buying an entity such as an LLC, land trust or corporation.

WHEN TO PAY ASSIGNMENT FEES

When I began assigning contracts, I was advised to collect assignment fees upfront. However, with all of the homes that I have assigned, I have never received my assignment fee before the home settled. No sophisticated investors would consider paying an assignment fee without knowing they were going to get clear title to the property and neither should you. The only way to be certain you will receive clear title is to be at the settlement table ready to walk away with the deed. Every assignment fee, cash or cash and second mortgage, should be paid at the settlement table.

SECOND MORTGAGES

On occasion, a wholesaler will take back part of their fee as a second mortgage. This allows them to control the deal so it proceeds to settlement regardless of a low appraisal from a lender. This also allows them to help their buyers conserve cash, which breeds loyalty since they put buyers into homes with little or no money down.

When looking to conserve cash, stay within reason, structuring deals so your wholesaler can pull some profits out in cash. Remember, you are trying to create win-win situations, meaning that both you and your wholesaler should end up satisfied.

LOW APPRAISALS FROM LENDERS

There are times when the amount a lender will lend on a particular property isn't enough to cover the original purchase price + your profit + closing costs + rehab costs. Sometimes, you will know this upfront. After speaking with your buyer's lender and determining the LTV percentage they are willing to finance, multiply this LTV percentage by a conservative after repaired value to get an idea of the anticipated loan amount. Even after this calculation, a lender may come back with an appraisal lower than you expected. In either case, your buyer will need to bring money to the table or you will need to take back part of your profit in the form of a "second mortgage." Just like the lender's first mortgage, your second mortgage will be a note secured by the property. However, stand behind the first mortgage holder with regard to payment. If the property is ever sold, the first mortgage holder gets all of their money before you collect anything owed to you. If the buyer stops making payments and the first mortgage holder forecloses, you will be wiped out along with any other subordinate liens.

EXAMPLE 1: FULL CASH PROFIT

Imagine getting a property under contract for $35k. The conservative after repaired value of the property is $100k, needing $20k in repairs, closing costs when you sell will be $5k, and you would like to sell it for $45k. After talking to your buyer's private lender, you find out that he will lend 70 percent of the after repaired value including $50k for purchase and $20k for repairs. At closing, there will be $70k from the lender on the table, which is enough to cover everything—$20k for repairs, $5k for closing costs, $10k for your profit and $35k to the original seller. No one needs to bring or leave any money on the table.

EXAMPLE 2: SECOND MORTGAGE FOR PARTIAL PROFIT

Say you get the same property for $35k, but the lender will only lend 65 percent of the after repaired value including $45k for purchase and $20k for repairs. At closing, there will be $65k from the lender on the table, but you will need $70k to cover everything. You know that the original seller needs $35k, so that leaves $30k cash on the table. Now assume that $20k is placed into a repair escrow, which leaves $10k cash on the table. At this point, you are owed $10k and closing costs of $5k must be paid. Ideally, your buyer will bring $5k cash to the table for the closing costs and you can walk away with the $10k cash that remains. However, every time your buyer lays out cash, it makes them less able to buy another house from you. One of the reasons my buyers keep coming back is that I get them into a home with as little cash out of pocket as possible. In this case, I would take back as much as $5k of my profit as a second mortgage to conserve my buyer's cash. The other advantage is that the deal closes rather than falls apart as a result of a low appraisal or LTV.

ADVANTAGES AND DISADVANTAGES

Second mortgages aren't necessarily bad, but they are risky. Given the risk of non-payment, I prefer my profits in the form of cash rather than a second mortgage. If I do take back a second mortgage, I name the terms and they typically mirror the terms of the private lender's first mortgage.

CHAPTER 28

CLOSING A RETAIL DEAL

Y͏OU HAVE REHABBED THE property, put it on the market and received several offers from buyers that you or your real estate agent has pre-qualified. Below will help you with the next few steps.

OFFERS RECEIVED, NOW WHAT?

First, evaluate the offers you've received. Realize that not all offers are created equal. Several key factors exist to impact the probability of each offer making its way through the financing and settlement process successfully. In the past, I ignored these factors and accepted the highest offer without a second thought. As a result, I ran into more difficulty selling my properties than I should have. Unfortunately, I see most beginning investors repeating the same mistakes.

When I review the offers today, I take into consideration several factors that affect a successful closing. First, I prefer offers with conventional loans as opposed to FHA Loans since conventional financing eliminates the need for an FHA inspection. Second, I weigh the need for an FHA inspection against the seasoning issues that some conventional lenders might raise. FHA doesn't have a problem with title seasoning, but some conventional lenders do. Third, I prefer to receive detailed prequalification packages from my buyers including a prequalification letter, provisions for a quick closing, financial statements, a decent earnest money deposit, no inspection contingencies, etc. Good real estate agents typically obtain as much information as they can from their buyers so they can build a case for their client when presenting an offer.

If I have a couple of contracts that appear solid and ready to close, I go for the most money by asking for the best offer from all parties. Sometimes I'll make a counteroffer at the same time, but my main goal isn't to get every last dollar for my house but rather to accept a fair offer with the highest probability of settlement. I'll take a sure $20,000 before gambling on $22,000 any day of the week. -

GETTING THE CONTRACT SIGNED AND COLLECTING A DEPOSIT

Just as with wholesaling, once you have an interested buyer, get a contract signed. You do not have a deal without a signed contract.

It is imperative for you to obtain fully ratified contracts when selling homes. It would be great if we could go back to the days when a handshake was all it took to seal a deal, but the bottom line is that a handshake will not hold up in court if you ever had to take a deal that far. Make sure all of the terms you discuss with your buyer are in the copy of the contract that you sign, including whether or not you will be contributing toward the buyer's closing costs, what inspections you agree to let them perform, what repairs you agree to make, the settlement date, the correct sales price, whether or not you are going to provide any financing, etc.

If you are selling through a Realtor, they will take care of obtaining a signed contract from the buyer and collecting a deposit. If you are selling your home as a FSBO, you will have to do these things yourself. Once you have an interested party, set up a time to get together and review/sign the contract. When selling FSBO, I always met my buyers at the home or a neutral place such as a restaurant. When we make an appointment, I always remind them to bring their checkbook and all of their documentation if I'm helping with financing. As soon as I told them to bring their checkbook, they knew the purpose of the meeting was to sign a contract and give a deposit.

Even if you trust your buyer, you will sleep better knowing they have something at stake. My success ratio without getting a check is zero. My success ratio at getting a deal closed after getting an earnest money check is probably around 98 percent. Make it perfectly clear that your home is still for sale until you have a check from them in the amount of $1,000. I usually make my buyers give me what I put down on the home. Most people who can't come up with earnest money on a home will not be capable of completing their purchase and you are better off letting them get away now than finding out they can't buy the home right before settlement.

CONVENTIONAL VS. FHA

I'm somewhat indifferent to the type of loan my buyers get. Conventional and FHA both have their pros and cons. One of the biggest drawbacks with FHA financing from a seller's point of view is that sometimes your current project may have inherent flaws that will prevent it from passing an FHA inspection. In these cases, your buyer needs to get conventional financing. For this reason, it is worth having a discussion with a knowledgeable home inspector to find out what is involved with an FHA inspection to determine that your renovations meet the minimum requirements.

All other things being equal, if I have a home that meets the FHA's minimum requirements, I prefer this method of financing. It doesn't take long to obtain, the buyers need little down and FHA allows me to contribute up to 6 percent for the buyer's closing costs. It's easy to make deals with buyers who have FHA financing.

LOAN PROCESS

This is where the adventure begins. It is easy to find and renovate a home as well as find a buyer. With these things, everything is out in the open. The loan process, on the other hand, is more mysterious. You never know if it will go smoothly, if it will happen at all or how long it will take. Usually, you can have an idea, but I have seen the best deals go south during the loan process. This is when you hold your breath and pray settlement will arrive without an issue.

You can improve your chances of smooth financing by dealing with buyers who have good credit. However, as soon as you find a buyer seeking a sub-prime conventional loan (or down payment assistance and/or closing cost assistance through low-interest loans or grants from the government or a non-profit organization), your transaction is more likely to run into some speed bumps. This happens because these deals take more time, involve more paperwork and include more moving parts.

Sub-prime loans don't conform to the government loan guidelines used by FHA and most conventional lenders (for prime loans). Similarly, grant and loan programs for closing cost assistance or down payment assistance involve playing a totally different game with a totally different set of rules. Finally, if you are dealing in the sub-prime market, you will be required to take back second mortgages on most deals, something that doesn't always complicate a deal but does impact your bank account.

Due to this uncertainty, I don't actively pursue the use of any programs involving closing cost or down payment assistance. I don't use any of them and really don't want to take the time to learn about them. However, I know investors who will use grant programs with every buyer and they do very well. This is your decision to make.

WORKING WITH MORTGAGE BROKERS / LOAN OFFICERS

Mortgage brokers call themselves all sorts of things these days—loan officers, loan specialists, customer service rep, mortgage bankers, account executive, etc. Regardless of the title, they usually represent many lenders. Alternatively, loan officers work for one company. Despite this difference, they both serve the same purpose and the terms "mortgage broker" and "loan officer" are interchangeable.

A good loan officer is vital when retailing and selling homes. It is time consuming to manage a renovation, market your completed homes, look for new projects and take buyers through the financing process on your own—having a good loan officer to obtain financing for your buyers can go a long way to ease the burden.

A good loan officer isn't necessarily someone who knows every single loan program inside and out. Over time, they have done numerous deals with certain underwriters and established really good relationships. They understand what they can and can't push through and can use their relationships with underwriters to their advantage.

Alternatively, inexperienced loan officers tend to use you as a guinea pig while they learn the ropes with different lenders. They may shop your buyer's loan to a number of different lenders, receiving a great education at your expense. Now I know that everyone has to start somewhere and I'm not putting down beginners, but even a rookie loan officer should be honest and let you know when things aren't going well rather than dragging out your deal for several months.

LOAN DOCUMENTS

There are various pieces of financial and credit information that a lender will require from a potential borrower. These include but are not limited to: pay stubs, W-2's, past two years' tax returns, (all three verify income), canceled rent checks to prove rental history, bank statements showing the source of their down payment funds, bankruptcy papers if applicable and anything relating to bad credit on a credit report (letter from a creditor showing that an account has been paid).

If you are dealing with buyers directly, your mortgage broker may ask you to help collect some of this information from your buyer, especially if you referred your buyers to the mortgage broker. This can be time consuming, but it is good for you to learn this part of the process since it helps you understand the process of packaging a loan, including what differentiates a good package from a bad package. However, you should be very careful when interacting this much with your buyers. It becomes more difficult to deny fraud if you were investigated for it.

APPRAISALS

In this business, appraisals are a necessary evil. They are required by lenders but can get you into trouble if you aren't careful. As logical as it might sound to establish a relationship with an appraiser, this may cause HUD to single you out during an investigation for illegal flipping. When reviewing their files, if HUD sees one investor continually selling homes with the same appraiser performing each appraisal, it immediately raises a red flag. I have always stayed away from the appraisal process. I have never had an appraiser in my back pocket and I never order the appraisal on my buyer's behalf. Rather, I have always chosen to allow my buyer's lender to pick the appraiser so no one can ever point a finger at me.

Almost all appraisers do their best to establish a value that equals or exceeds your sales price. They don't want to get in the way of closing a successful deal. Otherwise, they won't get much work from the lender in the future. I have only ever had my sales price knocked down once by an appraiser. My contract with the homebuyer was for $94,000 and the appraiser knocked it down to $91,000. I couldn't complain seeing as the highest sales price in the neighborhood prior to mine was $87,500.

INSPECTIONS

I pride myself on quality renovations but I try to avoid having inspections on my homes. Some inspectors are good but others are not. In many areas of the country, training and licensing are not required to be a home inspector, so some inspectors do not have a clue. One buyer hired an inspector who said the basement needed to be waterproofed because the floor was damp. The reason was that we had just mopped the basement floor. If the inspector was more knowledgeable, he would have checked the condition of the sump pump (a device installed below floor level to pump out water before flooding the basement). In this case, the sump pump was actually dusty. This inspector forced me to bicker with my buyers for two weeks before I resolved the "waterproofing" issue. I didn't do anything to fix the "problem." Instead, I told the buyers I would relist the home if they didn't want it.

I'm not skipping over items that need repairs. I go all out with my renovations and have nothing to fear from a legitimate inspection. What bothers me is inspectors who don't know the basics. In another instance, I put a two-month old roof on a home and the inspector estimated it to be fifteen years old. He told the buyers to have me replace it because its life expectancy was only five years. A bad report from a hack inspector not only wastes my time, but is infuriating when I'm trying to close a deal with a legitimate buyer.

DEALING WITH FHA

I don't mind dealing with FHA lenders. FHA does not have a seasoning requirement. The lenders finance my buyers without issue, allowing me to sell my homes three to four months after I bought it for substantially less. They usually scrutinize the appraisal in greater detail and request a scope of the work that I have completed, but the deals aren't any different from those that I do with a conventional lender. I don't care for their inspections, but I do such a good job with my rehabs that they really aren't an issue anyway.

WORKING WITH TITLE COMPANIES

If you are marketing properties, control the whole process, including leading your buyers to a title company. I usually ask the lender for a preference since they probably have a relationship with someone and I just want the deal to run smoothly. As soon as the lender gives approval, saying they can complete the deal successfully, the lender or myself start the title work. It doesn't hurt to have the lender make the arrangements since they know how to time everything and if the deal doesn't go through, they are liable if the title company wants to be reimbursed for any out of pocket expenses. When using a Realtor, I don't get involved in this process at all.

WAITING FOR SETTLEMENT

When using an agent to sell rehabs, the only thing to do after signing a contract of sale is to wait until you are asked to do something such as repairs as a result of an inspection, obtaining and providing payoff information from your private lender, or showing up at the settlement to sign the deed and pick up your check. On the other hand, if you are selling your homes yourself, once a contract is signed, you will have to start working through the following list:
- Collect credit and financial information from buyer
- Call mortgage broker / start financing process
- Get buyer's credit and financial information to lender
- Order appraisal, meet appraiser at house if necessary
- Make sure appraisal is done as scheduled
- Order inspection, meet inspector at house if necessary

- Make sure inspection is done as scheduled
- Order title work, including lien sheet
- Verify that title work is being done and that there are no title issues
- Schedule settlement

I get tired just thinking about it. Last but not least, you will need to attend settlement, sign the deed and pick up your check.

STAYING IN CONTROL OF THE SALE

Depending on rehab sale methods, the amount of control you need to maintain will vary. Since I use a Realtor, I exercise little control over my deals. Though my rehabs are nice and easy to sell, I let a professional Realtor handle the transactions and I pay their full commission to confirm a smooth deal. This gives me time to find more deals and manage my rehabs.

If you are doing your own marketing to save on commissions, you are responsible for everything my real estate agent does and more. Basically, it will be your job to find a qualified buyer and make sure the deal settles. You will have to advertise your homes, take calls, pre-qualify potential buyers, show your homes, get signatures, collect deposits, make sure that all contracts and addendums are completed properly, line up your buyers with mortgage brokers, help your buyers get qualified for financing, take them to a title company, etc.

After signing the contract but before settlement, coordinate the financing and settlement process by making sure inspections and appraisals are ordered and completed on time, making sure the lender and title company communicate properly, scheduling a settlement date with you, your buyers and the title company. If this sounds like a lot of work, it is, particularly if you are dealing with several prospective buyers per home or a multitude of homes.

In order to successfully sell your homes stay in control, put a good team together, the most important member is the loan officer or mortgage broker with whom you have experienced past success. Also, become knowledgeable about programs offered to low-income families that may provide down payment or closing cost assistance. Some of the most successful investors and Realtors are those who are patient enough to run buyers through these programs and prepare them to buy homes when no one else will give them the time of day.

Also, educate yourself on the types of financing programs available and identify which lenders will work with your buyers. Be very cautious about the type of financing your buyer intends to obtain. Know exactly where the money to purchase your home comes from and it's reliability. Avoid accepting what appears to be a good contract, but actually lacks title seasoning. When I was selling my homes alone, I needed to take my buyers to loan officers or mortgage brokers where I had already experienced success. The odds of the deal being completed fell dramatically.

At this point, some of you might be thinking that marketing your homes on a rent to own basis might save time. I can tell you from personal experience that it doesn't. You are still responsible for advertising, taking calls, meeting potential tenant/buyers, showing homes, taking applications, checking credit, reviewing job histories, and usually dealing with multiple prospects for each house. I was able to save some time in showing homes because my prospects were desperate for anything since they had exhausted all other options—not the types of people you want in your house since the chances of them cashing you out at some future date are very slim.

When selling as a FSBO, you deal with people who have already been through the real estate route and come to you because they couldn't qualify to buy a home through an agent. Next, if you do decide to market your home, be sure to keep everything above board. If your buyer were to default on their new loan, HUD might investigate you in the future and they will dig deeper than this transaction. Be sure to get all the information required from the buyer before they move into the home. Whenever I allowed a buyer to move in, getting information was nearly impossible.

TAKE A SECOND MORTGAGE TO MAKE A DEAL WORK

There is nothing wrong with taking back a second mortgage for profit, as long as you consider it to be a valid part of the sales price and fully intend to collect. When selling to wholesale buyers, it might be necessary to take back a second mortgage due to a low appraisal from the lender or the buyer's lack of funds. The low appraisal explanation printed in the last chapter is repeated here for your reference.

LOW APPRAISALS FROM LENDERS

There are times when the amount a lender will lend on a particular property isn't enough to cover the original purchase price + your profit + closing costs + rehab costs. Sometimes, you will know this upfront. After speaking with your buyer's lender and determining the LTV percentage they are willing to finance, multiply this LTV percentage by a conservative after repaired value to get an idea of the anticipated loan amount. Even after this calculation, a lender may come back with an appraisal lower than you expected. In either case, your buyer will need to bring money to the table or you will need to take back part of your profit in the form of a "second mortgage." Just like the lender's first mortgage, your second mortgage will be a note secured by the property. However, stand behind the first mortgage holder with regard to payment. If the property is ever sold, the first mortgage holder gets all of their money before you collect anything owed to you. If the buyer stops making payments and the first mortgage holder forecloses, you will be wiped out along with any other subordinate liens.

A NOTE ON "ILLEGAL FLIPPING"

First of all, I would like to make it perfectly clear that there is absolutely nothing illegal or unethical about buying a house cheap and selling it for more money. You can buy a home for $1 and sell it five minutes later for $1,000,000 without breaking any laws. Problems arise when investors falsify loan documents, manufacture supporting financial information, lie about a buyer's credit history or annual income, or submit fraudulently high appraisals to a lender. The end result is that the buyer ends up owing more money on a home than it's worth. Many times, the home hasn't been renovated properly and the buyer, who might not have been able to afford the house anyway, stops making payments causing the lender to foreclose. In today's investing environment, the fallout from unscrupulous investors "illegally flipping" properties in this manner to homeowners can be a major obstacle to the success of any investor. These people are going to jail for committing fraud within their retail sales transactions, but their actions are making life difficult for everyone, even everyday people selling their homes, due to all of the extra hoops that must be jumped through just to complete a transaction.

THE SCAM

I used to deal heavily with customers whose profile matched that of a potential victim of flipping fraud. Typically, the victims are unsophisticated homebuyers with challenged credit who can't qualify for A-credit loan programs. Criminal investors market their sub-par rehabs to these sub-prime buyers knowing they will only qualify for low LTV (loan to value) loans. The investors still want to cash out as if they had A-credit buyers, so they put together teams of mortgage brokers, appraisers, and title companies who are willing to go along with their plan—something like this:

Let's say an investor wants $70,000 for a home. However, their sub-prime buyer can only qualify for 70 percent financing and comparable sales indicate that the property is only worth $70,000. If shown the correct information, the lender would only be willing to lend $49,000—$21,000 short of the investor's desired price. With these criteria, the only way an investor can obtain $70,000 is to convince the lender that the property is worth $100,000 and that the buyer can afford a $70,000 loan. To do this, they have their appraiser issue a fraudulent appraisal that shows the value of the home at $100,000. This solves the LTV problem but leads to others.

By increasing the sales price, many buyers won't have the necessary down payment ($30,000 in this case) nor will they qualify for the larger loan amount. To "overcome" the down payment hurdle, the investor either takes back a $30,000 second mortgage and tears it up after closing or temporarily puts $30,000 into a bank account owned by a relative of the buyer and conspires with his mortgage broker to falsify a "gift letter" stating that the relative is actually gifting the money to the buyer for the purpose of purchasing this home. To "overcome" the annual income hurdle, the buyer mysteriously begins to make more money as the investor falsifies W-2's and other financial documents for the buyer and/or lists additional income from mythical part-time jobs. Finally, most lenders feel more comfortable if the buyer has a good rental history, so all of a sudden a Verification of Rent from some rental company is produced showing the buyer to be a stellar tenant.

In the end, you have a credit-challenged buyer with nothing at stake since they have no money invested into the purchase of their home and 100 percent financing from a bank who thinks they are protected because they only lent 70 percent of the purchase price. Needless to say, these deals have a very high rate of foreclosure.

HOW TO PROTECT YOURSELF

This takes place every day and people are going to jail as a result. I know ten people who have been investigated by HUD, and half of them (including some mortgage brokers and title company attorneys) are going to jail. These people did commit fraud, they did a lot of deals and they deserve to serve time. I think they were lucky to only receive sentences ranging from one to three years. These crimes are "white collar burglary," but they have done much more financial damage than someone who walks into a branch and demands money from a teller.

I recommend protecting yourself by avoiding all fraud at any cost, even if it means walking away from a profitable settlement. If you are selling homes, this is the best course of action. You may still be questioned, particularly if you are doing a lot of deals where you are still involved in the financing and selling process. However, whether you are doing one deal or one hundred deals, with the proper record keeping (keep all paperwork organized, save invoices and receipts, take before and after pictures) and fraud avoidance, you have nothing to worry about.

As soon as you become involved with the sales process, you are exposing yourself to the possibility of investigation. If the HUD investigators (who have the power of an IRS auditor) are having a bad day when they come across one of your deals, you could be investigated. I stay as far away from the marketing aspect of my homes as possible and let Realtors handle my sales from beginning to end. My involvement is limited to showing up at the settlement table, meeting the buyer for the first time, signing the deed, giving them the keys and picking up my check. I have nothing to do with the appraisals, the buyer or the mortgage company, and if anyone ever questioned me, I am so far removed they couldn't possibly charge me with anything.

Do deals honestly and ethically. Resist the temptation to break the rules regardless of the outcome. This can be tough, especially when profit is hanging in the balance. There will be times when people tell you all you have to do to make your money is bend one little rule. They'll say, "Don't worry about it. People do it all the time, and if you do it too, you'll walk away with a check for $15k. Otherwise, you'll get nothing." This is tempting, especially to the cash poor beginner. I walked away from a $15,000 profit when this same situation was presented to me. Later, I sold the house with owner financing to the same buyer. Then, I sold the note and made $13k. Sure, I made a little less and the deal took a couple extra months, but I did the deal honestly and I sleep peacefully because I don't ever have to worry about being investigated for committing fraud. I recommend you strive to uphold yourself to the same standard. It is easy to make money ethically, so don't risk jail time for a few shortcuts.

CHAPTER 29

SETTLEMENT PROCEDURES

THE HUD-1

The HUD-1, also known as the "settlement sheet" or "closing statement," is a breakdown of all costs related to a real estate transaction. Learn how to read one of these because a person prepares it and people make mistakes. For instance, you may have negotiated for a seller to pay some closing costs, say $500, but the person preparing the HUD-1 doesn't reflect this on the HUD-1. If you do not catch this error before the transaction is complete, you will end up paying this $500 yourself. Always check a settlement sheet before closing. Check the math and make sure it reflects your agreement with the seller or else you will have to pay.

SAMPLE HUD-1 — WHOLESALE DEAL

I purchased a property for $41,000 and assigned my contract for $4,000. My buyer borrowed $60,000 from a private lender where $41,000 went to the original seller, $11,500 went for repairs, $4,000 went to me for my profit and the remainder ($3,500) went for closing costs. My buyer only had to bring $430.35 to the settlement table. Immediately following the HUD-1 is a line item description of everything on the sheet.

DESCRIPTION OF SAMPLE HUD-1 — WHOLESALE DEAL

The first page of the HUD-1 is broken down into two sides, one for the buyer and one for the seller. Each side contains a summary of the participant's transaction. For the buyer, this includes the total amount they need (Section 100), the total amount, which is paid on their behalf by a lender or some other party (Section 200) and the difference, which is what they will bring or take from the table (Section 300). For the seller, this summary includes what they are owed (Section 400), what must be paid from the sales proceeds (Section 500) and the net amount to receive (Section 600).

The second page of the HUD-1 details the settlement charges to the buyer and seller. Section 700 calculates the commissions due to the real estate brokers, if the property was listed. This section is blank on the sample because the sellers did not sell the property through a Realtor. Section 800 details the expenses relating to any new financing. Section 900 details any items required by the lender to be prepaid. Section 1000 lists reserves deposited with the lender for taxes and insurance. Section 1100 outlines charges for title work completed. Section 1200 details document recording fees and real estate transfer taxes due to the local and state government. Section 1300 lists any additional settlement charges. Finally, everything is totaled at the bottom (line 1400) and reflected on the first page of the HUD-1 on lines 103 and 502. The following is a line-by-line description of each charge for the settlement sheet:

FIRST PAGE OF SETTLEMENT SHEET

101 Price at which the property was purchased from the seller

103 Total settlement charges paid by buyer. From line 1400 (first column) of second page.

104 Assignment fee paid to me in cash at settlement by buyer.

107 Prepayment of property taxes by buyer from the settlement date to the end of the tax year.

109 Reimbursement from the buyer to the seller for their prepayment of the water bill.

120 Total amount due from buyer

202 Amount borrowed from the private lender by buyer to pay for the purchase, rehab and closing.

213 Contribution by seller for payment of water bill from September 14, 2000 up to October 30, 2000, the settlement date.

214 Contribution by seller to pay for ground rent from October 15, 2000 to settlement.

220 Total amount paid for buyer

303 Takes line 120 (total due from buyer) and subtracts line 220 (total paid on behalf of buyer. If this is a positive number, then the buyer must bring that amount to closing ($430.35 in this case). If this is a negative number, then the buyer will receive that amount at closing.

401 Purchase price due to seller

407 Reimbursement to seller for property taxes from October 30, 2000 through June 30, 2001, which they had prepaid.

409 Reimbursement to seller for water bill which they had prepaid.

420 Total amount due to seller

502 Seller's portion of the settlement costs. Taken from line 1400 (second column) on the second page.

504 Seller pays off the remaining balance of their first mortgage.

513 Seller pays the amount owed to the county for the property's water usage from September 14, 2000 to October 30, 2000, the settlement date.

514 Seller pays the amount owed to the holder of the ground rent from October 15, 2000 to October 30, 2000.

520 Total amount that seller must use from the proceeds of the sale to pay settlement costs, satisfy existing mortgages and pay other bills.

603 Takes line 420 (total due to seller) and subtracts line 520 (total due from seller). This usually results in a positive number and, therefore, cash to the seller.

SECOND PAGE OF SETTLEMENT SHEET

805 Fees charged by the private lender to inspect the property before he releases a draw from the repair escrow. In this case, there will be two draws.

808 Fee charged by the lender for him to wire the money to settlement.

809 Amount going into the escrow for repairs.

810 Financing fee charged by the lender. Can be percentage points of the loan amount or a flat fee.

1103 Charge for title company to examine the title work.

1104 Charge for title company to prepare the title insurance binder.

1105 Charge for title company to prepare all of the settlement documents (deed, loan documents, settlement sheet, etc.).

1107 Charge for title company to handle the settlement.

1108 Charge for title insurance.

1109 Breakdown of cost for lender's portion of title insurance.

1110 Breakdown of cost for owner's portion of title insurance.

1111 Charge for lien certificate, which shows any outstanding liens on the property that need to be cleared up before settlement.

1112 Charge for judgment reports, which shows any judgments attached to the property which must be cleared up before settlement.

1113 Courier charge and charge required to have someone record the documents in person.

1201 Fees charged by local government to make deed, mortgage and any releases a part of public record.

1202 City and county transfer tax (deed stamps)

1203 State transfer tax (deed stamps)

1204 State mortgage stamps.

1205 Recording charge for Assignment of Rents and Leases, a document which allow a private lender to collect rents for the property if the borrower stops making the mortgage payments.

1303 Payment of property taxes.

1304 Release fee to settlement attorney.

1305 Seller's payment of October 15th ground rent payment.

SAMPLE HUD-1 — RETAIL DEAL

Included on the following two pages is an example of a HUD-1, or settlement sheet, from a renovation I recently completed. I sold the property for $91,000 (line 101) and walked away from settlement with a check for $39,456.04 (line 603), one of my best to date. My buyer borrowed $91,000 (line 202) from a conventional lender and brought $1,047.61 to the closing table including $547.61 in cash (line 303) and $500 (lines 201) in the form of earnest money deposit where he received settlement credit.

In addition, partly due to his participation in a closing cost assistance program, he received various credits totaling $2,520.19 (lines 204, 205, 206, 213, 214, 216 and 217) for a grand total of $94,567.80. Of this total, $40,293.94 (line 504) went to pay off my private lender, $10,475.25 (line 502) went for pay for my portion of the settlement costs (detailed on the far right hand column of page 2), $3,009.55 (line 103) went to pay the buyer's portion of the settlement costs (detailed on the left hand column of page two), $15.72 (line 513) went to pay my prorated portion of the water bill, $43.52 (line 514) went to pay my prorated portion of the ground rent, $1,003.78 (line 517) went to pay the property tax bill for 2001-2002 (part of which is pro-rated and credited to me on line 406), and $270.00 (line 518), or three years worth of ground rent, withheld in escrow to pay the holder of the ground rent (title companies will do this if they can't locate the ground rent owner). The balance, $39,456.04, was distributed to me. Immediately following is the HUD-1 from this transaction with a line item description of everything on the sheet.

DESCRIPTION OF SAMPLE HUD-1 — RETAIL DEAL

The first page of the HUD-1 is broken down into two sides, one for the buyer and one for the seller. Each side contains a summary of the participant's transaction. For the buyer, this includes the total amount they need (Section 100), the total amount paid on their behalf by a lender or some other party (Section 200) and the difference, which is what they will bring or take from the table (Section 300). For the seller, this summary includes what they are owed (Section 400), what must be paid from the sales proceeds (Section 500), and the net amount received (Section 600).

The second page of the HUD-1 details the settlement charges to the buyer and seller. Section 700 calculates the commissions due to the real estate brokers if the property was listed. This section will be blank if the seller does not sell the property through a Realtor. Section 800 details the expenses relating to any new financing. Section 900 details any items required by the lender to be prepaid. Section 1000 lists reserves deposited with the lender for taxes and insurance. Section 1100 outlines charges for title work completed. Section 1200 details document recording fees and real estate transfer taxes due to the local and state government. Section 1300 lists any additional settlement charges. Finally, everything is totaled at the bottom (line 1400) and reflected on the first page of the HUD-1 on lines 103 and 502. Following is a line-by-line description of each charge for both pages of the settlement sheet:

FIRST PAGE OF SETTLEMENT SHEET

101 Price at which the property was purchased from the seller

103 Total settlement charges paid by buyer. From line 1400 (first column) of second page.

106 Prepayment of property taxes by buyer from the settlement date to the end of the tax year.

109 Reimbursement from the buyer to the seller for their prepayment of the water bill.

120 Total amount due from buyer

201 Credit to buyer for earnest money deposited when the signed the contract to purchase.

202 Amount borrowed from the lender by buyer to pay for the purchase and closing.

204 Closing cost credit to buyer as a result of closing cost assistance program.

205 Closing cost credit to buyer as a result of closing cost assistance program.

206 Closing cost credit to buyer as a result of closing cost assistance program.

213 Contribution by seller for payment of water bill from October 26, 2001 up to December 14, 2001, the settlement date.

214 Contribution by seller to pay for payment of ground rent from June 20, 2001 up to December 14, 2001, the settlement date.

216 Closing cost credit to buyer as a result of closing cost assistance program.

217 Closing cost credit to buyer as a result of closing cost assistance program.

220 Total amount paid for buyer

303 Takes line 120 (total due from buyer) and subtracts line 220 (total paid on behalf of buyer. If this is a positive number, then the buyer must bring that amount to closing ($547.61 in this case). If

this is a negative number, then the buyer will receive that amount at closing.

401 Purchase price due to seller

406 Reimbursement to seller for property taxes from settlement, December 14, 2001, through July 1, 2002, which they had prepaid.

409 Reimbursement to seller for water bill which they had prepaid.

420 Total amount due to seller

502 Seller's portion of the settlement costs. Taken from line 1400 (second column) on the second page.

504 Seller pays off the remaining balance of their first mortgage.

513 Seller pays the amount owed to the city for the property's water usage from October 26, 2001 to December 14, 2001, the settlement date.

514 Seller pays the amount owed to the holder of the ground rent from June 20, 2001 up to December 14, 2001, the settlement date.

517 Seller pays the 2001-2002 property taxes to the city.

518 Title company escrows three years' worth of ground rent from the seller's proceeds in the event that the holder of the ground rent, whom they could not find, comes forward to collect. Three years is maximum rent that a ground rent holder can collect for back payments, though they may also try to collect attorney and title fees.

520 Total amount that seller must use from the proceeds of the sale to pay settlement costs, satisfy existing mortgages and pay other bills.

603 Takes line 420 (total due to seller) and subtracts line 520 (total due from seller). This usually results in a positive number and, therefore, cash to the seller.

SECOND PAGE OF SETTLEMENT SHEET

700 Calculation of total real estate commission.

701 Commission due to seller's agency.

702	Commission due to buyer's agency.
703	Total commission paid at settlement. Also shows who holds earnest money deposit.
704	Administration / paperwork fee to seller's agency.
802	Points paid to lender by seller on behalf of borrower.
803	Appraisal fee POC (paid outside of closing) by the lender.
804	Credit report fee POC by the lender.
805	Tax service fee POC by the lender.
809	Flood certification fee POC by the lender.
811	Fee paid to non-profit housing agency by buyer. Also POC.
901	Prepaid interest paid by buyer from settlement to the first of the month.
903	One year's hazard insurance premium POC by buyer.
1001	Three months' hazard insurance premium escrow collected by lender from buyer in advance.
1003	Three months' city property tax escrow collected by lender from buyer in advance.
1008	Miscellaneous credit.
1101	Charge for title company to perform settlement.
1102	Charge for abstracter to perform title search.
1103	Charge for title company to examine the title work.
1104	Charge to obtain lien sheet from Baltimore City listing any outstanding liens on the property that need to be cleared up before settlement. Also necessary to record deed.
1105	Charge for judgment report, which shows any judgments attached to the property that must be cleared up before settlement.
1106	Charge to record release of lien from private lender.
1108	Charge for title insurance.
1109	Amount of lender's title insurance coverage.

1110 Amount of owner's title insurance coverage.

1201 Fees charged by local government to make deed, mortgage and any releases a part of public record.

1202 City and county transfer tax (deed stamps). Equal to 1.5% of sales price.

1203 State transfer tax (deed stamps). Equal to 0.55% of sales price.

1204 State mortgage stamps. Equal to 0.25% of mortgage amount.

1301 Land survey of property required by lender.

1302 Pest inspection required by lender.

1303 Courier fees.

1304 Home warranty purchased by seller.

WHAT HAPPENS AT SETTLEMENT?

This takes place behind the curtain at a wholesale settlement and a retail settlement.

WHOLESALE DEAL

In the event of a cash deal, settlement is very easy. The seller signs over a deed to the buyer, all parties sign the HUD-1, monies exchange hands and the transaction is complete. This takes about ten minutes or less if everyone is organized.

If a lender is involved, the buyer has more documents to sign. Once all is signed, the lender or attorney makes the funds available to complete the purchase of the property and the seller signs the deed over to the buyer. This takes a little longer than a cash deal since there are more documents to sign, but not much longer.

RETAIL DEAL

When closing with new homeowners, it takes another forty-five to ninety minutes. It is amazing how much paperwork a homebuyer needs to sign to buy a home. The files are usually a couple of inches thick, and the buyer(s) must sign their name(s) about 100 times. In addition to the signature time, it takes time for the settlement attorney to explain all of the documents. Even so, waiting that excess time is understandable, especially because my reward is a nice payday.

SIMULTANEOUS WHOLESALE CLOSINGS

If you are in a simultaneous closing where you immediately buy and resell a property, the settlement process is performed twice and there will be a HUD-1 for each settlement. The first time, you act as the seller and the title attorney will collect funds from your buyers that are placed in escrow. The second time, you act as the buyer and the title attorney will distribute funds from the escrow to the initial seller for the purchase price of the property. They also cut you a check for profit that equals the balance of money in the escrow account. If necessary, it is possible to complete the first settlement hours or perhaps even a day before the second settlement, placing monies and documents in escrow until the second settlement is complete. Though not common, it is possible if you have a title attorney willing to cooperate.

GETTING PAID AS A WHOLESALER

When doing an assignment, the closing agent should have your assignment fee recorded as a line item on the HUD-1. It may simply state "Assignment fee to Steve Cook — $5,000". In this case, the closing agent would cut me a check for $5,000 out of the proceeds.

With a simultaneous close, there will be two separate HUD-1 statements. The difference between what you collect as the Seller on the second statement and what you pay as the Buyer on the first statement is what the closing agent will give you in the form of a check. Keep in mind that two settlements need to take place.

SETTLEMENTS ARE FUNDAMENTALLY SIMPLE

All things considered, settlements/closings are simple procedures. The seller signs a deed to the buyer, the HUD-1 is signed by all parties, monies exchange hands and the transaction is complete. Settlements are particularly easy when you are dealing with investors who pay cash. They get a little complicated when you have institutional lenders who require your buyer to sign about 100 documents, but even those settlements aren't complex. Mostly they are more time consuming than a settlement involving an investor paying cash for a home that usually takes ten minutes or less.

REAL LIFE EXPERIENCE

Portions of my settlements have mistakes on the HUD-1. Sometimes, the mistakes only amount to a few hundred dollars, but a few hundred dollars is still a few hundred dollars. On occasion, the mistakes are in my favor, but I always have those corrected as well. I once had a deal that looked like it would have made me a little over $3,000, but after correcting the HUD-1 errors, it only made me about $2,100. One could say that I lost a little over $900, but making the corrections was the right thing to do. I would have had to give the money back when the title company tried to balance their books and picked up the mistake. In addition, after bringing the mistakes to his attention, the attorney had much more respect for me. Basically, it pays to make corrections in both directions.

CHAPTER 30

CONTROLLING THE PROCESS

USING WHAT YOU HAVE LEARNED

There is a lot of information in this course. It is almost impossible to use it all immediately, but the important thing is that you do use it. You will learn more by getting out into the real world and doing deals, using the course as a tool to get started. I have recently received a number of e-mails from people who have bought my courses. They know all the processes and necessary steps but keep finding reasons not to take action. My favorite line has become, "Get out of your own way." No one is stopping you from achieving success as a real estate investor other than yourself. Even though the world is out there for the taking, nothing works until you do, While it's true that there will be obstacles in your path from time to time, if you don't succeed, the only person you can really blame is yourself.

STAYING IN CONTROL OF THE WHOLE DEAL

The reason this course contains so much information is that you need to know a lot in order to stay on top of your deals. Whether you are wholesaling or retailing, from the time that you sign a purchase contract to the time you pick up your check at settlement when you resell, you should always know where your deal stands.

THE PURCHASE

If you or your buyer are requesting financing from a private lender, follow up to get the results of the appraisal and determine the amount of money that you or your buyer need to bring to settlement, making sure the lender's attorney coordinates with your title company in forwarding the loan documents and wiring the money. Turn in the purchase contract to the title company and stay in touch to make sure that the title work is proceeding smoothly and there are no problems.

THE RENOVATION

If you are renovating the property for resale, start searching for a reputable contractor as soon as you sign the agreement to purchase the property. Once you settle and the contractor begins to work, make sure your job remains a priority until the work is complete. If you just hire the first contractor you see and let him loose on a property without any follow up, you will be unpleasantly surprised when you discover that not everyone follows through on their commitments.

THE SALE

When you sell a property as a wholesaler or a rehabber, stay in control of the sales and financing process, particularly if you are not using a real estate agent. If you collect earnest money deposits from buyers and walk away from the deal expecting everything to fall into place, you can expect trouble as people fail to keep their word. I caution you when wholesaling because many investors you encounter won't follow through if you don't hold their hand throughout the process. Similarly, when retailing, many people that you meet (contractors, mortgage brokers, title companies and real estate agents), won't follow through if you don't keep tabs.

When wholesaling or retailing, it's important to keep details such as where your buyer is obtaining their purchase financing, the timing and results of the appraisal, who is performing the settlement, when it is scheduled to close, the progress of the loan process, the progress of the title work, the timing and results of the inspections (usually only required when retailing), etc. After all, it's your money at stake and you need to identify potential problems before they become problems. Without specific attention, deals can spiral out of control in no time. Regardless, you need assistance in ensuring that deals go to closing successfully and your team can help this happen.

TURNING THE DETAILS OVER TO YOUR TEAM

If you have the right team in place—amazing employees—become the coach. Manage everyone on your team, making sure they are doing their part. Before long, everyone becomes familiar with your methods and they fulfill their duties extremely well. Consequently, your job as a coach becomes easier as you complete deals with the same team. On the other hand, if you are constantly changing your team, you will always be training and dealing with the bumps and bruises that result from having a team member who may make mistakes because they don't know how you like to do things. Put your team together, make offers, fix homes, sell homes and manage your team well. This is the key to being successful as an investor.

REAL LIFE EXPERIENCE

When I began, I believed everyone who signed a contract to buy a home from me. I believed everything they told me and took their word. I got burned a lot but it didn't take too many slaps in the face before I realized I needed to take control of the entire process. At that point, I decided to control every deal by lining up contractors, lining up the lenders, starting the title work myself through my attorney and mandating that my buyers use my attorney. Before taking control, about 25 percent of my deals didn't settle with my first buyer. Since taking control, that percentage has been reduced to about 5 percent of my deal. The next pages provide step-by-step details.

ANATOMY OF A WHOLESALE FLIP

I wanted to include a list, a summary, of all of the basic steps in a wholesale and a retail transaction. Here are the steps for a wholesale deal from start to finish:

Step 1) Make your offer.

Step 2) Offer is accepted. Sign contract to purchase property.

Step 3) Start title work.

Step 4) Begin marketing to find a buyer. Market property to your buyer's list and place an ad in the paper.

Step 5) Come to an agreement with a prospective buyer.

Step 6) Qualify the prospective buyer, making sure they have the cash or will be able to borrow the money from a private lender (preferably one whom you've used before) to purchase your property. Continue to market the property while qualifying your buyer.

Step 7) After verifying their source of funds, meet with your buyer, execute a sales contract or an assignment agreement with them, and collect a deposit. The sales contract serves as the receipt for their deposit. Either handwrite or include typewritten verbiage somewhere on your contract a statement such as the following, "Received $ (insert dollar amount) as an earnest money deposit on (insert date)" and initial it once you receive their deposit. You might also include their check number or write "CASH" if they give you cash.

Step 8) Submit both items–the executed contract with the original seller and the executed sales contract/assignment agreement with your buyer–to your title attorney and schedule a settlement date.

Step 9) Go to settlement, pick up your check, and celebrate!

ANATOMY OF A RETAIL FLIP

Here are all of the basic steps in a rehab transaction from start to finish:

Step 1)   Make your offer.

Step 2)   Offer is accepted. Sign contract to purchase property.

Step 3)   Start title work.

Step 4)   Start lining up contractors.

Step 5)   Settle on home.

Step 6)   Begin renovation, starting with exterior if you want to begin marketing prior to completion of project.

Step 7a) If you are marketing yourself, begin to call your buyers list and sell them. Offer to give them a choice of colors.

Step 7b) If you are marketing through a Realtor, have home ready to list upon completion of work.

Step 8)   Work through buying process for your buyer either directly or using an agent. This includes scheduling times for inspections, dealing with their loan officer, making the home available for appraisal, etc.

Step 9)   Make all final repairs, as requested by inspector or appraiser.

Step 10) Go to settlement, pick up your check and celebrate!

CHAPTER 31

TWO WHOLESALE DEALS

IN THIS CHAPTER, I am going to attempt to give you a step-by-step account, every single detail, of two wholesale deals that I was working on at the same time.

On September 19, 2000, I received a list of homes and decided to go take a look. There were about twenty homes on the list, but they were all over Baltimore so I decided to check the ones in the area where I had the best luck. By the end of the day, I had looked at eight homes and made offers on all of them. In addition to making offers on the homes I inspected, I also made offers on four other houses for a total of twelve offers. Four were made sight unseen, but my offers were ridiculously low. The twelve properties were a mix of HUD homes, bank-owned homes and a private party home. In terms of estimating values, I knew the neighborhoods very well so I didn't need to check comps. Two days later, two of my offers were accepted. I put the first home (Home #1) under contract for $55,000 and the second home (Home #2) under contract for $23,000.

Home #1 was good except that it needed a lot of work. I felt the amount of repairs was in the neighborhood of $20,000 and I really wasn't in the mood for getting into such a large rehab at the time so I was hoping to wholesale. The neighborhood was desirable (#6 on the

Neighborhood Scale) and I estimated the after repaired value to be about $105,000. The bank was asking $69,000 for the home, but they accepted my offer (sight unseen) of $55,000. After having my offer accepted, I drove to the home to inspect the interior, putting a lockbox on it before I left so my prospective buyers would be able to get into the property without having me there.

Home #2 was also purchased sight unseen. My purchase price was $23,000 and the seller (HUD) was asking $30,000. I knew the area (4 on the Neighborhood Scale) pretty well, having purchased two other homes nearby within the past year for $45,000 and $40,000, knowing that a nice home in the area retailed for $85,000-$90,000. Consequently, I knew that I could wholesale this property really quick.

I called one of my buyers, an investor I felt was the most likely person to purchase this home and told him to take a look. I said he could have the house for $35,000 (a great deal in the neighborhood) but that he had to move quickly if he wanted it.

Most of the bank owned properties and HUD homes have master keys. On occasion, a buyer will have a key to one of the homes I have purchased so I won't have to meet there or put a lockbox on the home. Fortunately, my buyer was able to gain access without my involvement. I called the newspapers the same day my offers were accepted to get ads in the paper. I particularly wanted to place an ad for Home #1 because I wanted to wholesale that one quickly and it needed more marketing than Home #2. The ad I ran in the paper was as follows:

Catonsville* 4 BR $100k+ area only $60k. Financing Available (410)xxx-xxxx

Later that day, I received a return call from my buyer I sent out to inspect Home #2. He decided to purchase the home, so we agreed to meet the next day. The following day, my buyer and I signed the paperwork and I collected a deposit check from him in the amount of $500. Since I was bringing him to one of my hard money lenders, we also discussed the amount of work he was going to do so I might put together a financing request on his behalf.

After receiving the signed contract for Home #2, I took the contract to my title attorney's office (escrow company / title company) so he could start the title work. I also dropped off a check (from my buyer) for the appraisal as well as the financing request for the hard money lender, who always uses the same attorney to prepare his loan documents. Now, I just have to wait for the process to play itself out, get settlement scheduled and pick up my check.

Over the weekend, I got a number of calls on my ad for Home #1. I didn't keep an exact count, but I know I had quite a bit of calls from non-investors. I gave many people the address to the home, but I wasn't getting any calls back. By the end of the week, I still had the home and I had to place another ad in the Sunday paper. Home #1 was beginning to worry me. I had my hands full with rehabs and I really wasn't in the mood for taking on another. Perhaps I had missed the mark on my rehab figure. I knew the numbers were tighter than I liked. Nonetheless, I submitted another ad and waited for calls. The next weekend I received a number of calls again. One person was interested and someone from the previous week called back showing interest. I worked diligently with each of these people, trying to get one to bite. Because of the amount of work required, one of the parties was very skeptical while the other party didn't think it was so bad.

In addition to working with these two investors, I returned calls for other prospects and found another really interested party. Since he was a new investor who had never done a deal before, I actually went out to meet him at the property. He told me that he and his father, who had the cash, wanted to do a rehab and that this was the area where they wanted to invest. His sister had just sold her home, which was five blocks away and very similar to the one I was offering, for $135,000. He felt he could get $130,000 or better for this home after it was repaired. I didn't agree and I told him just that, but he seemed confident in his estimate. Anyway, he and I met at the home on two occasions. He brought his father out for a third time without me and they decided they wanted to buy the home. So we met and signed the contract and I collected a $1,000 deposit from him. Since I already had the title work in motion, I suggested that they use my attorney and they agreed.

Two weeks later this home settled and I walked away with a check for $3,714 from the settlement table. When you add this to the $1000 earnest money deposit that I received and subtract the $500 that I put down when I bought the home, you arrive at a total of $4,214 profit for this deal. Not a bad payday when you consider that I spent a total of approximately ten hours on this one. About a week after the settlement on Home #1, we received the numbers for Home #2 from my hard money lender. He was willing to lend my buyer $40k for purchase and $12k for rehab, so my buyer was able to give me my $35,000 and use the remaining $5,000 to cover his closing costs. The $12,000 for repairs would be put into escrow at settlement and released as the repairs were completed. Several days later, we settled and I walked away with a check for $12,000 ($35,000 sales price - $23,000 purchase price). This was a great payday since I had only invested a total of about ninety minutes in the deal.

As you can see, both of these deals were different. One was much better than the other, but neither was bad. Sometimes you have to work harder than others, but the deals are really easy like Home #2. Not all deals will be home runs, but every deal that makes you money is a good one. The more deals you do, the more home runs you will find. Keep in mind that you shouldn't always swing for the fences. Go for as many hits as you can get and the law of averages will produce home runs. If all you ever try to do is hit home runs, you will strike out more often than not.

My buyer for Home #1 renovated the entire home and did a beautiful job. He and his father had it sold within five months for $139,900. Personally, I was surprised that he got that much for it, but a few others in the area recently sold for about the same amount. He was happy, I was happy, the original seller was happy and his new buyers were happy. Everyone made out on the deal.

CHAPTER 32

SUCCESSFUL REHAB STORY

IN THIS FINAL CHAPTER, I am going to attempt to give you a step-by-step account, every single detail, of one of my recent retail deals.

In February of 2001, I purchased a three bedroom, one bath Cape Cod in a fairly nice neighborhood. The home was first listed at $22,900 and I offered $21,000 right away, figuring the home would be worth about $75-80k after it was fixed up—with my repairs running between $15k and $20k. The sellers responded with a counteroffer of $22,000 and we settled on that.

I decided to borrow money to purchase the home from one of my hard money lenders. He loaned me a total of $40,000, where $15,000 was held in escrow for repairs to draw out as the work was completed. I actually walked away from the settlement table with about $50 since my lender loaned me closing costs as well as the purchase and rehab funds.

After settling on the home, I immediately began the rehab by ordering the windows and having a new furnace and central air conditioning system put into the home. My contractor started to work on the exterior of the home by putting a new roof and siding on the house. Within a week, the exterior of the home was beautiful, though the interior still left a lot to be desired.

The home was somewhat small and I wanted to get more living space out of it. Immediately, we looked at the possibility of finishing the basement and decided on a plan that would create a family room, a bedroom and a half bath in the basement. In all, it cost me about $5,000 and the finished basement increased the total living space by 950 square feet. Partially due to the basement, I went a little over budget on the rehab, spending about $21,000 total. The end result, however, was a four bedroom, one and one half bath, with a family room in a good neighborhood.

Besides increasing the living area, we didn't have much to do on the interior of the home. It actually required a lighter rehab than most of my projects. Basically, we had to do a few little patches, trim work, painting and carpeting. We moved some plumbing in the kitchen to make it more functional and repaired some rotted wood damage around a window. Outside of these things, the interior was fairly easy.

This deal took longer than expected to complete because my contractor fell on hard times with some of his other jobs. The rehab took about eight months and this was one of the major reasons I went over budget. Finally, the house was done and I decided to ask $94,900 for it. This was a little bit of a stretch since the highest sale in the neighborhood to date had been $87,750, but my home was very nice.

Within a week, I had three contracts on it—one for $94,000 and two at $94,900. I accepted the $94,000 because it appeared to be the most solid of the three offers. The buyer was prepared, having already been through programs for closing cost assistance, requesting very little closing cost help from me. In the end, the appraiser knocked my sales price down to $91,000. I couldn't complain since mine was still going to be the highest sale in the neighborhood. I may have been able to fight for more, but opted to let it go. I was happy with the $91,000, but I still reflect on the fact that I had three people willing to pay $94,000-$94,900, which I believe is what determines the true value of a home. In December of 2001, we went to settlement and I walked away with a check for $39,456.

Not all deals are as good as this one, so don't feel like you have to make as much on your deals or that they aren't any good. There isn't anything wrong with turning homes quickly and making a $10,000-$15,000 profit. If I were working with homes in the $100k+ range, I would want to make a little more money per deal, but don't be greedy. Do solid deals, get them done and pick up your checks.

CHAPTER 33

QUITTING YOUR DAY JOB

Every beginning investor asks this question: "When do I start?" The problem is that the answer is "it depends." Many have asked me to put together a checklist of the first few steps as if every person goes down the same path. This would not be fair to everyone because investing is not a one-size-fits-all business. Past experiences, financial resources, relationships and where you live factor into how your business can be built. Personally, I had nothing going for me when I got started. There is no one reading this course that is in worse shape than I was when I decided to take the plunge. Some may be as bad off, but not worse off. Many of you are in better shape, particularly from a financial point of view.

VARIOUS SCENARIOS

I'm going to try my best to give a broad answer to different scenarios to help get you going in the right direction. Let's first explore someone who has little financial resources and trouble getting their hands on money. On one hand, you are at a disadvantage. Someone with a lot of cash is better equipped to take advantage of deals. They can compete where you cannot, but not all hope is gone. You can still find deals. You may need to work harder, where someone with money can let their resources do a lot of the work. Dig up that next deal, turn over every rock and find the deals that others are not. There is always money to be made.

Being broke forces you to become a better investor. Not having money was the best thing that could have happened to me when I was getting started in the business. It forced me not to trust in my financial resources. I had to get creative and work harder than everyone else. Being broke was the single greatest factor that led to my success. I feel like people who get started and have a lot of money make more mistakes. They take shortcuts and depend too much on their checkbooks. I had to create winning situations with my deals.

CLOSING THE FIRST DEAL

I hope you are not reading this course hoping that it will put money in your pocket in the next couple of weeks. Don't get me wrong, the methods that I teach can make you money almost instantly, but it's not probable. There is work to do to begin making money as a real estate investor. For some, it comes together very quickly and for others, it takes longer. It took me eight months to get my first deal. I have students who pick up nice checks in less then thirty days and others take longer than I did. However, once you "get it" and have momentum going, the next deal typically comes quicker than the first.

If you need to start making money to pay your bills now, you should probably not pursue rehabbing right out of the gate. On average, rehabbing doesn't produce paydays for about six months. The paydays can be very substantial and for many investors, two rehabs per year can replace their current incomes. If you need paydays sooner than later, consider wholesaling as your route to earning an income in real estate. In time, a combination of the two is great. Some earn substantial incomes as wholesalers without ever fixing a home. It is not uncommon for wholesalers to earn fees as large as those that some rehabbers make. I frequently have students that earn in excess of $30,000 on the properties they wholesale.

FULL-TIME JOB

In my opinion, rehabbing is easier for someone who has a full time job. Wholesaling requires more time if you are going to turn it into a business where you are constantly searching for the next deal. If you want to treat it as a business, you need to be looking for the next deal. Rehabbing, you can find a deal and stop looking. With a good contractor you can check on your projects before or after work a few days a week to check on the progress.

QUITTING YOUR JOB

This question always disturbs me because "it depends." Only you know when you are ready to invest full time. I would not advise most to do what I did. I dove in with both feet and didn't look back. I've seen others do the same with varying results. I'm not quite sure when someone is ready. I do have a formula that I like to put in place that you can use to determine when is the best time for you to quit your day job. My recommendation is that you determine what your needs are for one year (at least six months) and that you earn at least this much from your real estate investing efforts that you set aside into an untouchable account. This account is going to be the one that you use to pay yourself a paycheck every two weeks. This will sustain you while you build your business. Once you finish a deal, replenish this account and bring it to the level you started with and continue to live off of your paycheck and not off of the deal. Many investors live roller coaster lifestyles, going to Ruth Chris for dinner when a deal closes and three months later they eat Ramen Noodles. Many investors would be more disciplined if they would keep a payroll account and learn to live off of a paycheck rather than a deal. If you can set this up before leaving your job, you'll save yourself the agony of worrying when you're going to get a payday. I hope this gives you some direction on where and when to get started. I know this doesn't address every single situation. The advantage of my coaching program is that I can get to know each student on a more intimate level and help them to devise the best plan.

APPENDIX A

GLOSSARY

ACCEPTANCE - the act of accepting an offer that results in a binding contract.

AGREEMENT OF SALE - a written agreement between a purchaser who agrees to buy, and a seller who agrees to sell a specific property.

APPRAISAL - a market value estimate of real property, through the comparison of actual sales of comparable properties.

APPRAISER - a person licensed or certified to determine the market value of property.

ASSIGN - to transfer one's rights and obligations under a contract to another party.

ASSIGNEE - the party to whom rights of a contract are assigned or transferred.

ASSIGNOR - a party who assigns or transfers and agreement or contract to another.

BINDER - see "EARNEST MONEY."

BREACH OF CONTRACT - non-performance, default, or violation by a party to a contract of any of its terms.

CLOSING - the finalizing of the purchase and sale of a property.

CLOSING COSTS - the expenses incurred by the buyer and seller of a real estate transaction.

CLOSING STATEMENT / HUD 1 / SETTLEMENT SHEET - a statement used to itemize all of the costs for the buyer and seller of a real estate transaction.

COMPARABLES - recent sales of similar properties used to help determine the value of a particular property.

CONTINGENCY - a condition within a contract that must be met before the contract can become legally binding.

CONTINGENT - dependent upon the occurrence of a certain event.

CONTRACT - an agreement between two or more parties that becomes legally binding upon execution by the parties involved.

DEED - a legal document that conveys ownership of a property to another party.

DEED OF TRUST - a legal document that conveys title of a property to a neutral third party, usually for collateralization purposes.

EARNEST MONEY or "GOOD FAITH" DEPOSIT - consideration used to secure a contract, usually in the form of cash or check. Given by a buyer to a seller upon execution of a contract, this deposit shows the buyer's intent to act in good faith.

ESCROW - consideration held by a third party (usually an attorney) until the conditions of an agreement are fulfilled.

ESCROW AGENT (CLOSING AGENT) - a third party used by a buyer and seller to facilitate a transaction. Usually an attorney or a title company.

FAIR MARKET VALUE - the value of a property determined by current market conditions.

FANNIE MAE - Federal National Mortgage Association (FNMA).

FHA - Federal Housing Administration.

FINDER'S FEE - the fee a person is paid for their services of arranging a real estate transaction between two parties. A finder's fee is normally paid for finding a property for someone to buy, or for finding a buyer for a particular party.

FORECLOSURE - the sale of a particular property to satisfy the debt of a defaulting debtor. The proceeds of the sale are used to satisfy the debt to the lender.

FRAUD - the act of cheating or deceiving another party to gain some dishonest advantage.

FSBO – For Sale By Owner

FREDDIE MAC - Federal Home Mortgage Loan Corporation (FHMLC).

GNMA - Government National Mortgage Association

HUD - Department of Housing and Urban Development.

LINE OF CREDIT - a particular amount of money made available by a lender to a borrower. Lines of credit used to purchase real estate are usually secured by real property.

MARKET VALUE - the price that a buyer is willing to pay a seller for a property under normal market conditions.

MORTGAGE - a lien against a property given by the debtor to secure a debt to a lender.

MORTAGE BROKER - a person who gets paid to bring borrowers and lenders together.

MULTIPLE LISTING SERVICE (MLS) - the network of real estate listing used by real estate agents and brokers. Homes listed in the MLS are exposed to all agents and brokers who are members of the network. In addition to current listings, the MLS also contains information such as historical sales data of properties listed and sold. This data is useful in completing a comparable sales analysis that can be used to estimate the value of a subject property.

OPTION - an agreement that gives a party the right to purchase a particular property at a predetermined price within a specified period of time.

OPTION FEE - the payment paid by a party for the right to receive and Option.

PROMISSORY NOTE - a written agreement executed by a payor as their promise to repay a loan.

PUBLIC RECORDS - courthouse records relating to real estate and other topics (e.g., corporations) which can be accessed by the general public.

REAL ESTATE - land and anything permanently attached to the land.

REAL ESTATE BROKER - an agent who receives a commission by bringing a buyer and a seller of real estate together.

REO - stands for Real Estate Owned. Term used to describe real estate held by banks or institutions.

RECORDING - the act of entering legal documents into public record for the purpose of notifying anyone who may be interested of the rights and claims of the parties within the recorded instruments.

TIME IS OF THE ESSENCE - a requirement of punctual performance stipulated in most contracts including those used in real estate transactions.

VA - Veterans Administration.

APPENDIX B

FORMS

Forms can be downloaded from our website *www.Lifeonaire.com*

DISCLOSURE

The forms contained in this publication are intended for instructional purposes only. They are offered with the understanding that neither the publisher nor the author is engaged in rendering legal, tax or other professional services and that these forms should be reviewed by an attorney before being used by the reader. If legal, tax or other expert assistance is required, including but not limited to the review of these forms, the services of a competent professional should be sought (from a Declaration of Principles jointly adopted by a committee of the American Bar Association and a committee of the Publishers Association).

Forms are available for download at: *www.Lifeonaire.com*

LETTER OF INTENT

This Letter of Intent specifies general terms under which the Buyer may have interest in purchasing the specified property from the Seller. Should the Seller find the proposed terms generally acceptable, the Buyer may then direct the Agent to prepare a formal Residential Contract of Sale for the consideration by the Seller. This Letter of Intent is not an offer to purchase or to sell, as such an offer shall be made only on a standard contract from which shall also include those provisions required by law.

- Property Address:
- Buyers Name:
- Purchase Price:
- Earnest Money: $
- Settlement Date:
- Financing Contingency:
- Additional Contingencies:
- Other Terms:
- This Letter of Intent expires 48 hours from the date of this letter.

Submitted for consideration this _____ day of _____, _____

_____   _____

Buyer   Buyer

REAL ESTATE SALES CONTRACT

Seller, _____

agrees to sell to

Buyer, _____

the real property set forth below and all improvements thereon (Property), and Buyer agrees to purchase said Property from the Seller according to the terms and conditions in this contract.

LEGAL DESCRIPTION:

_____

_____

ALSO KNOWN AS THE FOLLOWING ADDRESS:

_____

_____

PURCHASE PRICE: _____

as follows:

- (a) Initial Deposit $ _____
- (b) Sum due at closing (not including proration's) $ _____
- (c) Proceeds from a new note and mortgage to be given by Buyer or any lender other than the Seller (new loan) $ _____
- (d) Existing mortgage on the Property which shall remain on the Property $ _____
- (e) Balance due the Seller by promissory note from the Buyer as detailed in this contract (seller financing) $ _____
- (f) **TOTAL PURCHASE PRICE** $ _____

IT IS AGREED that the Property will be conveyed by a General Warranty Deed, with release of dower and homestead rights.

THE SELLER WILL PAY FOR: Revenue stamps (State, county and local); Title commitment in the amount of the purchase price from a title insurance company to be selected by Seller in the County of the Property location; Title abstract; Title opinion letter; Satisfaction of mortgage and recording fee.

THE BUYER WILL PAY FOR: Recording fees, prepaid insurance, prepaid taxes, prepaid interest, termite Inspection, appraisal fee, survey, fees associated with the procurement of financing, Property inspection, all other closing fees charged by the title company.

TITLE AND TITLE INSURANCE: Within 15 days from Effective Date, Seller shall, at Seller's expense, deliver to Buyer or Buyer's attorney, a title insurance commitment with fee owner's title policy premium to be paid by Seller at closing.

PRORATED ITEMS: All rents, water taxes or charges, taxes, assessments, monthly mortgage insurance premiums, fuel, prepaid service contracts and interest on existing mortgages shall be prorated as of the date of closing. If Buyer is to accept the Property subject to an existing mortgage requiring an escrow deposit for taxes, insurance and/or other items, all escrow payments required to be made up to the time of closing shall be made to the escrow holder at Seller's expense and said escrow balance shall be assigned to the Buyer, without compensation to the Seller, it being expressly understood that said escrow balance is included in the Total Purchase Price. All mortgage payments required of Seller to be made shall be current as of the time of closing. If the exact amount of real estate taxes cannot be ascertained at the time of closing, Seller agrees to prorate said taxes on the basis of the actual tax bill when issued.

THE DATE OF THIS CONTRACT ("Effective Date") shall be the date when the last one of Seller and Buyer has signed this offer.

EXAMINATION OF TITLE AND TIME OF CLOSING: If the title evidence and survey as specified above disclose that Seller is vested with fee simple title to the Property (subject only to the permitted exceptions set forth above acceptable to Buyer), and unless extended by other provisions of this Contract, this sale shall be closed on or before _____ at the office of the attorney or other closing agent designated by Seller. If title evidence or survey reveal any defect or condition, which is not acceptable to Buyer, the Buyer shall, within 15 days notify the Seller of such title defects and Seller agrees to use reasonable efforts to remedy such defects and shall have 30 days to do so. Seller agrees to pay for and clear all delinquent taxes, liens and other encumbrances, unless the parties otherwise agree. Seller agrees to deliver good and insurable title to the property within 60 days of the effective date.

DEFAULT BY BUYER: If Buyer fails to perform the agreements of this contract, Seller may retain as liquidated damages and not as a penalty all of the initial deposit specified in paragraph 1 (a) above, it being agreed that this is Seller's exclusive remedy.

DEFAULT BY SELLER: If Seller fails to perform any of the agreements of this contract, all deposits made by Buyer shall be returned to Buyer on demand, plus reimbursement for any expenses incurred under paragraph (4).

ATTORNEY FEES AND COSTS: If any litigation is instituted with respect to enforcement of the terms of this contract, the prevailing party shall be entitled to recover all costs incurred, including, but not limited to reasonable attorney fees and court cost.

RISK OF LOSS OR DAMAGE: Risk of loss or damage to the Property by any cause is retained by the seller until closing.

CONDITION OF THE PROPERTY: Seller agrees to deliver the Property to Buyer in its present condition, ordinary wear and tear excepted, and further certifies and represents that Seller knows of no latent defect in the Property. All heating, cooling, plumbing, electrical, sanitary systems and appliances shall be in good working order at the time of closing. Seller represents and warrants that the personal property conveyed with the premises shall be the same property inspected by Buyer and that no substitutions will be made without the Buyer's written consent. Buyer may also inspect or cause to be inspected the foundation, roof, supports or structural members of all improvements located upon the Property. If any such system, appliance, roof, foundation or structural member shall be found defective, and the costs of such repairs shall exceed 10% of the total purchase price, Buyer may, at his option, elect to terminate this contract and receive the full refund of all deposits and other sums tendered hereunder. In addition, seller agrees to remove all debris from the Property by date of possession.

OCCUPANCY: Seller shall deliver possession to Buyer no later than the closing date unless otherwise stated herein. Seller represents that there are no persons occupying the Property except the following tenants of the Seller:

_____

_____

_____

Seller agrees to deliver exclusive occupancy of the Property to Buyer at the time of closing unless otherwise specifically stated herein. Seller agrees to provide true and accurate copies of all written leases to Buyer within 5 days after the date of acceptance of this contract. Said leases are subject to Buyer's approval. Seller shall provide such letters notifying tenants to pay rent to the Buyer after closing as Buyer may reasonably request. Seller warrants that any rent rolls and other income and expense data provided to Buyer are complete and accurate, all of which must be acceptable to buyer.

[ ] MORTGAGE OR THIRD PARTY FINANCING: According to paragraph 1(d) of this contract, it is agreed that Buyer will require a new mortgage loan to finance this purchase. The application for this mortgage will be made with a lender acceptable to Buyer, and unless a mortgage loan acceptable to Buyer is approved without contingencies other than those specified in this contract within 10 (ten) days from the date of acceptance of this contract, Buyer shall have the right to terminate this contract and at that time all sums deposited by Buyer shall be returned to Buyer and Buyer shall return any surveys and copies of leases received from Seller. Seller acknowledges that there is a new institutional mortgage being placed on the property and closing may be reasonably extended to accommodate the mortgage financing process.

[ ] SELLER FINANCING: According to paragraph 1(e) above, it is understood that the Buyer will execute and deliver at the closing a

Promissory Note to Seller which shall provide for full or partial prepayment without penalty and shall bear interest at the rate of _____ per annum beginning on _____ in the amount of _____ per month such that the amount of such payments shall amortize the debt due in _____ with all unpaid principal and interest due upon the last payment date, APPROXIMATELY _____. The said Promissory Note shall be secured by a mortgage acceptable to Buyer and providing for the full and free right of the mortgagor to transfer the Property, in whole or in part, subject to the mortgage; and the right of first refusal to the mortgagor if the mortgagee shall at any time sell its interest at a discount; future advances at the option of the mortgagee

TERMITE INSPECTION: Buyer shall be furnished at Buyers expense, an inspection report showing all buildings on the Property to be free and clear from visible infestation and free from visible dry or wet rot damage by termites and other wood-destroying organisms. This inspection report is to be furnished by a licensed pest control firm. If a report shows such visible infestation or damage, Seller shall pay all costs of treatment of such infestation and all costs of repair of such damage. If the costs of treatment and repair shall exceed 3% of the total price, Seller may elect not to make such treatment and repairs and Buyer may elect to take the Property in its then condition or, at Buyer's option, to deduct the cost of repairs from the total purchase price and complete the transaction Buyer may terminate this contract and receive a full refund of all deposits made buyer hereunder.

ZONING: Unless the property is properly zoned for residential and there are no deed restrictions against such use at the time of closing, the Buyer shall have the right to terminate this contract and receive a full refund of all deposits made by Buyer hereunder.

LEGAL USE: Seller represents and warrants to Buyer that all improvements on said Property conforms to all building codes and restrictions that may be imposed by any governmental agency either national, state or local or from a Home Owners Association, Seller also warrants that there are no building code violations on the Property and that Seller has received no notice of any building code violations for the past ten years that have not been fully corrected.

PERSONAL PROPERTY INCLUDED IN THE PURCHASE PRICE: (Strike items not applicable): storm and screen doors and windows; awnings; outdoor television antenna; wall-to wall, hallway and stair carpeting; window shades and draperies and supporting fixtures; venetian blinds; window treatments; electric, plumbing and other fixtures as installed; water softener; attached shelving; hardware; trees and shrubs; refrigerator; stove; air conditioner; any existing ceiling fans, and such other items as is listed on a rider attached hereto or below, all of which personal property is unencumbered and owned by Seller.

THIS OFFER SHALL TERMINATE if not accepted

before _____ o'clock pm, _____

R.E.S.P.A. COMPLIANCE: Seller agrees to make all disclosures and do all things necessary to comply with the provisions of the Real Estate Settlement Procedure Act of 1974 if it is applicable to this transaction.

ADDITIONAL TERMS AND CONDITIONS:

(a) Where the context requires, the terms Seller and Buyer shall include the masculine as well as the feminine and the singular as well as the plural.

(b) There are no agreements, promises, or understandings between the parties except as specifically set forth in this contract. No alterations or changes shall be made to this contract unless the same are in writing and signed or initialed by the parties hereto.

(c) The provisions of this contract shall survive the closing and shall not merge in any deed or conveyance herein.

(d) This agreement shall be construed under the laws of the State of _____

(e) A faxed copy of this signed agreement shall constitute a legally binding agreement.

(f) other

NOTICES: Any notices required to be given herein shall be sent to the parties listed below at their respective addresses either by personal delivery or by certified mail-return receipt requested. Such notice shall be effective upon delivery or mailing.

TYPEWRITTEN OR HANDWRITTEN PROVISIONS: Typewritten or handwritten provisions inserted herein or attached hereto as addenda shall control all printed provisions of contract in conflict therewith.

_____ date _____
BUYER

_____ date _____
BUYER

_____ date _____
SELLER

_____ date _____
SELLER

ASSIGNMENT OF CONTRACT

In consideration for the sum of _____

_____ ($_____) and other good and valuable consideration, _____,

Assignor, hereby assigns, transfers and sets over to

_____,

Assignee, all right, title and interest in and to the following described contract:

_____

(Address)

dated _____.

The Assignor warrants and represents that said contract is in full force and effect and is fully assignable.

The Assignee hereby assumes and agrees to perform all obligations of the Assignor under the contract and guarantees to hold the Assignor harmless from any claim or demand made thereunder.

Signed under seal this ____ day of _____, ____.

_____	_____
Witness	Assignor
_____	_____
Witness	Assignee

APPENDIX C

CREDIT APPLICATION

CREDIT APPLICATION

Name: _____

Address: _____

_____

_____

Previous Address*: _____

_____

_____

Birthdate: _____

Social Security Number: _____

Signature: _____

\- Only necessary if they've been at their current address less than two years.

www.ingramcontent.com/pod-product-compliance
Lightning Source LLC
Chambersburg PA
CBHW050622300426
44112CB00012B/1618